FOREIGN DIRECT INVESTMENT

Foreign Direct Investment

Firm and Host Country Strategies

Magnus Blomström

Ari Kokko

and

Mario Zejan

First published in Great Britain 2000 by
MACMILLAN PRESS LTD
Houndmills, Basingstoke, Hampshire RG21 6XS
and London
Companies and representatives throughout the world

A catalogue record for this book is available from the British Library.

ISBN 0–333–82012–2

First published in the United States of America 2000 by
ST. MARTIN'S PRESS, INC.,
Scholarly and Reference Division,
175 Fifth Avenue,
New York, N.Y. 10010

ISBN 0–312–23141–5

Library of Congress Cataloging-in-Publication Data
Blomström, Magnus, 1952–
    Foreign direct investment: firm and host country strategies / Magnus
Blomström, Ari Kokko, and Mario Zejan.
        p. cm.
    Includes bibliographical references and index.
    ISBN 0–312–23141–5 (cloth)
        1. Investments, Foreign.   2. International business enterprises.   I.
Kokko, Ari.   II. Zejan, Mario.   III. Title.
HG4538.B545   2000
332.67'3 – dc21   99-055732

This book is printed on paper suitable for recycling and made from fully managed
and sustained forest sources.

10   9   8   7   6   5   4   3   2   1
09   08   07   06   05   04   03   02   01   00

Printed in Hong Kong

Contents

v

List of Tables and Figures

Tables

Figures

Acknowledgements

We are grateful for permission to reprint, in part or in full, the contents of the following studies:

'New Ventures or Acquisition: The Choice of Swedish Multinational Enterprises', *Journal of Industrial Economics*, vol. 38, no. 3 (1990), pp. 349–55.

'Why Do Multinationals Seek Out Joint Ventures?', *Journal of International Development*, vol. 3, no. 1 (1991), pp. 53–63.

'Intra-Firm Trade and Swedish Multinationals', *Weltwirtschaftliches Archiv*, Band 125, Heft 4 (1989), 814–33.

'R&D Activities in Affiliates of Swedish Multinational Enterprises', *Scandinavian Journal of Economics*, vol. 92, no. 3 (1990), pp. 487–500.

'Foreign Firms and Structural Adjustment in Latin America. Lessons from the Debt Crisis', in Göte Hansson (ed.), *Trade, Growth and Development* (Routledge, 1993), pp. 109–32.

'Multinational Corporations and Productivity Convergence in Mexico', in William Baumol, Richard R. Nelson and Edward N. Wolff (eds), *Convergence of Productivity: Cross-National Studies and Historical Evidence* (Oxford University Press, 1994), pp. 263–84.

'Technology, Market Characteristics, and Spillovers', *Journal of Development Economics*, vol. 43 (1994), pp. 279–93.

'Local Technological Capability and Productivity Spillovers from FDI in the Uruguayan Manufacturing Sector', *Journal of Development Studies*, vol. 32, no. 4 (1996), pp. 602–11.

'Productivity Spillovers from Competition between Local Firms and Foreign Affiliates', *Journal of International Development*, vol. 8, no. 4 (1996), pp. 517–30.

'Policies to Encourage Inflows of Technology through Foreign Multinationals', *World Development*, vol. 23, no. 3 (1995), pp. 459–68.

'Host Country Competition, Labour Skills, and Technology Transfer by Multinationals', *Weltwirtschaftliches Archiv*, Band 130, Heft 3 (1994), pp. 521–33.

Preface

This book is based on a number of articles on foreign direct investment and multinational corporations written by us over the past few years. Although the individual chapters focus on several different topics, they are all part of a common research agenda. For well over a decade we have tried to understand the differences in the observed behaviour of multinational corporations, as well as the differences in the apparent impact of foreign direct investment (FDI) on host countries. What has emerged is a picture where the outcome – in terms of firm behaviour or effects on host economies – is typically the result of an intricate interplay between firm strategies and host country strategies.

We have collected the articles as the chapters of one volume for reasons of complementarity and completion. Although they have been edited to avoid unnecessary repetition, it should be possible to read each of them separately from the others. Apart from updating some descriptive statistics, we have therefore not made any attempts to change the original content. Hence, they are presented more or less as they appeared in journals or conference volumes.

In writing this book, we have profited from the ideas of and criticism by many colleagues and friends. We owe particular thanks to Robert Lipsey, co-author of Chapter 7, whose invaluable contributions are too numerous to identify separately, and to Ruben Tansini and Edward Wolff, who have participated as co-authors in Chapter 11 and Chapter 9, respectively. In addition to these colleagues and friends, we would like to thank Renato Aguilar, Lennart Flood and Sanjaya Lall for valuable comments on various chapters.

Several of the chapters in the book are based on data for Swedish multinationals collected by the Research Institute of Industrial Economics (IUI) in Stockholm. We are grateful to the Institute for giving us access to these data.

Finally, financial support from the Swedish Council for Research in the Humanities and Social Sciences (HSFR) is gratefully acknowledged.

MAGNUS BLOMSTRÖM
ARI KOKKO
MARIO ZEJAN

1
Introduction

The central theme of this book is that the behaviour of multinational corporations (MNCs) and their affiliates, and the impact of inward foreign direct investment (FDI) on the host economy, will vary between industries and countries. Multinationals decide their strategies depending on the characteristics of their technologies and products as well as the characteristics and policies of the host countries. The MNCs' strategic decisions then determine how FDI affects the host economy. We know that some host country governments try simultaneously to influence the behaviour of the foreign MNCs operating in their territory, either directly – through regulations – or indirectly, by affecting the environment in which the MNCs operate. To the extent that these interventions affect the behaviour of the foreign MNCs, they also determine the effects on the host economy. This intricate interplay between firm and host country strategies is that FDI may contribute significantly to growth and development in some circumstances, but may also have insignificant or even negative effects on the local economy in others. Our research agenda since the late 1980s has largely been devoted to attempts to understand this interplay. This volume summarizes the results of these efforts.

It is obvious that our approach to FDI issues belongs in the structure–conduct–performance paradigm of industrial economics. One of the purposes of this brief introduction is to outline this theoretical starting point, since it will not always be discussed explicitly in the individual chapters. The following paragraphs will therefore provide a rough summary of our understanding of why FDI and MNCs exist, and how views on the effects of foreign direct investment have changed over time. The other purpose of the introduction is to summarize the chapters that follow, in two sections, to reflect the structure of the book. The first examines some determinants of MNC strategies, and the second turns to the impact of FDI on host countries, and our analysis of host country strategies.

1

1.1   A theoretical background

Stephen Hymer's nowadays well-known thesis from 1960 – which was not published until 1976 – was the first study to introduce foreign direct investment into the field of industrial organization. The point of departure for Hymer's analysis was the observation that indigenous firms have advantages over foreign enterprises in the domestic market, because of their better knowledge of the local environment. In order to compete with local firms, foreign enterprises must therefore have some advantages that compensate for the disadvantage of operating in a foreign environment. Furthermore, some market imperfection must also impede the local firms' access to the foreign enterprises' advantages. Thus the theory of perfect competition is not likely to apply in cases where FDI and multinational corporations are present.

Subsequent developments within the industrial organization approach have centred on analyzing the special characteristics that make foreign firms competitive and the nature of the market imperfections surrounding foreign direct investment. Kindleberger (1969) has presented a taxonomy of the monopolistic conditions that induce direct investment, based on departures from perfect competition in goods and factor markets, internal and external economies of scale, and government regulations. Caves (1971) distinguished between horizontal and vertical FDI and emphasized the importance of product differentiation in the first case. The ability to differentiate products, including advertising, and the concomitant skills developed to serve markets, are, in his view, the crucial monopolistic advantages behind horizontal FDI. Other advantages, such as technological expertise derived from investment in research and development (R&D), are expected to be strongly correlated with differentiation capabilities, since the bulk of these investments is directed to the development of new products and the improvement of existing ones. Thus the product differentiation capabilities emphasized by Caves can be seen as both comprising technological intensity and advanced marketing.

Another important step in the development of a theory of the multinational enterprise was taken by the internalization theory, which has an historical antecedent in Coase (1937) and an immediate precedent in the work of McManus (1972). McManus emphasized the role of transaction costs in the development of foreign operations. His analysis recognizes the existence of important interdependences between activities conducted in different countries and the need to coordinate the activities of the interdependent parties. There are three ways in which to coordinate economic agents: (i) decentralized decision-making leading to transactions at arm's length, making use of the price mechanism; (ii) contractual agreements; and (iii) the internalization of transactions within a single institution, through the establishment of an international firm. However, the price mechanism cannot be used without cost. There are transaction costs arising from the need to specify the attributes of the good to be exchanged, or from the difficulties in quantifying the flows of services or assets being exchanged. When the transacted commodity is information (for example, in the form of technological expertise or marketing skills), transaction costs can be expected to be high or perhaps even prohibitive. The multinational corporation, then, arises as a response to market failures, as a way to increase allocative efficiency in the presence of high costs of coordinating economic activity between independent economic agents.

McManus's ideas were further developed by Buckley and Casson (1976), who were the first to give an explicit presentation of the so-called internalization theory. The point of departure of this theory is that different business activities are linked by flows of intermediate products, embracing not only ordinary semi-processed materials, but also knowledge and information in the form of technological expertise and skills embodied in goods and human capital. The theory further postulates that external markets are often inefficient, particularly with regard to transactions in intermediate products that embody firm-specific intangible assets. This is because specification and pricing of these products is particularly difficult. Moreover, external markets in knowledge-intensive products are difficult to organize and usually do not cover the multiple eventualities given rise to by transactions in information. Thus, when appropriate external markets do not exist, or when the costs of operating in them are higher than the benefits, there are incentives for the MNC to develop its own internal organizational structure to achieve internal coordination of activities.

Hence the internalization theory sees the MNC as the outcome of a process in which firms attempt to secure rents from their intangible assets in the presence of market imperfections. The emphasis is no longer, as in earlier theories, on the possession of firm-specific advantages leading to market imperfections; but rather on the nature of markets, their weaknesses and limitations, and the organization of firms as a response to market imperfections.

A further contribution to the theory of the multinational corporation was made by J. H. Dunning (see, for example, Dunning, 1981). Arguing that no single theory could explain the existence of foreign direct investment, he proposed an eclectic approach in order to reconcile the different approaches and hypotheses discussed above. According to Dunning, international production is the outcome of a process in which ownership, internalization and localization advantages work together. The ownership advantages are firm-specific in the sense that the firm has control over them. They embrace patents, expertise, labour skills and other forms of superior production technology, control over markets and trade monopolies, scale advantages, managerial capabilities and so on. These factors determine a firm's competitive position in relation to other firms. The internalization advantages arise from the existence of market imperfections, and have been discussed above. They explain the firm's reluctance to engage in licensing agreements. Location advantages are those associated with the availability of inputs for all firms established in a certain country. They comprise natural resources, location, cultural and political environment, factor prices and transport costs, but also government policies such as trade barriers (quotas, tariffs) and local content requirements. These circumstances explain, for example, why a firm could undertake production abroad instead of producing for export from the home country.

The theories on direct investment and the multinational firm surveyed above focus on the determinants of foreign direct investment. Other aspects related to the behaviour of MNCs have received less attention, at least as far as empirical work is concerned. Yet it is obvious that MNCs will differ in their behaviour, depending on the characteristics of their technologies and products, and the characteristics and policies of their host countries (or, in the terminology of Dunning, depending on differences in ownership, location and internalization factors). Chapters 2 to 7 of this volume examine some of these neglected aspects in detail.

The first serious discussions about the effects of FDI on host countries date back to the late 1950s, when neo-classical economists started to analyze the implications of capital movements in standard models of international trade. Treating foreign investment simply as a capital flow between countries, it was shown that foreign investment and trade could be substitutes for each other and that both were welfare-improving (MacDougall, 1960). The liberal attitude towards FDI during the immediate post-war period was consistent with this theoretical understanding.

The unreservedly positive picture of the impact of FDI on host-country welfare changed dramatically by the end of the 1960s. Academic literature began to emphasize the connection between market imperfections and foreign investment, with focus on market structure issues. In line with Hymer (1960), foreign direct investment was often seen as a result of oligopolistic home-country markets, and it was feared that FDI would spread the market imperfections of the industrialized countries to the rest of the world. The earlier discussions of potential gains from the inflow of foreign capital in terms of tax revenues, economies of scale and external economies gave way to analyses of transfer pricing, uneven development, and 'dependency' in general. Host country governments also began to regulate the operations of foreign multinationals, and many foreign-owned firms, particularly in the primary sector, were nationalized during this period.

With the failure of import substitution in Latin America and Africa, the apparent success of the more outward-orientated Asian NICs, and the debt crisis of the early 1980s, attitudes towards multinationals changed again. More attention was directed to research suggesting that various positive external effects or 'spillovers' of foreign investment were important determinants of the development of host country industry (see Blomström, 1989). The importance of multinational corporations for the international diffusion of technology, as well as their central role in world trade, was emphasized. A general conclusion of this change in focus has been that foreign direct investment is now perceived as being an important determinant of economic growth in developing countries.

However, as we have argued above, there is reason to believe that the positive effects of FDI postulated in much of the recent debate are not automatic, although FDI is connected to *potentially* significant welfare gains. The reason is that the strategies of foreign MNCs – and thereby the effects on the local economy – will differ between host countries and host industries, depending on the local environment. Chapters 8 to 14 of this volume examine effects of FDI on host countries and host country policies in closer detail.

1.2   Outline and brief summary of Part I: firm strategies

Part I is concerned with differences in firm strategies. The first three chapters examine some of the choices facing a company that has decided to establish overseas production. In Chapter 2, we investigate to what extent Swedish multinationals choose majority or minority ownership when they go abroad. The results show that they rely heavily on majority-owned subsidiaries, both in developed and developing countries, and that their involvement in equity sharing is limited. In fact, Swedish firms have a lower proportion of foreign investment held in the form of joint ventures than do multinationals from the USA. This finding is noteworthy. It has been argued that equity sharing of MNCs varies with their national origin, and that multinationals from other (that is, smaller) countries than the USA tend to be more tolerant towards sharing of ownership. Although it is beyond the scope of this chapter to analyze why this is so, our findings indicate that one should look for explanations in the character of activities undertaken by the firms rather than in their nationality. Furthermore, our results suggest that factors such as firm-specific experience and skills, R&D intensity, degree of product differentiation, size of the project, and host country government regulations are of importance in the Swedish multinationals' choice between majority-ownership and joint ventures. In particular, it should be noted that MNCs tend to be unwilling to enter into ownership-sharing arrangements when their foreign operations require them to use their most modern or profitable technologies.

Chapter 3 includes an econometric analysis of the factors that make the MNC accept minority shareholder status in overseas manufacturing ventures. The concept of joint ventures in which MNCs have a minority stake has given rise to (in our opinion) exaggerated expectations of 'technology transfers' from the MNCs to local companies. This kind of presumption has also led to legislation that limits the extent of their ownership and control over local firms. Our econometric tests suggest that companies that are less insistent on majority ownership are often those lacking long production experience abroad and pursuing a strategy of industrial diversification. This, in turn, suggests that the companies that would, because of their experience, be of most interest for the host economies, appear to be the ones that are least interested in minority ownership.

There also seem to be systematic differences between investments in developed and developing countries. In particular, two variables were of interest: market size and the degree of economic development of the host country. The MNCs' propensity to opt for majority control appears to decrease with market size, but only for investments in developed countries. For developing countries, results suggest that the higher the income per capita of the host country the more likely it is that the MNC will insist on majority ownership. This suggests that the less developed – and less familiar – the host country's market, the higher the need for local partners.

In Chapter 4, we try to identify the factors that induce the MNC to enter a new market through the acquisition of an existing firm. This method of entry has been the subject of a heated debate, particularly in developing countries, where local authorities are afraid that acquisitions lead to increased foreign control without providing the benefits in terms of higher employment, investment and productivity expected from foreign greenfield investment. However, little is known about why an MNC would choose to acquire an existing firm rather than set up a new plant. To examine this issue, we use information on the overseas production affiliates of Swedish multinationals established between 1969 and 1978, and try to identify the factors determining whether the MNC will enter a new market by acquiring an existing firm, or through a greenfield investment. The results indicate that the propensity for acquisitions increases significantly with the diversification of the parent company. Rapid growth in the host in the relevant segment of the country's market, on the other hand, appears to be a disincentive for acquisitions. Our results also show that acquisitions have become more common over time. A number of other variables appear to be less important in explaining the choice of acquisitions versus new plants. For example, the size of the host market, two alternative measures of the multinational company's experience in managing foreign subsidiaries, and a measure of stock market conditions were not statistically significant in our models.

In the next three chapters, we turn our interest to various aspects of the behaviour of MNCs' subsidiaries. One such issue is the amount of R&D undertaken in a multinational's foreign subsidiaries. The conventional view is that MNCs undertake most of their R&D at home, with the R&D carried out in subsidiaries being of minor importance. The latter is assumed to consist mainly of applied work, involving product and process modifications. Chapter 5 examines the factors that determine the R&D intensity in the subsidiaries of Swedish multinationals. Since the focus is on R&D in specific parts of international multi-plant companies, the determining factors differ considerably from those for an independent firm. We assume that the R&D intensity in the subsidiaries depends on three categories of variable: characteristics of the multinational; the type of subsidiary; and the host country. The empirical analysis of Swedish multinationals suggests that the subsidiaries' R&D investments are influenced positively by the research intensity and labour skills of the parent company, as well as by the proportion of the parent's R&D expenditures devoted to the development of new products and processes. The size and level of development of the host country also have a significantly positive influence on the subsidiary's R&D investment. Moreover, our results suggest that a high degree of imports from Sweden discourages the subsidiary from undertaking research, while the extent to which the foreign affiliate supplies regional markets has a positive impact on its R&D commitments.

Chapter 6 focuses on an issue that has received considerable attention in recent research on international trade: the existence of international trade flows within one company (intra-firm trade). Part of the interest stems from the fact that this type of trade sustains transfer pricing, a subject of heated debate, particularly in developing countries, where some multinationals have been accused of using the practice to evade restrictions on profit repatriations. To shed further light on the transfer pricing debate, Chapter 6 studies the factors that influence Swedish MNC subsidiaries' imports from their parent companies. The findings suggest that the affiliates' imports from their parents depend on the technological intensity of the traded goods. This appears to confirm one of the basic tenets of the theories about MNCs: that imperfections in the market for information and technology are key factors in explaining the internalization of transactions within a company. The way in which the subsidiary was incorporated into the MNC (for example, by acquisition or through a new venture), and the size of the MNC network to which the subsidiary belongs are other factors that determine the import dependence of the subsidiaries. Our results also indicate that these imports increase with the level of development of the host economy. Thus the subsidiaries located in developing countries are not those with the highest import intensities. Furthermore, a variable introduced in order to capture possible incentives for transfer price manipulation – a proxy for balance of payment deficits – showed inconclusive results.

Chapter 7 examines the reactions of foreign firms in Latin America to the structural adjustment that followed the debt crisis of the 1980s. One distinctive feature of the affiliates of US MNCs in heavily-indebted Latin-American countries was their sharp shift from sales in host country markets to exporting after the debt crisis. The affiliates' exports grew significantly faster than the exports of their host countries, and their export propensities increased faster than the export propensities of their host countries. Thus the MNC affiliates were able to increase their exports and to shift focus from domestic sales towards exports when the local markets became less attractive or more risky as a result of the debt crisis. The results also suggest that multinationals carry a potential to export from production facilities that were largely set up to serve local markets in host countries (that is, those in Latin America), and that these firms are better equipped to convert import-substituting industries to exporting than are local firms.

1.3   Outline and summary of Part II: host country strategies

In analyzing how MNC activities affect host countries it is useful to distinguish between direct and indirect effects of foreign investment. By investing abroad, firms will influence directly macro variables such as capital formation, employment, tax revenues and trade. Indirectly, foreign investment may also influence the structure of the host economy, as well as the conduct and performance of locally-owned firms. Although the direct effects of foreign direct investment may be important in certain situations and/or countries, it is generally accepted that a significant share of the long-run impact of FDI is likely to occur in the form of indirect effects or 'spillover'. This is because FDI, apart from being a financial capital flow, also involves the capitalization of technology, knowledge, skills and other resources that represent the MNCs' intangible assets. Our discussion about host country effects of FDI is therefore focused on the transfer and diffusion of technology – broadly interpreted to include product, process and distribution technology, as well as management skills – from foreign multinationals to their host countries.

Spillovers can occur because MNC affiliates import and demonstrate technologies that are not well known in the host country, and because their operations (or mere presence) may increase the level of competition and force local firms to search for more efficient methods of production. Among many possible channels for technology spillovers, the most concrete may be linkages with foreign MNCs and the hiring of employees trained in MNCs. Chapter 8 provides a detailed survey of the various channels for technology spillovers from FDI. The survey confirms that the nature and significance of spillovers appear to vary between countries and industries, and that the positive effects of FDI are likely to increase with the level of local capability and competition.

As a check of whether spillovers are significant enough to leave a mark on the aggregate performance of host countries, Chapter 9 examines the impact of FDI on productivity growth of Mexican manufacturing industries. The results suggest that the presence of MNCs has acted as a catalyst to Mexican productivity growth, and speeded up the convergence process between Mexico and the USA. However, the chapter also concludes that it may not be possible to generalize this result to all other countries. In particular, there may be no spillovers to host countries that lack the technical skills needed to respond to the foreign challenge.

Chapter 10 investigates technology spillovers in various Mexican manufacturing industries, and tries to determine whether differences in observed spillovers are related to the technology gap between foreign MNCs and local firms. The conclusion of the chapter is that factors related to technology *alone* are not likely to inhibit spillovers, but that large technology differences and large foreign market shares *together* appear to mark sectors where spillovers are absent or particularly small. Chapter 11, focusing on detailed plant-level data for the Uruguayan manufacturing sector, comes to a slightly different conclusion. There, spillovers appear to be present only in plants with moderate technology gaps *vis-à-vis* foreign firms, but not in the group of local plants facing large technology gaps.

The focus of Chapter 12 is on the role of competition as a determinant of spillovers. The chapter tests two hypotheses about relations between foreign and domestic firms: first, that the productivities of foreign and domestic firms are determined simultaneously because of competition; and, second, that competition from foreign MNCs has a spillover effect on the productivity of local firms. The results support both hypotheses, but only after the exclusion of suspected 'enclave' industries, where foreign operate in isolation from local competitors. The policy conclusion suggested in the chapter is that host countries should pay more attention to the competitive environment in industries where foreign MNCs operate.

The last two chapters examine the determinants of the MNC affiliates' technology imports, which define the maximum potential for technology spillovers to local firms. In Chapter 13, we examine the behaviour of US affiliates in thirty-three host countries, while Chapter 14 looks at all foreign firms in 144 Mexican manufacturing industries. In spite of significant differences in data and variables, both chapters reach very similar conclusions. The technology imports of MNC affiliates consistently seem to increase with various proxies for the competitive pressure and the level of education in the host market. However, technology transfer requirements do not appear to have any positive impact on the affiliates' technology imports. The policy conclusions suggested by these findings are that government policies aiming to create a competitive climate and improve labour quality are relevant alternatives to formal technology transfer requirements. Policies focusing on the environment in which foreign firms operate may, in other words, sometimes be preferable to regulations focusing directly on the MNCs.

Part I
Firm Strategies

2
Modes of International Investment

2.1 Introduction

The role of technical progress as a key to economic growth is widely recognized today. New technologies can be developed domestically through investments in research and development (R&D), they can be imported in various ways from abroad, or generated through some combination of the two. Since R&D activities are normally very costly, many countries rely heavily on imports of modern technology from abroad. In most cases they must turn to multinational corporations, who have become the most important actors in the generation of technology.

Multinationals have traditionally exploited their technologies overseas by creating or acquiring foreign affiliates (foreign direct investment). The pros and cons for the host countries of such arrangements have been widely discussed (see, for example, Blomström, 1989). Over the years, however, this traditional form of technology diffusion has tended to give way to more complex business arrangements, in which the costs and benefits of the venture are shared between the foreign firm and the host country. In many cases, countries have forced the MNCs into such arrangements with the intention of speeding up the rate of technology diffusion. By forcing the multinationals to 'unbundle the package' of inputs that they bring to the host country, it is believed that the host country can enable local firms to gain access to these inputs without the traditional foreign investment.

The effects of policies like this are still, however, comparatively little known. For example, would a tighter control of technology transfer lower its costs, or would it also reduce the inflow of advanced techniques? Are the various channels of technology transfer equally effective and rapid? This chapter attempts to add to the sum of knowledge in this field of research by examining what determines the willingness of multinationals to accept equity-sharing in their foreign affiliates. The chapter explores the forms of international activities

15

undertaken by Swedish firms and suggests some explanations as to why firms use different forms of investment when they go abroad.[1] It concentrates on two organizational choices – majority- and minority-ownership – and adds a few observations on non-equity forms of involvement.

The chapter is organized in the following way. The next section gives a short theoretical discussion on why firms choose different organizational forms when they go abroad. Section 3 presents Sweden's foreign investment activities. Section 4 examines to what extent Swedish multinationals choose joint-venture agreements abroad and provides some hypotheses regarding the determinants of this choice. Finally, Section 5 concludes the study.

2.2 The analytical framework

Theory suggests that foreign direct investment and multinational corporations arise because of shortcomings in arm's-length markets for intangible assets (see Caves, 1996). These assets can be found in knowledge, technology, organization, and managerial and marketing skills. Given that a firm possesses some intangible asset, and that it has decided to exploit it by foreign production,[2] there are several ways to do so. We may think of three such stylized modes for organizing the activity: subsidiary production; joint ventures;[3] and licensing agreements. The first two involve varying degrees of equity participation, while the third implies arm's-length transactions in the market for technology and other skills.

The three organizational forms or modes of technology transfer represent different advantages and disadvantages for a firm. If production is internalized in a subsidiary, firms may keep more rents from their intangibles than if they choose some other form. On the other hand, there are normally differences in costs associated with the alternatives. Set-up costs, for example, are involved in subsidiary production, but not in licensing activities.

A useful model of the determinants of the firm's organizational choice is given in Teece (1982). There, the choice between affiliates, joint ventures, and licensing is assumed to depend on transaction cost issues (abstracting from the host country's policy), and the principal determinants of these costs are the degree to which the technological know-how (that is, the intangible asset) involved is proprietary, complex and tactical, and the frequency of contemplated transfers. Frequency matters, since set-up costs are involved in subsidiary production, and these can be spread over a large number of transfers.

An illustration of Teece's reasoning is given in Figure 2.1. The position of the 'indifference curves' in that figure will depend on country factors such as attitudes towards foreign ownership in the host country. Hostility, for example, would tend to move the schedules away from the origin. Thus, a firm's organizational choice is located along a continuum, where the relative advantages and disadvantages of subsidiary production, joint ventures, and non-equity participation determine where one stops and the other starts. This approach suggests several important determinants of the level of equity ownership in the foreign affiliates.

The nature of the multinationals' intangible assets seems to be such a determinant, since these assets enable firms to operate efficiently in foreign countries where local firms have various advantages (such as superior knowledge of consumer and factor markets). However, different kinds of asset are likely to motivate different organizational choices. For example, technology-orientated multinationals can be expected to be relatively unwilling to share information, and to insist on full control or majority-ownership of their foreign affiliates in order to limit the diffusion or spillover of their proprietary knowledge.

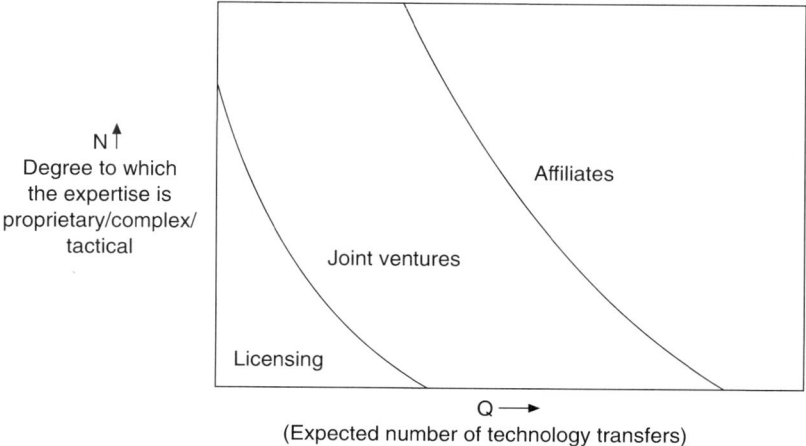

Figure 2.1.   Determining coefficient boundaries for horizontal foreign direct investment

Source: Teece, 1982.

Multinationals with a lot of experience of foreign operations are also likely to exploit their rent-yielding assets by internalizing their production abroad. 'Learning by doing' occurs in international technology transfers, in the sense that the transfer costs decrease with the number of transfers (see Teece, 1982). Furthermore, uncertainty levels decline as the firms become more familiar with international operations in general, and with their individual markets in particular (Davidson, 1980). This reduction should affect decisions regarding organizational choices.

On the other hand, there are several factors that might encourage multinationals to seek out joint ventures. For example, the economic environment may be unfamiliar to the multinational firm and it may therefore find it advantageous to take on a host country firm as a partner. A local firm may bring the joint venture some intangible assets of its own, such as knowledge of local marketing and production conditions.

Another reason for equity sharing and non-equity forms of involvement has to do with risk aversion. If a project is risky, the multinational may wish to shift some of the risks to firms in the host country, or to other multinationals. The same argument holds when the project is large in relation to the investing firm, which is particularly common in extractive industries. Therefore, equity sharing can be expected when foreign projects are large or risky.

Some characteristics of the host country may also influence the forms of international activity undertaken by the multinationals, one of them being the size of the host country market. It may be difficult for a multinational firm to enter a large foreign market on its own, if such an investment requires many resources for local sales networks, after-sales services and so on. This should be of particular importance if the MNC is based in a small country such as Sweden, because we know that Swedish firms are typically smaller when they venture abroad for the first time than are firms from, for example, the USA (Swedenborg, 1979). Thus we expect that joint ventures become more prevalent as multinationals establish presence in larger host countries, all other things being equal.

Furthermore, the willingness of MNCs to seek joint ventures should be influenced by the extent to which the host country can provide specific resources that are of interest to the multinationals. The higher the income level of the host country, the more likely that the local partner possesses technology, capital and knowledge about local marketing.

Finally, host government policy should make local equity participation relatively more common in developing countries than it
otherwise would have been, since the demand for local equity
participation is more common there. The same is true for certain
industries.

In sum, the choice between different forms of foreign involvement
by multinationals is expected to depend on a number of identifiable
firm, industry and country characteristics. Before analyzing such characteristics in order to suggest some explanations as to why Swedish
firms use different organizational forms abroad, a short description of
Sweden's foreign investment activities is warranted.

2.3   International investment by Swedish firms

Sweden is a small, highly industrialized country that has relied heavily
on international exchange for its economic development. More than
30 per cent of the country's GNP, and half of the production of manufactured goods, is exported. Despite the small size of the country (no
more than 3.5 per cent of the US population or income), Sweden
ranks as the seventeenth largest international trader in the world, with
about 1.5 per cent of total world trade.

In relation to the size of the economy, Sweden is also a significant
foreign investor, ranking as the world's tenth largest foreign investor
in absolute terms and as the fifth most multinational country, if foreign
investment is related to GNP. The rank would be even higher if the
comparison was limited to the manufacturing sector, since foreign
investment by Swedish multinationals is heavily concentrated to that
sector.[4]

Although international investment by Swedish firms has a long
history,[5] Sweden's position as a relatively sizeable net foreign investor
has been accentuated strongly only during the last few decades.
This investment activity can be traced back to two main factors
(Swedenborg, 1985). First, as an industrialized, high-income country,
Sweden is relatively well endowed with capital, especially 'human
capital'. Its industry is therefore technologically advanced, and
technological expertise is an important factor underlying the foreign
investment process.

Second, the small size of the Swedish market forces Swedish firms
to export at an early stage of growth in order to reap economies of
large-scale production. It also compels them to produce abroad, when

Firm Strategies

that is the more profitable way of serving foreign markets, to reap economies of large firm size (economies of firm size are related to the large fixed cost of investment in R&D, advertising, and sales and distribution networks). Thus small Swedish firms are more export-orientated and more likely to invest abroad than are, for example, US firms of comparable size (Swedenborg, 1979).

As shown in Table 2.1, Swedish manufacturing production abroad is concentrated in a few industries, of which the two machinery industries are by far the most important. In 1994, the latest year for which data are available, these activities accounted for 32 per cent and 20 per cent, respectively. The chemical industry decreased somewhat in importance during the 1970s, but has recovered since then.

Although over 200 Swedish companies have wholly-owned manufacturing subsidiaries abroad, a few (large) firms dominate foreign investment activity. About two-thirds of Swedish production and employment abroad originate from twenty companies (among them Volvo, Scania, SKF, Ericsson, Electrolux and Astra). Most of these firms produce high-grade goods for international markets where quality is more important than price.

Table 2.2 shows that Swedish foreign investment is heavily concentrated in the developed countries. Given the types of product produced by the Swedish multinationals, this is not surprising. Cost advantages in production are seldom the reason for foreign

Table 2.1   Employment in Swedish majority-owned manufacturing affiliates abroad, 1965–94, by industry (%)

Industry	1965	1974	1978	1986	1994
	0.4	0.7	1.0	1.5	2.8
Textiles	0.5	2.6	2.0	1.0	0.3
Pulp and paper	1.1	2.9	3.8	2.6	8.1
Paper products	1.0	3.0	5.4	8.0	4.6
Chemicals	16.3	10.5	7.5	11.1	10.9
Metals	7.8	11.3	12.5	8.8	9.7
Non-electrical machinery	49.0	34.1	34.1	34.1	31.7
Electrical machinery	17.8	23.7	21.4	21.6	19.9
Transport equipment	2.0	5.1	8.0	6.9	7.7
Other manufacturing	4.1	6.1	4.3	4.4	4.3
Total manufacturing	**100**	**100**	**100**	**100**	**100**

Source: Braunerhjelm and Ekholm (1998).

production by Swedish firms (Blomström and Kokko, 1997). More often, their foreign investment is made to circumvent transportation costs, tariffs and various regulations in the host countries. Outside the developed countries, Latin America is the region where Swedish industry has concentrated most of its efforts. Before the 1960s, Latin America was an important export market for Swedish industry. But when the import-substitution era began, these markets were largely lost and many Swedish firms chose to start subsidiary production instead. This partly explains the rapid increase in the importance of Latin America as a host region for Swedish foreign investment between 1965 and 1978.

Swedish multinationals have so far had relatively little interest in Asia, with India being the exception. However, with the numerous foreign exchange regulation acts in India, overall Swedish investment there has declined markedly. On the other hand, this has been partly compensated by a growing interest in the Asian newly industrialising countries (NICs). The modest foreign investment in Africa is because of the relative backwardness of the countries in this region. Africa provides neither geographical advantages nor markets big enough to attract Swedish multinationals (except for a few Swedish projects in the extractive sector).

2.4 Majority versus minority ownership

Traditionally, Swedish MNCs have relied heavily on majority-owned subsidiaries (see Table 2.3). In 1965, 89 per cent of the manufacturing

Table 2.2   Employment in Swedish majority-owned manufacturing affiliates abroad, 1965–94, by region

	1965	1974	1978	1986	1994
Developed countries	120196	175375	182112	214927	232539
Developing countries	27096	45736	45037	44894	33474
of which:					
Africa	574	612	156	491	957
Asia	13565	15590	5907	13222	13089
Latin America	12957	29534	38974	31181	19428
All countries	**147292**	**221111**	**227149**	**259821**	**266013**

Source: Braunerhjelm and Ekholm (1998).

Firm Strategies

Table 2.3   Number of Swedish joint ventures as a percentage of all manufacturing associates, 1974 and 1978, by industry

Industry	1974	1978
Food	n.a.	11
Textiles	n.a.	4
Pulp and paper	29	47
Paper products	13	20
Chemicals	8	7
Metals	15	10
Non-electrical machinery	12	19
Electrical machinery	14	24
Transport equipment	12	12
Other manufacturing	12	12
Total manufacturing	19	18

Source: Unpublished IUI surveys.

affiliates abroad were majority-owned. Between 1965 and 1974, joint ventures grew in importance, and by 1974 they made up 19 per cent of the total number of affiliates. However, between 1974 and 1978 this share remained roughly the same. The employment figures seem to follow the same route, although here the data are more shaky.[6]

Swedish multinationals have, in fact, a lower proportion of foreign investment in the form of joint ventures than have US multinationals (see Lipsey, 1984, for comparable US figures). This contradicts the notion that the large US firms are the least tolerant to sharing ownership, but the reason for this difference may be that US firms have a higher overall propensity than Swedish firms to invest in industries and countries where equity sharing is more common (resource extraction and LDCs).

Industry, firm and country determinants

Table 2.3 also shows the relative importance of joint ventures, as measured by number of firms, in different industries. Apparently, equity sharing is most common in the pulp and paper and electrical machinery industries. The pulp and paper industry is characterized by large investment requirements and economies of scale in production. This tends to make joint ventures the preferred mode of foreign investment.

The story behind the electrical machinery industry is different. Joint ventures in this industry emanate mainly from two large firms. There is a simple and straightforward explanation for the relatively large minority interests only in the case of one of them; namely, a large MNC in the telecommunications industry. It is clear that this firm has abandoned majority control in its foreign affiliates only when it has been pressured to do so by host country policy. This firm accounted for some 20 per cent of joint venture employment in the industry in 1974, but as much as 80 per cent in 1978.

In the food industry, as well as in chemicals (which includes pharmaceuticals) and textiles, joint ventures are rare. In food and chemicals, firms rely heavily on product differentiation, and the arguments that explain why firms are intolerant of joint venture agreements may also explain why they use subsidiaries instead of arm's-length contracts: the internalization of economic activities within the firm is the most efficient mode for organizing the specific economic activity. The reason why Swedish companies hold such high fractions of equity in the textile industry is probably that the foreign affiliates are largely export-orientated to the Swedish market, and that Swedish MNCs in this industry are mainly located in relatively 'familiar' countries, such as Finland.

In the non-electrical machinery industry, which is by far the biggest Swedish foreign investor, firms are relatively disinclined towards ownership sharing. There are several reasons for this. The first has to do with the nature of the intangible assets controlled by the firms. The competitive advantage of Swedish MNCs in this industry is strongly related to continuous R&D by the parent companies, and we expect that the more technologically-orientated a firm, the less the willingness to share information, and thus the greater the insistence on control. Second, firm-specific advantages are often based on learning-by-doing that is not easily dissociated from the overall management of the firm. It is specific to each firm. A final reason why there is less need for equity-sharing in the Swedish non-electrical machinery industry is that each subsidiary is small relative to the size of the parents. Thus, the parents can afford to support the investment.

Table 2.4 shows the relative importance of joint ventures for Swedish firms in 1974 and 1978 in different regions. Evidently, equity sharing is more common in LDCs than in developed countries, although Swedish parent companies are relatively reluctant to share ownership of affiliates in the LDCs as well. However, it can be seen that there was no general trend towards equity-sharing in developing

Table 2.4 Number of Swedish joint ventures as a percentage of all manufacturing associates, 1974 and 1978, by country

	1974	1978
Developed countries	17 (486)	14 (567)
EEC	13 (261)	11 (306)
EFTA	13 (107)	16 (114)
North America	19 (48)	15 (68)
Developing countries	28 (109)	27 (132)
Africa	62 (8)	71 (7)
Asia	38 (26)	39 (34)
India	33 (12)	64 (11)
Thailand	0 (1)	0 (2)
Philippines	0 (1)	0 (2)
Malaysia	50 (2)	40 (5)
Hong Kong	0 (0)	0 (2)
Singapore	0 (2)	0 (3)
Latin America	20 (75)	14 (91)
Argentina	10 (10)	0 (12)
Brazil	23 (31)	21 (38)
Colombia	37 (8)	25 (8)
Mexico	20 (15)	21 (14)
Peru	25 (4)	0 (4)
Rest of Latin America	0 (7)	0 (15)
All countries	19 (595)	18 (699)

Note: Total number of manufacturing affiliates in parentheses.
Source: IUI surveys.

countries between 1974 and 1978, despite the pressure in this direction from many host country governments. In Latin America, for instance, where this pressure has been strong, the proportion of joint ventures fell from 20 per cent to 14 per cent. On the other hand, the efforts by the Indian government to gain equity shares in foreign (including Swedish) affiliates seem to have had some success. This has been at the expense of the overall volume of foreign investment, however. India's share of Swedish foreign investment has declined markedly.

Another factor that may be of importance in this context is the geographical and 'cultural' distance between Sweden and the developing countries. Swedish multinationals are, in general, more likely to choose majority ownership in European countries, where they have more experience and a better knowledge of local conditions, than elsewhere. Distance increases communication and transaction costs, and it seems that joint ventures become more prevalent as MNCs look towards more unfamiliar countries.

However, the high proportion of joint ventures in India and Latin America, compared to more liberal developing countries, may not only be a result of host country policies. Another explanation is found in the activities undertaken by foreign subsidiaries. It has been shown that MNCs hold significantly higher fractions of equity in export-orientated subsidiaries than in local-market-orientated ones (Blomström, 1990). This difference arises partly from public policy, and partly from the multinationals' own preferences. If a project aims at serving the host country market, a local firm with some capacity or competence to make the investment succeed may serve as a useful ally. On the other hand, if a subsidiary is export-orientated and produces components for the parent or other affiliates, we can expect resistance to joint-venture agreements.

The high proportion of joint ventures in Africa could possibly be traced to the fact that the few Swedish firms there are involved to a large extent in large projects in the extractive industry. Both because of local requirements and because of the risks involved in such projects, we expect MNCs to seek equity-sharing. However, given our data, we are not in a position to say with whom the Swedish firms share equity. It may be the case that the partners they seek are primarily other MNCs, and not host country firms.

In Table 2.5, the proportion of joint-venture agreements is calculated both in terms of the number of ventures and employment. If we define the size of a firm in terms of employment, this table shows that the joint ventures tend to involve larger projects than the majority-owned affiliates. Table 2.5 also shows similar figures for the twenty largest Swedish companies with manufacturing activities abroad in 1974. For these large firms, which in general are the oldest and most experienced ones, the joint ventures tend to involve more equally-sized projects. This suggests that small and medium-sized Swedish multinationals tend to be more tolerant towards equity-sharing than the larger enterprises when the size of the projects increases. While the bigger Swedish MNCs are able to handle large projects on their own, the smaller ones are not, mainly because of their limited financial and managerial resource base.

Table 2.5   Swedish joint ventures in different countries, 1974

	Number of joint ventures as percentage of all manufacturing affiliates		Employment in joint ventures as percentage of total employment in manufacturing affiliates	
	All MNCs	**20 firms**	**All MNCs**	**20 firms**
Developed countries	17	21	25	26
EEC	13	14	24	24
EFTA	13	29	42	53
North America	19	23	6	5
Developing countries	28	40	27	29
Africa	62	78	88	97
Asia	38	38	16	26
India	33	20	8	8
Malaysia	25	0	30	0
Latin America	20	35	24	23
Brazil	23	23	27	27
Colombia	37	50	43	20
Mexico	20	20	21	20
All countries	19	26	25	27

Source: IUI surveys.

In sum, our findings suggest that Swedish parent companies are reluctant to share ownership in affiliates. In fact, Swedish MNCs have a lower proportion of investment in joint ventures than have multinationals from the USA, although the latter are relatively larger. Our findings also suggest five factors that influence the multinationals' choice of sharing ownership:

(i)   *Experience and knowledge within the firm*   Firms lacking experience and knowledge of foreign production, or of production in a specific market, may seek a joint venture instead of starting up alone.

(ii)   *Research intensity*   The more technologically-orientated a firm is, the smaller the willingness to share information and the greater the insistence on control and ownership.

(iii)   *Product differentiation*   Firms relying heavily on advertising and ownership advantages in their marketing operations are also reluctant to share information and try to avoid equity sharing.

(iv) *Size of the project* The larger and riskier the project, the more tolerance there is towards equity sharing.

(v) *Government regulations* Governments may force the MNCs into joint-venture agreements.

Bearing in mind the reluctance of Swedish multinationals to share ownership in foreign affiliates, it is not surprising to find that they are also very little involved in non-equity forms of technology transfer (such as licensing agreements, technical-assistance contracts, management contracts, turnkey agreements, and franchising). We expect the same factors making a firm intolerant towards equity-sharing to be important also in the decision-making in non-equity forms of arrangement. Swedish MNCs' income from sales of licences, patents, "know-how" and management contracts was only SEK 557 million in 1978, and most of this came from their majority-owned affiliates abroad (Swedenborg, 1982).

2.4 Concluding remarks

This chapter has investigated to what extent Swedish multinationals choose majority or minority ownership when they expand abroad. The results show that they rely heavily on majority-owned subsidiaries, in both developed and developing countries, and that they are only to a small extent involved in equity sharing. In fact, Swedish firms have a lower proportion of foreign investment held in the form of joint ventures than have multinationals from the USA. This finding is noteworthy. It has been argued that equity sharing of MNCs varies with their national origin, and that multinationals from other (that is, smaller) countries than the USA tend to be more tolerant towards the sharing of ownership. Although it is beyond the scope of this chapter to analyze why this is so, our finding indicates that one should look for explanations in the differences in activities undertaken by the firms rather than in the nationality of the firms.

We have also tried to identify some factors that are of importance in the Swedish multinationals' choice between majority ownership and joint ventures. Our results suggest the following five factors to have at least some influence:

(i)   Experience and knowledge within the MNCs.
(ii)   Research intensity.
(iii) Product differentiation.
(iv)   Size of the project.
(v)   Host country government regulations.

These findings do not allow any definitive policy conclusions for host countries, but a few speculative comments on the policy implications of the study seem to be in order.

Many countries try to force multinational corporations into joint ventures or licensing agreements on the assumption that they will obtain access to foreign technology without the traditional involvement of direct investment. However, our findings suggest that MNCs will not give away their most important intangible assets under such conditions. In particular, it seems that it is not possible to obtain the more advanced technologies through means other than foreign direct investment in subsidiary production. For less advanced technologies, however, there certainly seem to exist alternative transfer modes to the traditional foreign direct investment. That does not mean, however, that governments should force multinationals into such alternative arrangements, since neither the costs nor the benefits for host countries of the alternative channels of technology transfer have been studied in detail. It is clear that much research remains to be done in this area.

Notes

1.   In this study we use the data on Swedish multinationals that have been collected by the Research Institute of Industrial Economics (IUI) in Sweden. The IUI surveys are unique in that there exists no comparable information on MNCs from other countries. The surveys contain much more detailed information on majority-owned foreign manufacturing affiliates than on other affiliates. Still, they cover enough information on joint ventures, particularly for 1974, for the purposes of this paper. For a presentation of the data, see Andersson *et al.* (1996) or Braunerhjelm and Ekholm (1998).
2.   We exclude the possibility of producing at home for export, since we are not interested in that case here.
3.   A joint venture or minority-owned affiliate refers to a subsidiary in which the parent company's equity share is 50 per cent or less.
4.   The reason why foreign investment in extractive industries is so modest may be that Sweden is rich in raw materials and it has no colonial ties. Multinationals in extractive industries generally originate from countries lacking a specific raw material and/or from former colonial powers.

5. The earliest Swedish direct investment was carried out in the USA by Alfa Laval in 1883.
6. The availability of data explains why we are not going beyond 1978 in this section. The employment figures are available for 79 per cent of the joint ventures in 1974, but only for 37 per cent in 1978. In order to correct for this, the number of employees in 1978 has been increased by 14 300. This was the number of employees in 1974 in the firms that gave information for that year, but not for 1978. Because of this manipulation, the data for 1974 are more reliable than those for 1978.

3
Why Do Multinationals Seek Out Joint Ventures?

3.1 Introduction

Over the years, we have witnessed an increasing desire in a number of developing countries to exercise greater control over the activities of multinational corporations. Many countries have started to frame the environment within which these firms operate and have introduced various performance requirements for their behaviour. Special attention has been given to policies regarding the transfer of technology. A number of measures intended to encourage multinational firms to transfer more technology have been introduced over the years, including requirements for a certain degree of local participation in the ownership of the MNCs' affiliates. By forcing the multinationals to 'unbundle the package' of inputs they bring to the host country, it is believed that a host country can enable local firms to obtain access to these inputs without the traditional direct investment.

Before conclusions about such effects can be drawn, however, one has to know the costs of the 'unpacking'. For example, policies aimed at forcing multinationals into joint-venture agreements may impede the inflow of advanced technologies, since firms may choose not to invest rather than to accept local equity participation. In this chapter, we take a first step towards understanding these costs by analyzing the characteristics of multinational firms that insist on majority-ownership of their foreign affiliates, and the characteristics of those that do not. We thus focus on the determinants of the different patterns of ownership of foreign affiliates of MNCs and ask why multinational firms seek out joint ventures.

Previous studies of the strategy alternatives for potential multinational firms have focused mainly on why a company would choose to become multinational rather than exploiting its firm-specific advantages by exporting (see Caves, 1996, for a review). However, given that a firm has decided to invest abroad, it can do so with varying degrees of equity participation. The main investment alternatives are majority-owned affiliates and minority participation or joint ventures. These alternatives offer different advantages and disadvantages for the MNCs, and the question is why they choose one over the other.

There have been only a few empirical analyses of this issue using comprehensive, quantitative, firm-level data. Apart from a few case studies, from which generalizations are dangerous, the regression analyses are either based on small samples of firms (Stopford and Wells, 1972; Fagre and Wells, 1982) or on small samples of host (developing) countries (Lecraw, 1984). Furthermore, none of these studies uses quantitative data for some of the most important explanatory variables. D. J. Lecraw, for example, uses a subjective ranking, as perceived by the affiliates' managers, for the 'technological leadership' of parent companies and for the 'attractiveness' of host countries.

This study uses unique data covering almost the entire population of Swedish manufacturing firms operating abroad in 1974. The data distinguish between majority- and minority-owned foreign affiliates, and we focus on the Swedish MNCs' choice between these two investment alternatives.[1] With these data, it is possible to describe the firms' behaviour analytically, using a model of dichotomous choice. The parameters of such a model, estimated using the maximum likelihood technique, help to distinguish the characteristics of firms that insist on majority ownership of their foreign affiliates from those of firms that do not, and thus to shed light on the potential benefits for the host developing countries of various forms of foreign investment.

The next section provides the theoretical framework for the study. In the third section the data and the statistical model are described. The fourth section presents the empirical results, and the fifth section concludes.

3.2   Theoretical framework

Theory suggests that in order to compete successfully in a foreign market, a firm must possess some ownership-specific assets in knowledge, technology, organization, managerial and marketing skills. A firm blessed with such assets enjoys several possible ways (apart from exporting) to claim the rents that they will yield in foreign markets, including subsidiary production, joint ventures, licensing, franchising, management contracts, marketing contracts, and turnkey contracts. Of these, subsidiary production and joint-ventures involve varying degrees of equity participation, while the others represent arm's-length transactions in the market for technologies and other skills.

Technology and similar rent-yielding assets can usually be transferred more efficiently and more cheaply within a firm than between independent firms. In fact, multinational firms often find it very difficult, sometimes impossible, to earn the same rent on their intangibles in foreign markets in forms other than through the establishment of an affiliate abroad. However, affiliate production is not without cost. It involves the commitment of both capital and managerial resources, the costs of which must, of course, be considered by the firm in its choice of how to exploit a foreign market.

According to Caves (1996), a firm's organizational choice is located along a continuum, where the relative advantages and disadvantages of subsidiary production, joint ventures, and non-equity participation determine where one stops and the other starts. This approach suggests several important determinants of the level of equity ownership in the foreign affiliates.

The nature of the multinationals' intangible assets seems to be an important aspect, since such assets enable firms to operate efficiently in foreign countries where local firms have certain advantages (such as knowledge of consumer and factor markets). In order to limit the diffusion or 'spillover' of such intangible assets, we expect technology- and marketing-orientated multinationals to be more unwilling to share information, and to insist on full control or majority-ownership of their foreign affiliates, since both product and process technologies are generally considered to be important intangible assets.

Multinationals with a lot of experience in foreign operations are also likely to exploit their rent-yielding assets by internalizing their production abroad. 'Learning-by-doing' occurs in international technology transfers, in the sense that the transfer costs decrease with the number of transfers (see Teece, 1976). Furthermore, uncertainty levels decline as the firms become more familiar with international operations in general, and with their individual markets in particular (Davidson, 1980). This reduction should affect decisions regarding organizational choices.

On the other hand, there are several factors that might encourage multinationals to seek out joint ventures. For example, the economic environment may be unfamiliar to the multinational firm and it may therefore find it advantageous to take on a host country firm as a partner. A local firm may bring the joint venture some intangible assets of its own, such as a knowledge of local marketing and production conditions. In that way, MNCs might economize on the information requirements of foreign direct investment (Beamish, 1988).

Another reason for equity sharing and non-equity forms of involvement has to do with risk aversion. If a project is risky – which many projects in developing countries undoubtedly are – the multinational may wish to shift some of the risks to firms in the host country, or to other multinationals. The same argument holds when the project is large in relation to the investing firm, something that is particularly common in extractive industries. Equity sharing can therefore be expected when foreign projects are large or risky. Minority ownership is also more likely when the subsidiary's output is diversified from the parent's (Stopford and Wells, 1972).

Finally, some characteristics of the host country may influence the forms of international activities undertaken by the multinationals, one of them being the size of the host country market. It may be difficult for a multinational firm to enter a large foreign market on its own, if such an investment requires a lot of resources for local sales networks, after-sales services and so on. This should be of particular importance if the MNC is based in a small country such as Sweden, because we know that Swedish firms are typically smaller when they venture abroad for the first time than are firms from, for example, the USA (Swedenborg, 1979). Thus we expect that joint ventures become more prevalent as multinationals proceed towards larger host countries, all other things being equal.

The willingness of MNCs to seek joint ventures should also be influenced by the extent to which the host country can provide specific resources that are of interest to the multinationals. The higher the income level of the host country, the more likely that the local partner possesses technology, capital and knowledge about local marketing.

3.3 Data and statistical model

The data for this study come from the Research Institute of Industrial Economics (IUI) of Stockholm, supplemented by official GDP and GNP per-capita figures from the United Nations. The IUI has completed seven surveys of Swedish multinationals (1965, 1970, 1974, 1978, 1986, 1990 and 1994), which cover virtually all Swedish manufacturing firms operating abroad. We used the 1974 survey, mainly because it offers much more detail on the minority-owned affiliates than do the other surveys. Another reason for going back to the early 1970s is that many host countries (particularly developing countries) had not at that time begun to demand local equity participation.[2] Thus the 1974 survey is better suited to our purposes, which are to isolate the factors causing firms to seek out joint ventures.

In the data, it can be observed whether or not the foreign affiliates are majority-owned. Labelling this characteristic as 1 in the case of a majority-owned affiliate, and 0 otherwise, we obtain a dichotomous dependent variable which requires an appropriate statistical technique.

We postulate the existence of a continuous variable $y*$, linearly dependent on a vector of explanatory variables X – corresponding to a set of parent company, affiliate and host country attributes – and a vector of parameters β. That is:

$$y* = X'\beta$$

The variable $y*$ could be interpreted as an index of the utility that majority ownership generates to the parent company. When the index is positive, the parent chooses a majority ownership strategy.

We cannot observe $y*$, but we assume that there is a certain threshold value (we can assume this threshold to be zero without loss of generality), such that $y*$ is greater than this threshold value for majority-owned subsidiaries.

On the other hand, we do observe the outcome of this process, that is, if a subsidiary is majority-owned or not. Labelling the event 'majority-owned' with 1 and 'minority-owned' with 0, we get a proxy variable for $y*$. We assume that the probability of a given subsidiary to be majority-owned is given by:

$$p(y* > 0) = p(y = 1) = F(X'\beta)$$

where (F) is the standard normal cumulative distribution function. This case is known as the *probit model*, and maximum likelihood estimates can easily be computed.

The explanatory variables for the model were suggested in the previous section. They are:

R&D   = R&D expenditure as a percentage of sales for the parent firm. We expect technologically-orientated multinationals to insist on control, and thus the probability of majority-ownership increasing with R&D expenditure.[3]

AGE = The age of a multinational firm's oldest foreign manufacturing affiliate (in log), as a measure of 'experience' of producing abroad.[4] The more experience a firm has of foreign production, the less tolerant we expect it to be towards equity sharing.[5]

DIV = A dummy variable taking the value 1 if an affiliate belongs to a different 2-digit industry from its parent company's principal one, and 0 otherwise. If an affiliate's output is in a different industry from the parent's, minority-ownership is expected to be more likely.

MIX = 1 minus a Herfindahl index of the distribution (over 6-digit industries) of a firm's industrial activities, as calculated by Swedenborg (1979).[6] MIX equals 0 if a firm produces only one product, and 1 if it produces an endless number of products. A high value of this index is thus supposed to reflect a high degree of product differentiation, which in turn is expected to result in more tolerance towards minority ownership.

SIZE = The size of the parent firm, measured by its world-wide sales. We expect larger firms to be able to take higher risks in the form of majority-owned subsidiaries.

GDP = Host countries' GDP in 1974, as a measure of market size. The larger the host country market, the more resources needed for a successful entry. Thus we expect the likelihood of minority-ownership to increase with the size of the market.

GNPC = Host countries' GNP per capita in 1974, as a measure of income level. The sign of this coefficient, however, cannot be determined a priori. On the one hand, the income level might capture the extent to which host country firms can bring a joint venture certain intangible assets of their own. If that is the case, we expect the probability for joint venture agreements to increase with the level of income in the host country.[7] On the other hand, the demand pattern in countries with higher *GNPC* can be expected to be more similar to that of Sweden, which decreases the need for the contribution of a local partner. This would imply a positive sign for *GNPC*.

3.4 The empirical results

The probit model was estimated, using the maximum likelihood method, first with data on the fifty host countries of Swedish MNCs, and then for the twenty-three developed and twenty-seven developing countries, separately. The reason for the separation of the data is that the status of being a developed country may have some meaning beyond per capita income (for example, the investment risks may be lower). The main findings from these .estimations are shown in Tables 3.1 and 3.2 (see Appendix) for correlation matrices.

The results seem to confirm most of our prior expectations regarding the determinants of the patterns of ownership of the MNC affiliates. The importance of capacity and competence as an underlying reason for joint venture agreements is certainly suggested by the performance of the variables *AGE, MIX* and *DIV*. The *AGE* variable consistently performed well, with the expected positive sign. In other words, firms that have been in international business for a long time seem to become more experienced and interested in exploiting their rent-yielding assets in majority-owned affiliates. The variables *MIX* and *DIV* had, as expected, negative signs in front of their coefficients, although these were not always significantly different from zero. Still, the result suggests that MNCs that are diversifying in product (*MIX*) seem to find it advantageous to take on a domestic firm as a partner. A similar situation arises if an affiliate's output is diversified from the parent's (*DIV*). In both these cases, the parent may lack the capacity or competence for majority ownership of foreign affiliates.

The same argument should, of course, hold for the size variable as well.[8] We expect larger parent companies to have more resources of various kinds and thus to be able to take higher risks, but *SIZE* turned out to be strongly negative. In other words, the probability of minority-ownership seems to increase with the size of the parent company. The reason for this is unclear, but one might speculate whether large Swedish MNCs prefer to create joint ventures as an option to expand in response to future technological and market developments.

Another result that deserves a comment is the insignificance of the *R&D* variable, particularly since it has been shown elsewhere that ownership sharing in high-tech industries is rare (see, for example, Lipsey, 1984). The explanation for this finding may be connected to the construction of the dependent variable. The most technologically-

Table 3.1   Regression results for the determinants of majority ownership in affiliates of Swedish multinationals

Explanatory variables	All countries (497 observations) probit β
Intercept	1.22***
	(3.53)
R&D	−2.21
	(0.54)
AGE	2.87 E-01***
	(2.98)
DIV	−2.52 E-01*
	(1.62)
MIX	−1.21***
	(2.85)
SIZE	−3.83 E-05***
	(5.82)
GDP	−5.05 E-07**
	(2.32)
GNPC	7.49 E-05**
	(1.94)
Wrong predictions as percentage of total observations	16.6
Wrong predictions of majority ownership (%)	0.96

Notes: t-statistics in parentheses.
***   Significant at the 1 per cent level; **   Significant at the 5 per cent level;
*   Significant at the 10 per cent level.

orientated firms may not accept any ownership-sharing at all, while firms that are less technology-intensive but still dependent on their proprietary technology, may accept only limited joint participation (less than 50 per cent) in foreign ventures. Unfortunately, we were not able to examine this hypothesis in detail because of the lack of data on ownership studies.

Finally, the performance of the two host country variables adds some interesting information to the problem at hand. The size of a host country market (*GDP*) seems to be an important determinant of different patterns of ownership of foreign affiliates only in the developed countries. The likelihood of joint ventures thus seems to increase with the size of the host country market, but only after the market has reached a certain size. The income level variable (*GNPC*) turns out

Firm Strategies

to be significant only in the regressions with data for developing countries, and with a positive sign. The income level may therefore not be
a very good proxy for the comparative advantages of local partners.
Instead, this variable seems to reflect the degree of similarity in the
demand patterns of Sweden and the host countries.

Earlier work has also suggested that it may be important to distinguish between export-orientated and local-market affiliates. It has, for
example, been shown that MNCs hold significantly higher fractions of
equity in export-orientated affiliates than in local-market-orientated
ones (Reuber *et al.*, 1973; and Blomström, 1990). Unfortunately, we

Table 3.2   Regression results for the determinants of majority ownership in
affiliates of Swedish multinationals in developed and developing countries

Explanatory variables	Developed countries (403 observations) probit β	Developing countries (94 observations) probit β
Intercept	1.64***	−5.68 E-01
	(3.56)	0.64
R&D	−2.37	−6.88
	(0.52)	(0.71)
AGE	2.50 E-01**	5.77 E-01**
	(2.37)	(2.17)
DIV	−1.93 E-01	−5.39 E-01
	(1.09)	(1.54)
MIX	−1.32***	−8.60 E-01
	(4.00)	(0.88)
SIZE	−3.81 E-05***	−3.84 E-05***
	(4.00)	(2.71)
GDP	−4.23 E-07**	−1.04 E-06
	(1.90)	(0.29)
GNPC	2.05 E-05	9.65 E-04***
	(0.31)	(2.74)
Wrong predictions as percentage of total observations	14.9	20.0
Wrong predictions of majority ownership (%)	0.29	4.1

Notes: t-statistics in parentheses.
***   Significant at the 1 per cent level; **   Significant at the 5 per cent level;
*   Significant at the 10 per cent level.

cannot test for this in our study, since we do not have any export data for the minority-owned affiliates.

It has also been suggested that the joint-venture participation of MNCs varies with their national origin (see, for example, Vernon, 1977). Multinationals from other (that is, smaller) countries than the USA are supposed to be more willing to share ownership. Of course, we cannot test this hypothesis here, but it is worth noting that in Chapter 2 we found that Swedish firms had a lower proportion of foreign direct investment held in the forms of minority ventures than did US multinationals. From this we conclude that one should look for explanations to openness for ownership sharing in factors such as the age, size and the differences in activities undertaken by the firms, rather than in their national origin.

3.5 Concluding remarks

The particular concern of this chapter has been to investigate what drives multinational firms to enter into minority venture agreements, rather than to invest in majority-owned affiliates. Comprehensive firm-level data, covering almost the entire population of Swedish multinationals, have been used in a model of dichotomous choice, where the firms can choose between majority or minority ownership of their foreign affiliates. The results suggest that this choice is strongly influenced by the firms' capacity and competence. Firms with brief experience of foreign production and highly diversified product lines turned out to be the most likely to choose minority ventures. There was also some support for the hypothesis that multinationals choose minority-ownership for affiliates producing different (2-digit) output from their parents.

The size of the host country market also turned out to be an important determinant for the firms' choice. However, the likelihood of seeking out joint ventures seems to increase with the size of the host country market only when it has reached a certain size, judging from the fact that the variable was not significant in separate regressions on developing countries.

Our findings are of interest for the current debate on the transfer of technology to developing countries. The abundant literature analyzing the costs of such transfers by multinational corporations sometimes claims that developing countries, which are often in a weak bargaining position *vis-à-vis* the multinationals, are paying too much for foreign technology by accepting subsidiary production. This implies that joint-venture agreements between local and foreign firms should be better alternatives for the LDCs. However, before such conclusions can be drawn, it is necessary to examine whether wholly-owned foreign affiliates and joint ventures are really alternative ways for obtaining one and the same technology. Our study suggests that this may not always be the case. The MNCs that seek out joint ventures appear to be more diversified than those opting for wholly-owned foreign production.

Notes

1. See Chapter 2 for a discussion of Swedish FDI.
2. For example, India introduced its Foreign Exchange Regulation Act in 1973, which placed a 40 per cent ceiling on foreign equity participation (with some exceptions). In Malaysia, the Industrial Co-ordination Act of 1975 required all manufacturers to apply for licences to start or continue operations. In some Latin-American countries, various regulation policies are even older. In Mexico, for example, some regulations have been in force since 1944, but it was not until the Law to Promote Mexican Investment and to Regulate Foreign Investment, which came into force in 1973, that majority Mexican ownership in all foreign ventures was required. The law was applied mainly to firms starting up after 1973. Many of these regulations have been relaxed during the 1990s.
3. It was not possible to analyze whether other rent-yielding assets, such as managerial and marketing skills, were of importance or not, since data were not available. An interesting additional variable would have been advertising expenditures, but no such information has been collected for Swedish MNCs.
4. It seems realistic to assume that firms gain more experience in the first year of operation than in, say, the fifteenth, but that they always gain something. This is why we use this variable in its logarithmic form.
5. An alternative measure of experience, defined as the parents' number of foreign affiliates (also in log), was tried, but it did not change the results in any significant way.
6. $MIX = 1 - \dfrac{\sum_i^n x_i^2}{\left(\sum_i^n x_i\right)^2}$; $0 \leq MIX \leq 1$ where x_i is a firm's output in industry i.
7. Here we assume that all joint ventures are with host-country firms. They could, of course, be with other investors, but the data do not show who the partners are.
8. A dummy variable equal to 1 if an affiliate belonged to natural resource intensive industries, and 0 otherwise, was also tried, to take care of generally risky and big projects in extractive industries. Since it never turned out to be significant it is not shown in the tables.

Appendix

Table A-3.1   Simple correlation coefficients for independent variables

	R&D	**AGE**	**DIV**	**MIX**	**SIZE**	**GDP**
All host countries						
R&D	1.00					
AGE	0.348	1.00				
DIV	−0.107	0.089	1.00			
MIX	−0.054	0.427	0.405	1.00		
SIZE	0.245	0.317	−0.026	0.143	1.00	
GDP	0.058	0.092	0.033	0.094	−0.051	1.00
GNPC	−0.051	−0.138	0.064	0.024	−0.092	0.371
Developed countries						
R&D	1.00					
AGE	0.357	1.00				
DIV	−0.099	0.094	1.00			
MIX	−0.012	0.453	0.424	1.00		
SIZE	0.222	0.336	−0.027	0.206	1.00	
GDP	0.086	0.143	0.036	0.113	−0.020	1.00
GNPC	0.025	0.027	0.072	0.081	0.062	0.356
Developing countries						
R&D	1.00					
AGE	0.226	1.00				
DIV	−0.149	0.068	1.00			
MIX	−0.292	0.264	0.324	1.00		
SIZE	0.273	0.101	−0.035	−0.126	1.00	
GDP	0.042	0.093	−0.173	−0.121	−0.069	1.00
GNPC	0.211	0.125	0.022	−0.035	0.062	−0.101

4
MNC Entry Strategies: New Ventures or Acquisitions?

4.1 Introduction

Multinational firms may initiate affiliate activities abroad in two different ways; either by building a new establishment (greenfield investment) or by taking over an already existing firm (acquisition). The two methods can be expected to yield different costs and benefits for the host economy. Some argue, for example, that acquisitions have few positive effects on productive capacity, employment or market concentration, and that foreign purchases of local firms should therefore be prevented. Others are less pessimistic and point to possible long-run effects on the host economy, such as improvements in technology and management practices.

Few empirical studies have focused on the choice between new ventures and acquisitions in the internationalization of companies. Most of the available work concentrates on parent-firm characteristics and does not take into account the characteristics of the host country markets. One of the few studies that incorporates market characteristics in the analysis of the penetration of MNCs into a market is that of Caves and Mehra (1986). However, their work only looks at entries by foreign MNCs into US markets. Since the USA may have particular characteristics as a host country (see Lall, 1982), studying entry patterns into other markets may be valuable.

This chapter provides such a study. By including host country market characteristics in an analysis of Swedish MNCs' expansion into thirty-five countries we are able to analyze the influence of market size, market growth and the host country's level of development on the MNC's entry decisions.

4.2 The choice of new venture or acquisition

The theoretical framework for our analysis of the determinants of an MNC's choice between establishing an affiliate by building a new plant or acquiring an existing facility is provided by Caves (1996). The point of departure for the analysis is the hypothesis that acquisitions offer a lower, but less uncertain rate of return. The risk is lower, because the acquired firm is already established in the market, having a definite market share, established manufacturing skills, management with knowledge of local conditions, and a distribution network. The rate of return is arguably lower because competition in the market for firms sets the price of the target firm at such a level as to yield a competitive rate of return.[1]

On the basis of this, we can postulate some hypotheses about why MNCs would choose a low-risk entry strategy, and prefer the acquisition of existing firms rather than greenfield entry when expanding abroad. Specifically, firms with long experience in overseas production are expected to have accumulated ample knowledge about conditions in foreign markets and to be more reluctant to pay an acquisition premium which reduces the rate of return on the investment.

On the other hand, results from early studies (Wilson, 1980; and Caves and Mehra, 1986) give strong support to the statement that 'diversified companies set up a process of expanding via acquisition, whether in their national markets or abroad' (Caves, 1996, p. 71).

As for host countries, two groups of factors require attention: (i) those affecting the probability of finding suitable firms for acquisition (for example, the size of the host country's stock market); and (ii) the possible effects on local output and prices of acquisitions and new ventures. Entry through a greenfield investment implies an increase in the industry's overall capacity. As long as market demand is not perfectly elastic, this increase in capacity, and subsequently in output, causes the market price to fall. However, the effects on prices (and revenues) may be mitigated if market demand is increasing. Consequently, an MNC expanding into a local market may be influenced by the structure of the host market and the nature of demand. More precisely, we expect the probability of entry by acquisition to be greater the higher the degree of market concentration and the lower the growth and elasticity of demand.[2]

4.3 Data and the model

The data used in this chapter are from the 1978 survey of Swedish foreign investment, conducted by the Research Institute of Industrial Economics (IUI) in Stockholm, covering virtually all Swedish manufacturing firms investing abroad. In 1978, there were 118 Swedish manufacturing MNCs with 570 majority-owned foreign affiliates (MOFAs) involved in productive activities.[3] This left us with a sample of seventy-seven parent companies and 250 MOFAs established in thirty countries between 1969 and 1978.[4] This data set was supplemented by official statistics on host country variables.

Our dependent variable, *ACQ*, is a dummy which takes on values of 1 for 'takeovers' and 0 for 'greenfields'. The dependent variable is thus a binomial random variable. An appropriate statistical estimation technique is in this case the probit model, which can be estimated by the maximum likelihood method.

The independent variables are as follows:

AGEPAR   A measure of the MNC's stock of experience, measured as the length of time (in years) that a company has been operating abroad (the date of entry minus the date of establishment of the oldest, still operating, subsidiary). This variable was introduced in logarithmic form, since we expect years to have a decreasing impact on a firm's stock of experience and knowledge. The smaller the international experience and knowledge of the MNC, the greater the incentive to reduce risk by choosing an acquisition. A negative sign is predicted.

MIX   The degree of diversification of an MNC, measured by 1 minus a Herfindahl index constructed from the relative shares of the parent's sales in different 6-digit industries in 1978 (see Swedenborg (1979) for a description of the method of deriving this variable, which is clearly related to Berry's (1971) index of diversification). The corresponding data for the degree of diversification at the time of entry are not available. A positive sign is expected, since diversification is often accomplished by the acquisition of firms.

DIV   A dummy variable equal to 1 if the market entered does not belong to the same 2-digit industry as the parent's prime product line. When the parent is diversifying into other product markets, risk may be higher, which should be an incentive to pay an acquisition premium and reduce risk. Thus, a positive effect is expected for DIV.

ΔIND A measure of the growth prospects facing the foreign investor, which is defined as the growth of industrial production in the 3-digit ISIC sector into which entry took place, calculated over the two years preceding entry.[5] We expect demand growth to facilitate the establishment of new productive capacity in an industry and, accordingly, to encourage new investments. Thus, the expected sign is negative.

GNPCAP The host country's GNP per capita in 1978, as an indicator of the level of the economic and technical environment in which locally based firms operate. The higher the level of development, the easier it is to find firms that fit the acquisition requirements of a MNC from a developed country such as Sweden. Hence, a positive relationship is expected between the host country's per capita income and the choice of acquisitions.

GDP The size of the host market, measured at current market prices in 1978. It is difficult to predict how market size will influence the form of entry. On the one hand, the larger the market, the smaller the disturbances that an entry via new investment causes in both the existing market shares and the revenue of existing firms. On the other hand, a large market raises the likelihood that the prospective entrant will find a suitable plant for acquisition. Hence, the sign of the coefficient remains to be determined empirically.

T Time of entry (1969 = 1 to 1978 = 10). There are indications of a rapid increase in the use of acquisitions, not only in the case of Swedish MNCs, but for multinational companies from other countries as well. This may partly be explained by the increased risks in international market operations in the 1970s (the first oil price shock, fluctuations in exchange rates), but also by the increased liquidity and the low real interest rates prevailing in those years. All these circumstances are expected to increase the MNCs' propensity for acquisitions. Thus, we expect the variable *T* to have a positive coefficient.

4.4 Empirical analysis

Table 4.1 reports the results of our probit estimations. The results serve to confirm some of the hypotheses advanced above, while others are rejected. *MIX*, an indicator of the degree of product line diversification of the parent company, has a strong positive effect on the dependent variable. This finding conforms with those of previous studies and suggests that differentiated firms tend to rely on takeovers when they expand abroad. The variable Δ*IND*, which shows the

Table 4.1   Determinants of the probability that a Swedish MNC enters a market by the acquisition of an already existing firm

	(1)	(2)
Constant	−3.874 E-01	−1.388***
	(3.939 E-01)	(5.143 E-01)
AGEPAR	−1.369 E-02	−2.978 E-02
	(3.098 E-02)	(3.197 E-02
MIX	1.528***	1.532***
	(0.413)	(0.421)
DIV	−1.843 E-01	−9.008 E-02
	(2.044 E-01)	(2.127 E-01)
ΔIND	−1.437 E-02	−6.415 E-03
	(7.027 E-03)**	(7.577 E-03)
GNPCAP	4.848 E-05	7.414 E-05**
	(3.459 E-05)	(3.631 E-05)
GDP	−1.576 E-04	−2.146 E-04
	(1.773 E-04)	(1.853 E-04)
T		1.215 E-01***
		(3.844 E-02)
n	224	224
Wrong predictions as percentage of total observations[a]	25.89	24.55
Wrong predictions as percentage of ones[a]	7.27	7.27

Notes: Standard errors in parentheses.
Levels of significance (two-tail test) are: ***, ** and *   significant at 1, 5 and 10 per cent, respectively.
[a]   A critical probability of 0.5.

growth of industrial production in the particular industries considered, has a statistically significant negative effect when used without the time of entry: high growth rates of production in the host market immediately before entry appear to decrease the probability of entry by acquisition. This finding is compatible with our hypothesis that high growth promotes investments in new productive capacity, while takeovers seem to be favoured in low-growth markets.[6]

The results also indicate that the probability of entry through acquisition has increased over time (variable *T*). This finding is consistent with the hypothesis that increased risks in the 1970s had a positive influence on the propensity to choose takeovers as an entry method.

Furthermore, we see that *GNPCAP* has the expected positive sign, but that it is only significant when used without *GDP* or ΔIND, or when this is introduced together with *T*. This result gives some support to our hypothesis that acquisition activities are more common in developed countries, arguably because it is easier to find takeover candidates there that embody the technological or managerial attributes that would suit Swedish MNCs.

One set of variables denoting factors usually considered to influence the choice between takeovers and greenfields performed poorly. This was the case of the variable *DIV*, a dummy for the similarity of the parent's and the affiliate's principal product line. A similar, though not identical, variable was also used by Caves and Mehra (1986) without success. Furthermore, market size, as indicated by the *GDP* variable, does not appear to have any significant influence on the choice of form of entry. One reason could be that the two opposing effects discussed earlier balance each other. The same is true for the two variables reflecting the MNC's stock of experience in foreign operations. It is worth noting that this last result is in accordance with findings in previous studies.[7]

4.5   Conclusions

The results of our empirical examination of the factors influencing MNCs' choice between takeover and greenfield investment when expanding abroad can be summarized as follows. The probability of choosing takeover as an entry method was significantly influenced by the degree of industrial diversification of the parent company. The more diversified in products a firm is, the higher the probability of choosing the takeover option. The probability of takeover also seems to increase with the host country's income per capita, and to decrease with the rate of growth of the host country's GDP and the growth in industrial production in the industry entered. Furthermore, we found takeovers to be used increasingly by Swedish MNCs as a means of entry. However, some caution is necessary. The variable for the time of entry was highly correlated with several of the host country variables, so the effect of each of them cannot be distinguished clearly. None of the variables standing for the size of the host market or the degree of experience of the MNC showed any significant effect on the choice of entry form.

Notes

1. This might not apply to the MNC: by using its specific assets the MNC may be able to obtain a higher rate of return than a national firm. This hypothesis is not tested explicitly here.
2. Lack of data prevents us from examining the influence of concentration and other aspects of market structure on MNC choice, nor do our data provide information on the subsidiary's initial scale or earlier activities.
3. See Swedenborg (1982) for a description of the data.
4. Given the purpose of this study, we excluded those subsidiaries that developed out of already existing sales affiliates. We also left out investment made before 1969, because some of the explanatory variables related to the market structure in the host countries were unavailable.
5. More precisely, the variable indicates total growth in the 3-digit industry entered, calculated for the two years preceding entry, and was constructed using the index numbers of industrial production of the industry concerned.
6. We also considered the hypothesis, proposed by Caves and Mehra (1986), that acquisition is also favoured when the entered market is growing very rapidly (probably because entry by acquisition is quicker) or very slowly (probably because the prices of existing assets are depressed). Thus they predicted a positive effect on acquisitions of both high and low growth. We followed the procedure used by them and introduced a variable equal to the absolute value of the deviation of the host country's annual precentage change in gross domestic product at constant market prices from its sample mean, divided by its standard deviation. This transformed variable was insignificant in all the cases in which it was introduced, and was therefore dropped from the tables.
7. We also tried incorporating a variable for the state of the host country's stock market at the year of entry. A dummy for the difference between actual and predicted share prices was used but not found to be significant.

5
R&D Activities in Affiliat
of Swedish MNCs

5.1 Introduction

The fact that multinational companies do not undertake all their research and development activities at home has become a matter of recent concern, both in the home and host countries of these companies. Some empirical work has been done on the question of why MNCs decentralize their R&D activities (see Mansfield *et al.*, 1979; Lall, 1979a; Håkansson, 1980; and Hirschey and Caves, 1981).[1] The study by Håkansson (1980) is one of the few that deal with the determinants of the R&D intensity of MNC affiliates, but it is confined to subsidiaries that carry out R&D, while foreign affiliates that do not are excluded.[2] Furthermore, the analysis does not take into account the characteristics of the MNC to which the affiliates belong.

Our study investigates the factors that explain the R&D intensity of foreign subsidiaries of Swedish MNCs, using data for 1978. Following Håkansson (1980), we concentrate on the technological capabilities developed at the subsidiary level, but also take into account affiliate, host country and parent company characteristics. Furthermore, our sample includes those foreign affiliates that do not perform R&D, which leads us to use a Tobit model.

The chapter proceeds as follows. Section 2 focuses on some factors of importance in determining the amount of research activity carried out by foreign affiliates. In Section 3 we present the data and describe the model and method of estimation used. The empirical results are presented in section 4, and we draw the main conclusions in Section 5.

5.2 The theoretical framework

R&D constitutes a strategic activity, since it creates important assets on which the multinationals' future competitiveness is built. There-

der the direct control of head-
ome countries. This implies that
dent on the innovation and R&D
amount of resources spent on R&D
epends on a combination of factors.
n the multinationals' willingness and
D function, while others depend on the
untry, or stem from the performance and
elf.

The ~~~~~~~~~~~ only mentioned in favour of centralization of
R&D is ~~ ~~~~~~~~~~~ scale economies in the production of technological knowle~~~~ fficulties in project coordination, as well as the
dispersion of resources for executing parallel projects in different
places, may also call for centralization of R&D. Other factors working
in the same direction are the need to control the diffusion of knowledge and protect industrial secrets. Some of these factors promote concentration of R&D to the home country, while others merely promote
centralization of it somewhere (see Hirschey and Caves, 1981).

Other factors, however, encourage decentralization of R&D. Examples include the need to adapt production processes and characteristics of products to local market conditions and regulations. It is
sometimes necessary to reduce the scale of production or modify
products to suit local prescriptions, local consumers' tastes or some
other specific conditions. In general, factors which promote decentralization are related to the choice of location of production, to
industry-specific factors, and to some aspects regarding the performance of production units abroad. R&D units abroad could also serve
as recruiting stations for local scientists and technicians, and as points
of contact with the scientific community in the host country. Furthermore, the cost of skilled labour, such as engineers and technicians,
might be important when choosing a location for R&D activities (see
Lall, 1979a).

Earlier studies suggest the existence of a time sequence in the
development of foreign R&D units (see Ronstadt, 1977). This
sequence begins with the establishment of a production subsidiary.
Should technical problems arise at the outset of the operation, the
parent sends its own technical staff to assist (see Behrman and
Fischer, 1980). However, when the subsidiary is located in a large
market, with promising growth prospects and satisfactory technical
and scientific infrastructure, then conditions for the establishment
of a team exclusively dedicated to R&D tasks are fulfilled. When the

subsidiary grows gradually, the research departments may also grow, both in terms of the staff employed and the complexity of tasks (see Ronstadt, 1977). This sequence suggests that, after some time, the R&D departments of some affiliates might establish themselves as centres of technology production which could be commercialized in regional markets. This is particularly the case for subsidiaries that base their activities on knowledge of specific local conditions, different from those of the MNC's home country.

The conventional idea about the composition of foreign affiliates' R&D expenditure is stated by Mansfield *et al.* (1979), who point out that there is a predominance of adaptive tasks of short-term maturity over long-term projects. This does not mean that investments in innovative tasks in the subsidiaries are negligible. In the case of Swedish foreign affiliates carrying out R&D in 1978, more than 25 per cent of them dedicated more than half of their R&D investments to the development of innovations.

It seems reasonable to expect that the determinants of investments in adaptive or innovative R&D will differ, since the tasks of improving and adapting products and/or processes are not subject to the same degree of uncertainty as other types of research activities. The uncertainty is lower concerning both the characteristics of the results and the chances of success. Furthermore, adaptive R&D is a complement to the production process. The conjunction of actual production and improvements through adaptations, after-sales services, better quality control, and special customer design may give rise to additional benefits. The outcome of this type of research is also easier to appropriate, as it is embodied in products. We therefore expect the leakage risks of doing research outside the MNC's central units to be outweighed by a greater capacity to appropriate the research outcomes. On the other hand, innovative R&D competes with actual production for economic resources. This type of R&D is aimed at generating new technological assets that might give rise to a stream of additional income in the future, and has a more uncertain outcome. The reasons for promoting this type of activity in the subsidiary will therefore necessarily differ from those for adaptive R&D.

5.3 Data, estimation method and model

The data for this study are from the 1978 survey of Swedish investments abroad compiled by the Research Institute of Industrial

Economics (IUI) in Stockholm. The survey covers virtually all Swedish manufacturing firms that invest abroad and provides data for parent companies and majority-owned foreign affiliates. Of the 118 multinationals in the sample, forty-three undertook R&D abroad.[3] There were 570 majority-owned foreign subsidiaries, of which 420 responded to questions regarding their research activities. The fact that 70 per cent of the affiliates reported no expenditure on R&D calls for caution in the choice of statistical model. The appropriate statistical technique in this case is the Tobit model.

The earlier discussion on the determinants of research activities in foreign subsidiaries of multinationals may now be used to build a cross-section model that relates the R&D intensity of Swedish multinationals' foreign subsidiaries to affiliate, host country, parent firm and industry characteristics.[4] First, we analyze the determinants of total R&D expenditure. The dependent variable, *R&DAFF*, is defined as the ratio of total R&D expenditures to total sales in a subsidiary.[5] Second, we look at different types of R&D activities by using two other dependent variables. One is *R&DADAPT*, which is defined as the ratio of the amount of R&D expenditures of the affiliates devoted to adaptations, product improvements, process and quality control to their total sales. The other, *R&DNEW*, is defined as the ratio of the amount devoted to the development of new processes or products to the subsidiaries' total sales.

In Section 2 we suggested several factors that may influence the affiliates' R&D expenditures. Let us begin with those factors that are related to the subsidiaries themselves.

Factors related to subsidiaries

Size.   Although there is no empirical evidence that larger enterprises spend proportionally more on R&D than smaller ones (see Kamien and Schwartz, 1982), size may be of importance when studying the research intensity of firms with limited autonomy. The affiliate's size might reflect such factors as managerial talent, the relative position of a subsidiary in the MNC's hierarchy, and the affiliate's capacity to generate its own financial resources. We measure the size of an affiliate (*SIZEAFF*) by the number of its employees and expect this variable to have a positive influence on the affiliate's research intensity.[6]

Age.   The age of an affiliate represents an aspect of the time sequence discussed in Section 2. Given that other conditions such as the size and growth rate of local market are favourable, the longer the affiliate has been operating, the more research activities we expect to observe. We use the age of an affiliate (*AGEAFF*), measured in years, and expect it to be positively related to the dependent variable.

Import intensity. To some extent the subsidiaries act as sales offices and after-sales service agencies for their parents. If this is the main purpose of the foreign investment, we expect the degree of autonomy to the affiliates, and their need to develop specific technological solutions, to be limited. The affiliates' imports from their parent companies as a proportion of total sales in the affiliates (*IMPAFF*) is therefore expected to have a negative influence on the affiliates' R&D activities.

Export performance. The variable *EXPAFF* is defined as the ratio of an affiliate's exports to destinations other than Sweden to its total sales. A high level of this kind of export is supposed to promote some degree of research and adaptation in the affiliate. This might be explained by the existence of incentives for local research aimed at the adaptation of products to regional conditions. This would particularly be the case if the difference in technological level between the subsidiary and its export markets is less than the technological gap between the latter and the parent company. Consequently, we expect EXPAFF to have a positive sign.

Form of incorporation into the MNC. The literature suggests that the level of R&D activity in a subsidiary is related to the form in which it is incorporated into the MNC. When an existing firm that carries out some R&D is acquired by the MNC, we expect these research activities to continue for a time, although they are usually not incorporated into the parents' R&D programme (see Ronstadt, 1977). In order to control for this kind of phenomenon, we introduce a dummy variable (*BEFORE*) which is equal to 1 if a firm was taken over and integrated into the multinational no more than five years before 1978, and 0 otherwise.[7] A positive sign is expected for the coefficient of *BEFORE*.

Factors related to parent companies

Technology. The attitude of an MNC towards innovations, and the technological characteristics of the industry to which it belongs, are expected to have allocative consequences for its R&D investments. If the MNC is already R&D-orientated, we expect the affiliates to be encouraged by the corporation's open attitude to research tasks. A high degree of product sophistication may also promote more adaptations to local conditions, and thus more R&D activities in the affiliates. We take the research intensity of the parent company (the ratio of R&D expenditures to total sales), *R&DPAR*, as an indicator of the MNC's technological intensity. This variable will also reflect industry characteristics, as a high level of research in the firm might be explained by the technological opportunities which arise in these activities. The proportion of the parent's R&D expenditures invested in new processes or products, *NEWPAR*, is also used as an index of the firm's strategy regarding technological performance. We expect both *R&DPAR* and *NEWPAR* to have a positive influence on the affiliates' R&D activities.

International experience of the corporation. Accumulated experience of foreign production may lead to the development of appropriate control and information systems that allow geographical decentralization of R&D without loss of control. The variable used as a measure of experience is the age of the oldest, still active, subsidiary. Since we expect this relationship to be non-linear, because of decreasing returns to age, we used a logarithmic transformation (*AGEPAR*) as a measure of the MNC's experience in production overseas. A positive sign is expected for the coefficient of this variable.

Factors specific to the industry

Scale economies. In their study of the international allocation of R&D by US multinationals, Hirschey and Caves (1981) showed that scale advantages promote concentration of R&D activities to one location, usually in the home country. Similarly, we are forced to use a measure of scale in production as a proxy for the minimum efficient scale in R&D. We are sceptical of this procedure, but considered it interesting to test the method by applying it to our data. Our variable, denoted *SCALE*, was calculated by Swedenborg (1982) from the average value added in each Swedish 5-digit industry. She then took the weighted mean of these averages with weights corresponding to the product mix of the parent companies. Thus, *SCALE* reflects the average value added of a hypothetical industry producing the same product mix as the parent company considered. This variable is somewhat different from the two most commonly used approaches: one based on the slope of the industry's cost curve, and the other using the average taken over the largest firms in the industry. Data availability, however, prevented us from using either of these methods. A negative sign is expected for the coefficient of this variable.

Adaptive needs. We use a dummy variable (*DUMMY*) for affiliates in the machine tool industry. This industry is characterized by close technological cooperation between producers and consumers, product specialization to meet the purchasers' specific design needs, the need to adapt products to local conditions, and the provision of after-sales services (see UNIDO, 1983). All this works in favour of the development of a technological capability at the affiliate level. Thus, a positive sign is expected for *DUMMY*.

Host country characteristics

We use two host-country variables that may be of importance in the MNC's decision to decentralize R&D: the country's GDP and its per capita income (*GNPCAP*). The *GDP* variable is a rough indicator of the size of the local market. We expect it to be positively correlated with the dependent variable, since a large host market encourages adaptive research and development of new products suited to local demand patterns. *GNPCAP* is a proxy for the level of development in the host country, and for the scientific resources potentially available there. Access to scientific staff and the possibility of using affiliates as 'research windows' are supposed to be reflected by *GNPCAP*, so we expect this variable to show a positive sign.

We can now summarize the preceding discussion as follows:

$$R\&DAFF = f(SIZEAFF, AGEAFF, IMPAFF, EXPAFF,$$
$$(+) \qquad (+) \qquad (-) \qquad (+)$$

$$BEFORE, R\&DPAR, NEWPAR, AGEPAR,$$
$$(+) \qquad (+) \qquad (+) \qquad (-)$$

$$SCALE, DUMMY, GDP, GNPCAP)$$
$$(+) \qquad (+) \qquad (+) \qquad (+)$$

where the variables employed are those discussed above. The signs below the variables show the expected signs in the regressions.

5.4   Statistical results

The results with *R&DAFF* as the dependent variable are presented
in Table 5.1. Collinearity problems forced us to use the independent
variables selectively (a correlation matrix for the independent variables is presented in the Appendix). For the same reasons, the variables *AGEPAR* and *BEFORE* are never used together with
AGEAFF. As its inclusion considerably reduces the number of observations, the variable *NEWPAR* is used in only two models (4 and 5).
The variables were standardized by dividing them by their corresponding sample means.

The results lend support to many of the hypotheses presented
above. The research intensity of the parent company, *R&DPAR*, as
well as the proportion of the parent's R&D expenditures devoted to
the development of new products and processes (*NEWPAR*), seem
to have a strong positive influence on the affiliate's research intensity.
The host country variables, *GDP* and *GNPCAP*, are also both significantly different from zero with positive coefficients. Moreover, our
results suggest that a high degree of imports from Sweden discourages the subsidiary from undertaking research (see *IMPAFF*), while
the extent to which the affiliate supplies regional markets (proxied by
EXPAFF) has a positive and significant effect on the subsidiary's
R&D commitments.

The variables *BEFORE* and *AGEAFF* were not statistically
significant in any of the equations. Thus, the recent incorporation
of a foreign branch into the MNC by a takeover (*BEFORE*) or
the age of the affiliate (*AGEAFF*) do not seem to be related to
research activity in the affiliate. In contrast to Hirschey and
Caves (1981) our *SCALE* variable is not statistically significant. There
may be two reasons for this. Either the scale advantages in production may not be a satisfactory proxy for the scale advantages in
R&D, or there are simply no scale advantages in R&D. There is
some support for the second hypothesis in the literature on
technological innovations. Kamien and Schwartz (1982), for example,
concluded that the existence of scale advantages in R&D has
not achieved conclusive empirical corroboration, and that the
innovation process seems to be characterized by constant or even
decreasing returns to scale. Our results, however, do not allow us
to present clear evidence against the existence of these kinds of
advantage in the production of innovations. More empirical evidence
is necessary.

Table 5.1 Results of Tobit estimations of determinants of Swedish subsidiaries' R&D intensities

	Dependent variable: R&DAFF				
	(1)	**(2)**	**(3)**	**(4)**	**(5)**
Constant t	−2.704*** (0.598)	−2.829*** (0.526)	−2.100*** (0.443)	−2.635*** (0.644)	−4.122*** (1.023)
R&DPAR	0.351*** (0.112)	0.401*** (0.105)	0.441 (0.113)***	0.477*** (0.149)	0.445*** (0.157)
AGEPAR	0.499 (0.425)				0.536 (0.520)
SCALE	−0.094 (0.110)	−0.161 (0.114)	−0.059 (0.115)	−0.061 (0.164)	
DUMMY	0.087 (0.061)				
AGEAFF			0.126 (0.223)	0.050 (0.132)	
SIZEAFF	0.058 (0.043)	0.113*** (0.041)	0.065 (0.044)	0.077 (0.048)	
IMPAFF			−0.325** (0.131)	−0.340* (0.180)	−0.419** (0.185)
EXPAFF	0.311*** (0.073)		0.290*** (0.073)	0.209** (0.100)	0.108 (0.100)
BEFORE	0.003 (0.061)	−0.021 (0.059)			
GNPCAP		1.295*** (0.311)			1.418*** (0.435)
GDP	0.274*** (0.076)		0.296 (0.077)	0.246** (0.097)	
NEWPAR				0.711** (0.323)	0.756** (0.322)
$\bar{y}$	1.04	1.01	1.04	0.99	0.99
$\hat{\bar{y}}_1$	1.32	1.29	1.33	1.40	1.40
$\hat{\bar{y}}_2$	1.03	1.06	0.99	0.97	0.94
1-ratio	140.93	153.72	92.53	106.24	215.62
$y = 0$	268	279	267	166	166
$y > 0$	114	118	112	80	80

Notes: Standard errors are given in parentheses. Significance levels of coefficients are: *** = 1 per cent; ** = 5 per cent; * = 10 per cent (Two-tail test). $\hat{\bar{y}}_1$ predicted value evaluated at each observation. $\hat{\bar{y}}_2$ predicted value evaluated at sample mean.

The coefficient of the variable for the size of the foreign branch (*SIZEAFF*), is positive in all regressions, but is significantly different from zero in only one equation (when used without *EXPAFF* and *GDP*). The experience of the parent company, *AGEPAR*, has the expected positive coefficient in all cases, but is not significant.

To sum up, the R&D intensity in foreign majority-owned subsidiaries of Swedish multinationals seems to be related to some characteristics of the host country (*GDP* and *GNPCAP*), to the degree by which the affiliate carries out productive tasks and supplies third markets (*IMPAFF* and *EXPAFF*), and to the intensity and composition of the research activities of the parent firm in Sweden (*R&DPAR* and *NEWPAR*). With the exception of *IMPAFF*, all variables have positive signs.

We now use the information available on the composition of R&D in the affiliates to carry out another set of regressions. Though the quality of the data has some weaknesses, we believe that these regressions throw some additional light on the issues at hand.[8] The new dependent variables are *R&DADAPT* – that is, the affiliate's amount of R&D expenditure devoted to adaptations, product improvements, process and quality control – and *R&DNEW*, the amount devoted to the development of new processes or products. Both variables are normalized by the affiliates sales, and we analyze them according to the models used in regressions 1–3 in Table 5.1.

The results of the estimations shown in Table 5.2 suggest that the different types of research in the affiliates are affected by different variables. The affiliates' investment in innovative R&D is positively correlated with the research intensity of the MNC in Sweden (*R&DPAR*), but this variable is not significant for adaptive R&D. On the other hand, adaptive R&D seems to be affected by a group of variables that lack significance in the estimations of innovative R&D. In particular, the subsidiary's imports from the parent company in Sweden, *IMPAFF*, discourages adaptive R&D. The *DUMMY* variable for the machine tool industry, which was not significant for total R&D expenditure, is now positive and significantly different from zero at the 5 per cent level. This suggests that in the case of the machine tool industry, we can expect a higher degree of adaptive activity in the affiliates. This is in accordance with previous evidence that the machine tool industry often finds itself forced to adapt designs to purchasers' special requirements and offer after-sale technical services.

Table 5.2 Results of Tobit estimations of determinants of Swedish subsidiaries' R&D intensities (adaptive and innovative R&D)

	Dependent variable: R&DADAPT			Dependent variable: R&DNEW		
	(1)	(2)	(3)	(1)	(2)	(3)
Constant	−2.953***	−2.722***	−1.913***	−2.427***	−3.981***	−3.599***
	(0.699)	(0.587)	(0.486)	(0.678)	(0.790)	(0.710)
RDPAR	0.019	0.192*	0.178	0.620***	0.570***	0.555***
	(0.135)	(0.116)	(0.126)	(0.148)	(0.138)	(0.141)
AGEPAR	0.696			−0.751		
	(0.479)			(0.496)		
SCALE	−0.090	−0.197	−0.069	−0.097	−0.078	−0.014
	(0.125)	(0.132)	(0.134)	(0.128)	(0.127)	(0.129)
DUMMY	0.151**			−0.055		
	(0.069)			(0.076)		
AGEAFF			0.0007			0.400
			(0.251)			(0.283)
SIZEAFF	0.030	0.095**	0.057	0.089*	0.104**	0.049
	(0.048)	(0.045)	(0.048)	(0.050)	(0.048)	(0.050)
IMPAFF			−0.435***			−0.105
			(0.165)			(0.143)
EXPAFF	0.302***		0.278***	0.405***		0.394***
	(0.084)		(0.083)	(0.096)		(0.096)
BEFORE	0.028	−0.016		−0.084	−0.045	
	(0.068)	(0.065)		(0.079)	(0.075)	
GNPCAP		1.104***			1.552***	
		(0.336)			(0.414)	
GDP	0.219***		0.239***	0.412***		0.414***
	(0.083)		(0.085)	(0.096)		(0.097)
$\bar{y}$	1.07	1.03	1.06	1.07	1.05	1.07
$\hat{y}_1$	1.66	1.61	1.66	1.27	1.24	1.28
$\hat{y}_2$	1.33	1.42	1.28	0.83	0.92	0.83
l-ratio	104.42	80.77	45.88	70.18	131.04	112.33
$y = 0$	279	290	278	295	308	293
$y > 0$	93	96	92	77	78	77

Notes: See Table 5.1.

5.5 Summary and conclusions

The aim of this chapter has been to investigate the determinants of R&D activities in foreign majority-owned affiliates of Swedish MNCs. The results suggest that the affiliates' research activities are positively influenced by certain technological characteristics of the parent company such as its R&D intensity, the share of R&D expenditures that the parent devotes to the development of new technological assets, and its level of labour skills, which is a proxy for the technological capabilities not reflected by a firm's expenditures on R&D. Certain characteristics of the affiliates also have an influence on their technological creativity – that is, the extent to which they are dedicated to production (as opposed to being a sales office) and the degree to which their production is intended for export to third markets. The less the affiliates import from the parent, and the more they export, the more research they carry out. Finally, two host country factors: the size of the local market, measured by its GDP, and its level of development, measured by GNP per capita, also favour the development or research in the affiliates.

The statistical model was also estimated for two kinds of research activity; those directed toward the improvement of products or processes already developed – that is, adaptive R&D, and those aimed at developing new products or processes – that is, innovative R&D. The question raised was whether the same set of variables explains the two types of R&D expenditure. The results suggest that this is not the case, and that different factors determine different kinds of R&D. In particular, innovative R&D in the subsidiaries is positively influenced by the technological level of the parent company. One possible explanation for this difference is that the degree of uncertainty related to adaptive and innovative R&D differs.

If it is true that investment in research and development by subsidiaries of foreign firms constitutes a contribution to the host country, then which subsidiaries make the greatest contribution? On the basis of our results, we can speculate that the answer to this question is: subsidiaries which are (a) not heavily dependent on imports from their parents; (b) export-orientated, particularly toward countries other than that of the parent; and (c) subsidiaries of firms that invest heavily in R&D, and particularly in R&D of an innovative character. However, these are not likely to be the last words on the subject. Our understanding of the determinants of subsidiary R&D is still in its infancy. Further research is required to attain better comprehension of this aspect of international technology transfer.

Notes

1.   See also Ronstadt (1977) and Behrman and Fischer (1980) for presentations of case studies.
2.   For a summary in English, see Håkansson (1983).
3.   In 1978, Swedish industry spent SEK4.6 billion on R&D, of which 10 per cent was spent abroad. Investment in R&D abroad grew ten times between 1965 and 1978, with the largest increase being at the beginning of the 1970s. During the same period, the ratio of R&D expenditure to

value-added abroad increased from 0.7 per cent to 1.0 per cent, and the number of Swedish MNCs undertaking this kind of activity increased from fourteen to forty-three. The industry distribution of the R&D expenditures abroad was uneven: 49 per cent was spent in the non-electrical machinery industry; 14.5 per cent in the electrical machinery industry; and 12.6 per cent in the chemical industry. The geographical distribution was also uneven, with 58.5 per cent of the R&D expenditure abroad concentrated in the European Community (EC) and 19.5 per cent in the USA. Only 1.7 per cent of Swedish R&D expenditure abroad was found in affiliates in the LDCs; see Swedenborg (1982).

4. In principle, the R&D decision is taken along with many other decisions pertinent to the management of the company. The true model (if there is one) describing this whole process would be very complex. The state of theory, as will be evident from Section 2, does not provide us with any definite form for the equations to be estimated. Estimation of more complex systems of equations would entail considerable risks of mis-specification. We have therefore chosen to estimate the simplest, and intuitively most reasonable, equation.

5. An alternative measure of research intensity was constructed as R&D expenditure per employee in each subsidiary. However, the Pearson correlation coefficient between the two measures was high ($r = 0.68$), and since this alternative measure gave similar results, it was dropped.

6. We tried an alternative size measure – that is, the subsidiary's total sales, but since this variable was highly correlated with the employment variable, and gave similar results in the regressions, it was dropped.

7. The five-year term was chosen arbitrarily. We regard this time lapse as sufficient to permit complete integration of the affiliate into the corporation. We also believe that after this time period has elapsed, R&D activities in the subsidiary will respond to a decision taken by the MNC, and not to inertia. Other period lengths were tried without showing significant variations in the results obtained.

8. The classification used to differentiate between R&D expenditure applied to the improvement of existing processes or products and those directed toward the development of new technology leaves room for considerable arbitrariness; for a discussion of this, see Swedenborg (1982, appendix A). For example, the criteria pursued by the affiliates to classify their expenditure are probably not uniform. In spite of this, we consider the use of these data interesting.

Appendix

Table A-5.1 Correlation matrix

	R&DPAR	NEWPAR	AGEPAR	SCALE	DUMMY	SIZEAFF	AGEAFF	IMPAFF	EXPAFF	BEFORE	GNPCAP
R&DPAR											
NEWPAR	0.360										
AGEPAR	0.259	0.143									
SCALE	0.113	-0.064	-0.029								
DUMMY	-0.057	0.103	0.290	-0.210							
SIZEAFF	0.070	-0.021	0.188	0.125	0.172						
AGEAFF	0.102	-0.021	0.431	-0.066	0.062	0.273					
IMPAFF	0.162	-0.128	-0.198	0.265	-0.178	-0.089	-0.072				
EXPAFF	-0.047	0.064	-0.031	0.033	0.117	0.070	-0.034	-0.156			
BEFORE	-0.162	0.182	-0.106	-0.044	-0.017	-0.041	-0.406	0.154	-0.029		
GNPCAP	-0.145	-0.024	-0.183	-0.050	-0.001	-0.054	-0.079	0.020	0.212	0.148	
GDP	-0.016	0.047	-0.019	-0.013	0.044	0.062	-0.055	-0.009	-0.087	0.098	0.314

Sources: GDP and GNCAP were taken from *International Finance Statistics, Supplement on Output Statistics*, Supplement Series No. 8, IMF, Washington DC, 1984. The remaining data are from the IUI 1978 Survey of Swedish Multinational Corporations.

6
Intra-firm Trade and Swedish Multinationals

6.1 Introduction

International trade has always been an important aspect of economic development and there has been an increasing emphasis on trade as a mechanism for promoting economic growth. In almost every year since the end of the 1940s, the volume of international trade has grown faster than the volume of world production and, as a result, the degree of interdependence of the world economy has increased markedly. A large share of this rapid growth of international trade has been accomplished under the control of multinational corporations, and a good proportion of the MNCs' exports and imports consist of intra-firm or intra-corporate trade.

The present study deals with the determinants of intra-firm trade, or more precisely with the identification of the determinants of Swedish foreign affiliates' imports from their parents. Several observers have pointed out that such trade behaves differently from arm's-length trade. For example, Lall (1973) emphasizes that trade between related parties sustains transfer pricing which, if manipulated, can result in an unfair distribution of the gains of trade.[1] Helleiner (1979), while stressing the importance of transfer pricing, also claims that intra-firm trade is characterized by relatively low short-run price elasticities, which, in turn, lead to inflexible trade flows and reduce the effectiveness of exchange rate policies.

The shortcomings of traditional trade theory in dealing with intra-firm trade have been noted in the literature for a long time, and Lall (1973, p. 128), for example, stated that 'a strong attack may be mounted on both the positive and normative aspects of trade theory for that part of trade which is intra-firm'.

Although intra-firm trade is important when studying monopolistic trade practices, for example, vast gaps remain in our knowledge of it. As indicated above, we shall attempt to fill some of these gaps regarding affiliates' imports from their parents. For example, how do the different characteristics of multinational corporations influence their affiliates' propensity to import from their parents? Are these kinds of transactions more intense among affiliates in less developed countries (LDCs) than among those in the developed countries (DCs)? This chapter aims to answer these questions.

Earlier empirical investigations of intra-firm trade suffer from a high degree of aggregation. Most studies are based on industry-level data, and are therefore unable to incorporate attributes of the parent companies. In this study we use firm-level data. This allows us to test a wide range of hypotheses regarding the determinants of the affiliates' internalized imports which have not been tested before, and to shed some more light on the determinants of intra-firm trade.[2] By concentrating on affiliate imports from parents, our study differs somewhat from what is normally dealt with in the literature on intra-firm trade. We can, however, make use of this literature in formulating our hypotheses.

In Section 2 we discuss the determinants of the affiliates' internalized imports and offer a brief summary of previous studies in this area. Section 3 presents the data and the specification of the model used. Section 4 reports the empirical results, and Section 5 gives a summary and conclusions.

6.2 Intra-firm trade and affiliate imports

Firms are expected to react to various factors that promote internalization of their transactions. Earlier work has emphasized the role of market imperfections, which affect the transactions of information and other firm-specific assets, and induce multinationals to replace market transactions with internal operations (Buckley and Casson, 1976; and Casson, 1979). For example, technological know-how developed within a firm is not a free good, but can be used as an asset for the firm. The markets for such intangible assets are usually characterized by imperfections, or may simply not exist. The costs related to the establishment of contracts when markets are incomplete and imperfect will be so high that firms have incentives to avoid market contracts, resorting to internal transactions (Casson, 1979). Not only information in more or less intangible forms (experience, know-how, blueprints, catalogues and so on), but also goods embodying information such as managerial and marketing know-how or specific technological innovations will be internally transacted (Lall, 1978a).

Market imperfections are also expected to arise when future markets are involved. There, the cost of contracts at arm's length, covering disruptions, defaults, delays, price changes, quality alterations, and several other eventualities, may be very high. That, in turn, will discourage the use of external markets. Casson (1979) suggests two cases in which we can expect the incentives for internalization to be particularly intense: first, when the goods transacted embody proprietary information; and second, when the commodities are produced by multi-stage processes requiring intertemporal coordination. According to Casson, the second case is more likely to occur when very capital-intensive techniques are used.

Some risks and uncertainties are also related to the conditions prevailing in the host countries. The impact of recurrent crises in the balance of payments, exchange rate fluctuations leading to periodical over- or undervaluing of national currencies, or political and social pressures against foreign companies, may be mitigated if the corporations can resort to the use of internal prices. In these cases, real transactions may also be employed as an instrument for financial ones – that is, purchases of components and finished goods can be utilized to send dividends or royalties to the parent companies. Thus transfer prices make it possible to decapitalize subsidiaries when risks of nationalization are apparent, or to avoid regulations on profit remittances, royalties and management fees imposed by host country governments.

We expect factors inducing transfer price manipulation to have a positive influence on the extent of internal transactions performed by the corporations, since these transactions can generate financial flows that are difficult to control. Accordingly, the usual incentives to manipulate transfer pricing (namely, the existence of international differences in tariffs, taxes and subsidies, restrictions on financial flows, and multiple exchange rates regimes) will also encourage the internalization of trade. Several studies have discussed the possible LDC losses from the MNCs' discretionary pricing policies for intra-firm transactions (for example, Lall, 1973, 1979b; and Vaitsos, 1974). We do not have access to sufficient information to examine the price issue, but, in this context, it may be relevant to probe into the question of whether the extent of intra-firm imports is greater in the case of LDC affiliates than in other affiliates.

Several previous studies have dealt empirically with intra-firm trade. Among earlier contributions, the most directly germane to the subject of this study are the works of Lall (1978a), Helleiner (1979), Helleiner and Lavergne (1980), and Casson (1986).

Lall (1978a) examined the determinants of the exports by US multi-national corporations to their majority-owned foreign affiliates (MOFAs) by means of a regression analysis, performed on industry-level data for 1970. The dependent variables used by Lall were the intra-firm exports for each US industry, expressed both as a percentage of total MNC exports for that industry, and as a percentage of sales of the affiliates receiving these exports. He found that intra-firm exports were positively related both to an industry's research and development expenditures, and to its degree of internationalization (measured by the ratio of foreign to domestic assets). Dummy variables for after-sales service requirements and divisibilities of the production process also exhibited statistically significant positive influences on the intra-corporate export flows. On the other hand, the advertising-to-sales ratio showed a negative impact, suggesting that heavily advertised goods do not require highly specialized after-sales services provided by the foreign affiliates.

Further research performed by Sleuwaegen (1985) also found the positive correlation between intra-firm exports and the research intensity of parent companies to be strikingly high compared to that of exports to unrelated parties, suggesting that exports from US parent companies to their foreign affiliates consist of relatively high technology commodities.[3] Further estimates showed a high R&D content in trade of goods for resale, and an even higher R&D content in the case of intermediate goods.

Buckley and Pearce (1979) provided empirical tests of the so called internalization theory, developed in Buckley and Casson (1976). A more recent treatment of this theory can be found in Casson (1986). According to this theory, firms have incentives to internalize the markets for intermediate goods when external markets are imperfect. A high degree of market imperfections is expected in the case of technology transactions, because such transactions embody information. Thus, this theory predicts a high proportion of intra-corporate trade when the transacted intermediate goods have a large content of technological innovation. Empirical tests, using data from 156 of the world's largest enterprises, suggested a strong positive correlation between intra-firm exports and the size of the parents and the research intensity of the industry (no data on the research intensity of the parent companies were available).[4]

Pearce (1982), using a sample of the world's largest firms derived from Dunning and Pearce's (1981) survey, found an inverse U-shaped association between intra-firm exports and the degree of multina-

tionality of firms. His explanation was that a high level of multinationality leads to multilateral trade between different subsidiaries,
rather than between parents and affiliates. Bilateral trade in the form
of exports to and from the parent company shows the highest intensities in corporations with medium levels of international spread.

Helleiner (1979) analyzed the imports of US industries from
'related parties', which include not only US MNCs' imports from their
affiliates abroad, but also imports of foreign-owned subsidiaries in the
USA from their parent companies or other related affiliates abroad.
These two trade flows are, of course, very different, since US parents'
imports originate to a large extent from the LDCs and Canada, while
non-US firms' imports come mainly from other developed countries.
Helleiner found, however, a statistically significant positive impact of
R&D intensity, skill intensity (proxied by average wages), and average
firm size in US industries (as a measure of barriers to entry) on intra-
firm imports. Helleiner and Lavergne (1980) extended the analysis
further and used other data, where imports were disaggregated by
region of origin. Once again, research intensity showed a strongly
positive correlation with intra-firm trade, while firm size and skill
intensity had statistically significant positive effects only in the cases
of total intra-corporate imports and imports originating from OECD
countries.

Only one study, Goldsbrough (1981), presents empirical evidence
on the low responsiveness of intra-firm transactions to changes in relative prices. His findings suggest that both imports of US firms from
their MOFAs and exports from US affiliates in several countries to
their parents are less sensitive to relative price changes than are conventional trade flows. Additional tests indicated that the differences
in the price elasticities of the two types of trade flow cannot be attributed to differences in their commodity composition.

In studies by Swedenborg (1979 and 1982), using data from 1974
and 1978, respectively, the effects of production abroad on Swedish
exports were analyzed. To do this she estimated separately models
for exports from Swedish parents to their affiliates (which she called
complementary exports) and to other firms in the host country (called
substitute exports). Although the issue she addresses (and the independent variable and model specifications) is not the same as in our
case, some of her results are useful for our study. However, when
results from regressions across firms and countries, for the two sample
years, are compared, one finds that some variables are significant in
one case and not in the other. Nevertheless, for the following cases

she found similar results for both 1974 and 1978: complementary exports were positively influenced by the corporation's R&D/sales ratio and by the comparative advantages of Swedish firms in relation to the home country's resource endowments. The latter was measured by a dummy variable equal to 1 when the parent company is in the paper and pulp or iron and steel industries. The parent company's capital–labour ratio had a negative but statistically insignificant influence on its exports to the affiliates. Finally, the sign of the coefficient of the host country's GDP per capita was positive and significant in the 1974 sample, but insignificant in the 1978 one.

Of the studies referred to above, Swedenborg's are the only ones that look at inter-firm variations in intra-corporate trade. She has, however, not addressed the latter issue explicitly. The studies we have surveyed above suggest an extensive list of hypotheses that we test using the disaggregated firm-level data for Swedish multinational corporations. However, before we state these hypotheses, a few words on the specific characteristics of Swedish foreign investment and host countries' import restrictions are warranted.

Swedish firms investing abroad are mainly engaged in production for local markets, and not in off-shore production (see Blomström and Lipsey, 1989). This orientation conditions the pattern of relationships between parents and subsidiaries, and thereby the character of the affiliates' imports. First, these subsidiaries are, to some degree, simply used as sales offices for goods produced elsewhere. Second, their production is dependent on flows of intermediate and capital goods provided by the corporations. For many countries, particularly LDCs, imports are perceived as a burden to the balance of payments. In addition, the import of finished goods, and of technology in embodied form, is considered to weaken the extent of the technology transfer. For all these reasons, and because of the fear of transfer price manipulations, local authorities in many countries have tried to discourage foreign affiliates' imports through the imposition of regulations. Therefore, these policy measures have to be taken into account when studying the determinants of subsidiaries' imports.

6.3   Hypotheses and explanatory variables

The data used in this study are mainly from the 1978 survey of Swedish investment abroad compiled by the Research Institute of Industrial Economics (IUI) in Stockholm.[5] The survey covers virtually all Swedish manufacturing firms investing abroad and gives data for parents and their majority-owned foreign affiliates. In 1978 there were 118 Swedish manufacturing firms investing abroad and 570 majority-owned foreign affiliates (MOFAs) involved in production activities.[6] The data on these firms are supplemented by official statistics on a few host country characteristics, and data from the US Department of Commerce (1981) on the host countries' import requirements.

Our study concentrates on the Swedish foreign affiliates' intra-firm imports, or more precisely, on the MOFAs' imports from their parents, and our dependent variable, *IMPAFF*, is defined as the ratio of the foreign affiliates' total imports from their parents to the affiliates' total sales.[7] The variable thus not only includes semi-processed materials, but also finished goods. This is, however, in accordance with the wide definition of intermediate goods in this field (see, for example, Casson, 1986, p. 8). The subsidiaries' exports to their parents are neglected because for Swedish MNCs such exports are insignificant, except in the case of textiles and clothing (off-shore production in Portugal and Finland – see Swedenborg, 1982). We also neglect Swedish MOFAs' imports from other Swedish affiliates abroad, through lack of information.

As the discussion above indicated, there is much evidence in the literature suggesting that intra-firm trade is strongly related to an industry's R&D intensity. Specific technologies developed within a firm may be embodied either in capital goods or in intermediate products provided by the parent company. Imports from the parent companies may then be a channel for technology transfers within a corporation. High R&D expenditure is expected to indicate a high degree of technological innovativeness and/or a high degree of product differentiation in a firm, and according to the so-called internalization theory (Buckley and Casson, 1976), both these aspects encourage the internalization of transactions. We use the MNCs' total R&D expenditures as a percentage of their total sales (*R&DMNC*) as a measure of the technological intensity of the multinationals, and expect this variable to be positively related to our dependent variable.

A firm's managerial capacity is expected to be another important determinant of intra-firm trade. A firm with relatively good access to managers would probably be better equipped to coordinate purchases, sales and internal prices in different markets, and therefore more likely to engage in them. We use the ratio of white-collar workers to the total number of employees in the parent firm (denoted

MAN) as a proxy for this type of resources and also expect this variable to be positively related to the dependent variable.

Furthermore, we also include a variable (denoted *FA*) for the degree of multinationality of firms, measured as the ratio of the firms' foreign assets to their assets in Sweden (assets in book value). When such a variable, as in Lall (1978a), is based on industry data, and the dependent variable is the industry's total exports to related parties, it seems logical to expect the degree of multinationality to have a positive effect on internal transactions. However, the picture is different when, as in this study, firm-level data and affiliate imports from parents are used as the dependent variable. Then we expect trade between affiliates to become more intense the higher the degree of multinationality of the corporation. Thus it seems reasonable to assume that the subsidiaries' imports from the parent companies decrease when multilateral flows increase. Since we do not have any data on trade between affiliates, we use the degree of multinationality as a proxy for such flows. Hence, the variable *FA* is expected to have a negative impact on our dependent variable[8].

We also noted above that Buckley and Casson (1976) and Casson (1986) suggested that common ownership and centralized planning should occur when production in different stages calls for coordination. Through internalization, a firm can avoid the costs related to the operation of external markets covering diverse circumstances, or the establishment of forward markets insuring future deliveries or purchases. Since an intense utilization of durable equipment will characterize these kinds of production process, Buckley and Casson suggested the use of capital intensity as an adequate proxy for synchronization requirements. We use the ratio of the value of plant and machinery (book value) to the number of employees for each parent company (*KLPAR*) as a measure of capital intensity. To the extent that this variable really represents the complex processes suggested by Buckley and Casson, we expect it to be positively related to the affiliates' imports from their parents.

Another hypothesis is that subsidiaries founded by acquisition of local firms will not become as fully integrated into the network of the MNCs as firms created by greenfield investments. Hence the extent of internal transactions with purchased affiliates may be less than with new ventures. In the latter case, linkages between the new foreign branch and a MNC's network are planned from the beginning, leading to closer relationships and more intense flows of transactions. We therefore introduce a dummy variable (*ACQ*) that equals 1 if the subsidiary was integrated into the corporation through the acquisition of an already existing firm, and 0 otherwise.[9]

Finally, three variables describing certain host country traits are used in the regressions. First, we expect exchange-rate speculation, restrictions on remissions and profit repatriation, multiple exchange-rate regimes, price controls, and differences in tariffs and taxes between countries to encourage transfer price manipulations, and thus intra-firm transactions. Unfortunately, neither estimates of tariffs and tax levels for different countries, nor sophisticated measures indicating incentives for exchange-rate speculation were available. Furthermore, we do not have price data for the imports of the affiliates either. Instead, we used a country's balance of payments situation as a rough indicator of the existence of factors inducing the manipulation of transfer prices. In order to capture the structural, rather than the cyclical position of a country, we took the average yearly international reserves in 1976–8, measured in weeks of imports, as our independent variable (denoted *RESRV*). In this way we try to capture the possibility of transfer price manipulation by postulating that the larger the country's international reserves, the less the incentive for a firm to rely on transfer price manipulation and to increase the level of internal transactions. This is, obviously, a rough test. Still, it should at least allow us to test hypotheses about other determinants of the foreign affiliates' imports by controlling, to some extent, the possible influence of some incentives for transfer price manipulation. Thus, the expected sign for *RESRV* is negative.

Policy measures directly aimed at reducing the foreign affiliates' imports should also be of importance here. Ideally, one would like to know whether a particular Swedish subsidiary has been forced to limit its imports, but there is no such information available. Instead we use data from the 1977 Benchmark Survey of US Foreign Direct Investment (US Department of Commerce, 1981), and construct our variable *REQ* as the number of US foreign affiliates that were required to import no more than a certain amount, over the total number of US foreign affiliates answering the question in a host country. We then assume that each country can be characterized by a certain level of intervention, and that all foreign subsidiaries located there experience the same pressures. Thus the variable we construct is a measure of the degree in which the host country resorts to import restrictions. We expect the regression coefficient for *REQ* to be negative.

In the development literature, it is often claimed that the LDCs are the main victims of transfer pricing practices. It is therefore interesting to check whether affiliates located in developing countries import relatively more from their parents than do those located in developed countries. There are strong reasons to believe that this is not the case. Many studies have shown the importance of intra-industry trade between developed countries (see Pagoulatos and Sorensen, 1975; Havrylyshyn and Civan, 1985; Balassa, 1986; and Culem and Lundberg, 1986). Such trade generally takes place in differentiated goods produced in the presence of economies of scale, and a great proportion of it is accounted for by trade within MNCs. We therefore, expect the one-way transactions studied here to reflect this pattern of trade to some extent. The rationale for this is as follows. Economic growth generally leads to an increasing need for a wide range of products. As differences in income levels are associated with different patterns of demand, we expect the demand for imports of consumer goods to differ between LDCs and DCs. In particular, consumer demand in developed countries shows a strong preference for differentiated goods. In the presence of economies of scale, subsidiaries can satisfy consumer preferences with their own products only by completing their product ranges through imports from affiliate units. Differentiated goods, developed and produced by the parents in Sweden are thus expected to be exported to a larger extent to affiliates established in DCs. In order to test this hypothesis, we include the host country's GNP per capita in 1978, denoted *GNPCAP*, and expect its coefficient to show a positive sign.

6.4 Empirical results

On the basis of the considerations discussed in the previous section, our model is:

$$IMPAFF = f(R\&DMNC, MAN, FA, KLPAR, ACQ$$
$$(+) \qquad\quad (+) \quad (-) \quad (+) \qquad (-)$$
$$RESRV, REQ, GNPCAP)$$
$$(-) \quad\ (-) \qquad (+)$$

The dependent variable is constrained between 0 and 1, so a logistic model to constrain the predicted values to the expected range would be appropriate. However, since the proportion of predicted values outside the 0–1 range does not account for more than 4 per cent in any of the regressions, we chose a less sophisticated approach and used a linear model which was estimated with OLS, with known small-sample properties. The variables were standardized by dividing them by their corresponding sample means. This procedure transforms the values of the variables into indices, which allow us to compare directly the coefficients estimated.

The most important statistical findings are reported in Table 6.1 (see Appendix Table A-6.1 on page 80 for correlation matrices). With the assumption of normally distributed errors, the research intensity variable ($R\&DMNC$) registers a positive coefficient that is statistically different from zero at the 0.01 level. This result is in line with findings from earlier studies based on industry data, and suggests that R&D promotes the internalization of markets for goods.

Also, the FA variable, which shows the degree of multinationality of the corporation, and was introduced as a proxy for possible intra-firm trade between affiliates, is highly significant with the expected negative sign. The capital-intensity variable, on the other hand, plays an insignificant role in our regressions, as it did in Helleiner (1979). This variable was introduced to capture the influence of uncertainties and risks that arise when synchronization in production is needed. However, it may be the case that the variable is an imperfect indicator of these factors, and that the claims concerning the role of risk suggested by the internalization theory (Buckley and Casson, 1976) are, nevertheless, correct.

The variable ACQ, aimed at taking into account the influence of the form of incorporation of the subsidiary, shows the expected negative sign and is statistically significant. The balance of payments constraint, proxied by $RESRV$, turns out to be statistically significant. Thus the larger the host country's reserves, the lower the degree to which Swedish affiliates in this country import from their parents. To what extent this result can be taken to corroborate that these imports are influenced by transfer price considerations is, however, uncertain, since this variable is a very rough proxy for incentives to manipulate transfer prices. We shall return to this issue later. At this stage we shall only note that this result does not contradict Casson's conclusion from case studies, indicating that transfer pricing is not 'the principal motive for establishing intra-firm trade' (Casson, 1986, p. 59).

The REQ variable, reflecting host government's policies aimed at reducing the affiliates' imports, is significantly less than zero, suggesting that these measures have an impact on the affiliates' performance. This question will also be given further consideration below, when the

Table 6.1   Results of OLS estimations of determinants of the Swedish subsidiaries' intra-firm imports,
total sample

	(1)	(2)
Constant	2.258	1.778
	(10.173)***	(6.679)***
R&DMNC	0.259	0.244
	(4.516)***	(4.403)***
MAN	−0.519	−0.459
	(−2.707)***	(−2.554)***
FA	−0.253	−2.243
	(−3.013)***	(−3.070)**
KLPAR	0.014	0.032
	(0.200)	(0.495)
ACQ	−0.876	−0.889
	(−6.924)***	(−7.331)***
RESRV	−0.284	−0.261
	(−2.736)***	(−2.646)***
REQ	−0.139	
	(−2.325)***	
GNPCAP		0.293
		(2.081)***
$\bar{R}^2$	0.2146	0.1984
F	(13.768)***	(13.483)***
SSE	389.06418	405.60261
n	326	352

Notes: Dependent variable: *IMPAFF*. Figures in
parentheses are t-statistics. The asterisks *, ** and
*** indicate significance at the 10, 5 and 1 per cent
level of confidence, respectively.

differences between the results of the LDC and the DC samples are
considered.

Finally, the *GNPCAP* variable bears a positive and statistically significant coefficient. Thus, as in the case of intra-industry trade, the one-
way, intra-firm transactions studied here appear to be more intense
between high-income countries.

To sum up, the signs of nearly all coefficients are in agreement with
our predictions, and almost all the coefficients are statistically significant. Further, most of the point estimates are very robust to minor
modifications in the specification of the model and the sample size.[10]
The only variable that does not perform as expected is *MAN*, which

refers to the firm's managerial resources. This variable shows an unexpected statistically significant negative sign, and it is hard to find a reasonable explanation for this. It is worth noting, however, that Sleuwaegen (1985) found a similar result, although his variable was not significant.

To investigate the factors behind the affiliates' internalized imports more deeply, we applied our statistical model separately to the subsidiaries established in developed and developing countries. The idea behind such a separation is that differences between LDCs and DCs may not be sufficiently captured by the per capita income variable. Features common to LDCs, such as the countries' level of technological development, with its implications for the possibilities of subcontracting and the degree of development of infrastructure, could, for example, influence the affiliate's import behaviour in specific ways.

As Table 6.2 shows, there seem to exist some disparities between the two subsamples. One of these is the lack of differences, in the LDCs, between new ventures and subsidiaries incorporated through acquisitions, while this fact seems to be relevant for the import performance of affiliates in DCs. The reason for this is unclear, but one may speculate whether it has to do with the limited possibilities for subcontracting in the LDCs. That may force foreign subsidiaries to rely more heavily on their parent companies, no matter in what form they have been incorporated to the MNC.

Another difference is that the variable for the degree of multinationality, *FA*, loses significance in the case of developing countries. If this variable reflects the existence of intra-corporate trade flows other than those originated in the parent company, this may indicate that the subsidiaries in the LDCs are relatively more dependent on their parents for their imports, while affiliates in DCs are more integrated into the MNCs' overall networks, and more involved in triangular or multilateral transactions. The requirement variable (*REQ*) turns out to be significantly different from zero in the DC sample, but not in the sample for the LDCs. However, the reason for this seems to be a purely statistical one: the variation in the LDC sample is considerably lower than in the DC sample.

It is surprising that the variable *RESRV* is not statistically significant in the case of LDCs. We introduced this variable to capture some indirect effects on intra-firm trade, through the encouragement of transfer-price manipulation. The reasons for this lack of significance may lie in the fact that a large proportion of the Swedish subsidiaries in the LDCs were, in 1978, located in Latin America, with their activities directed mainly towards domestic host country markets. The development strategies pursued by the different Latin-American countries are similar, and could, in most cases, be considered as varieties of import-substitution policies. This being the case, short-term shifts in both the evolution of exchange-rate regimes and the regulatory policies would not have any significant effects on the MNCs' planned levels of internal transaction. Because of the peculiarities of our data, discussed above, further research using a broader sample might be necessary. We must, however, conclude that we have not found any strong support for the transfer pricing effect on the affiliates' imports. Finally, it is worth noting that the technological factors indicated by the variable *R&DMNC* appear to play an important role

Table 6.2   Results of OLS estimations of determinants of the Swedish subsidiaries' intra-firm imports

	DCs		LDCs	
	(3)	**(4)**	**(5)**	**(6)**
Constant	2.318	2.025	1.541	1.024
	(9.082)***	(6.526)***	(2.398)**	(1.839)*
RDMNC	0.262	0.250	0.336	0.283
	(3.842)***	(3.835)***	(2.915)***	(2.869)***
MAN	−0.512	−0.449	−0.760	−0.741
	(−2.445)**	(−2.283)**	(−1.441)	(−1.633)
FA	−0.267	−0.258	−0.193	−0.131
	(−2.836)***	(−2.934)***	(−0.997)	(−0.758)
KLPAR	0.007	0.021	0.055	0.040
	(0.092)	(0.300)	(0.191)	(0.154)
ACQ	−0.966	−0.956	−0.494	−0.422
	(−6.804)***	(−7.108)***	(−1.560)	(−1.539)
RESRV	−0.226	−0.206	−0.102	−0.118
	(−1.449)	(−1.397)	(−0.544)	(−0.664)
REQ	−0.289		−0.037	
	(−1.935)**		(−0.530)	
GNPCAP		0.093		1.765
		(0.498)		(1.306)
$\bar{R}^2$	0.2166	0.2008	0.1349	0.1173
F	(11.623)***	(11.659)***	(2.269)**	(2.044)*
SSE	335.66016	364.03462	46.71920	33.25432
n	269	297	57	55

Notes: Dependent variable: *IMPAFF*. Figures in parentheses are t-statistics. The asterisks *, ** and *** indicate significance at the 10, 5 and 1 per cent levels of confidence, respectively.

in explaining internalized imports of subsidiaries located in both DCs and LDCs.

The inability of the estimated model to capture the statistical structure in the sample of LDCs, may be attributed partially to the low number of observations available. However, there is a possibility that this result reflects a different structure in the two subsamples. In order to see whether the factors that explain the subsidiaries' propensities to import from their parents are the same in both cases, we performed a Chow test (Chow, 1960). According to the results of this test, the assumption that the coefficients for the two subsamples are equal cannot be rejected.[11] Thus, although we can speculate on the possible economic reasons behind the lack of significance of certain variables in the sample for LDCs, the test suggests that no significant differences necessarily exist between the two subsamples.

6.5 Summary and conclusions

This study has sought to shed some light on factors influencing intra-corporate trade. Firm-level data on almost the entire population of Swedish MNCs were examined, the focus being on the imports of the foreign majority-owned affiliates from their parent companies. We were able to take into account firm and host country characteristics, making the analysis more detailed than in previous industry-level work. The principal deficiency of our investigation is that we could not differentiate between imports of different types of product. However, a separate analysis was performed for affiliates located in DCs and LDCs.

The statistical analysis both confirmed several findings from earlier studies performed on more aggregated data, and identified other determinants of the propensity to internalize transactions within international corporations. The study shows, first, that the extent of the subsidiaries' imports from their parents increase with the parents' expenditure on R&D. Second, these imports are affected negatively by the parents' degree of multinationality. Here one may speculate whether the existence of a network of affiliates reduces the extent of the subsidiaries' imports from the parents, as triangular and multilateral trade between related units increase.

Our results also underline the importance of the way in which a subsidiary has been incorporated into the corporation. Affiliates founded by acquisition of already existing firms showed lower import intensities. Moreover, host country policies aimed at reducing the subsidiaries' imports appeared to have significant effects. Another finding was that the affiliates' internalized imports in 1978 were negatively correlated with the average yearly international reserves of the host country for the period 1976–8. This last variable was used as a proxy for possible structural balance of payment pressures in the host country, which were expected to increase the risks of regulations on the affiliate's financial flows. In order to circumvent these regulations through the use of transfer pricing, we expected that affiliates in countries experiencing foreign currency shortage should have higher levels of import from their parents. The evidence on this issue is, however, inconclusive, partly because of the rough measure we had to use, and partly because the variable aimed at capturing this effect was not significant in the case of the LDC sample.

We distinguished between subsidiaries located in DCs and LDCs, and applied the statistical model to them separately. The model's fit and the level of significance of many variables were considerably lower in the LDC case. This could be attributed partly to the low number of observations in this subsample, but some hypotheses on the economic reasons behind such results were advanced. Finally, a Chow test was performed and gave no statistical evidence to reject the hypothesis that no significant differences exist between the two subsamples.

The activities of the Swedish MOFAs are mainly directed towards local markets. This homogeneity regarding market orientation appears to affect the affiliates' pattern of imports in such way that no differences arise from the mere fact that they are located in developed or less developed countries.

Our study brings out some important results for the very topical issue of intra-firm transactions. First, they indicate that the internalization theory is a fruitful theoretical approach for the understanding of these transactions. Second, we did not find evidence that Swedish subsidiaries in LDCs import relatively more from their parents than affiliates established in DCs. Furthermore, we found that the extent of these imports seems to increase with the host country's per capita income.

Notes

1. In the literature, there seem to be two different ways of looking at transfer pricing. Although it is not our intention to evaluate them here, they can be illustrated by quotes from M. Casson, and A. Rugman and L. Eden, respectively. For a fuller discussion of transfer pricing, see Plasschaert (1979). 'Transfer pricing occurs when the accounting price

at which intra-firm transactions take place differs from the price that would prevail in an arm's length market. Opportunities for transfer pricing arise when customs authorities are lax in checking the prices of intra-firm exports and imports, or when the intermediate products are so specific that there is no arm's length price to check against. The incentives to transfer pricing stem from the opportunity it provides to reduce the firm's global tax liability by transferring accounting profits to low-tax countries. It is also possible to reduce ad valorem tariff payments by understating the value of imports, and to avoid exchange controls by disguising capital transfers as expenditure flows' (Casson, 1986, p. 17); 'A transfer price can be defined as the price used for internal sales of goods and services between the divisions of a business enterprise' (Rugman and Eden, 1985, p. 1).

2. By the affiliates' internalized imports we mean the affiliates' imports from their parents.

3. The dependent variable in Sleuwaegen's study was the ratio of each US industry's exports to affiliated foreign firms to the consolidated world sales of US-based MNCs for that industry.

4. Buckley and Pearce use two measures of intra-firm exports: parent exports to overseas affiliates (internal exports) in relation to parent production, and the ratio of internal exports to total parent exports.

5. See Swedenborg (1982) for a description of the data.

6. The intensity by which these affiliates import from their parents varies considerably between industries. In transport equipment and metals, 37 and 28 per cent, respectively, of the affiliates' sales were imports from the parents. In food, paper, paper products, non-electrical machinery and other manufacturing industries it was generally less than 10 per cent (Swedenborg, 1982, p. 104).

7. Another measure of the dependent variable is, of course, the ratio of intra-firm imports to total imports, but no data are available on the affiliates' total imports.

8. To test for the possibility of an inverse U-shaped relationship between the subsidiaries' internal imports and the parents' degree of internationalization, as suggested by Pearce (1982), a quadratic formulation for the variable *FA* was tried. Since it did not give significant results, this specification was dropped.

9. It seems likely that this effect should be stronger in the case of recent acquisitions. That turned out not to be the case. A dummy variable was set equal to 1 for acquisitions after a certain date (different dates were tried) and 0 otherwise, but they gave similar results to those obtained for the dummy *ACQ*.

10. As we have already pointed out, Swedenborg (1982) estimated the determinants of the Swedish parents' exports to their foreign affiliates. Although the dependent variable in that study differs from our variable, the results are generally consistent. In particular, she found the R&D variable to be significant, while the capital intensity variable was not significant (ibid., p. 178).

11. The null hypothesis to be tested is that the coefficients for the two sub-samples are equal. The test variable is:

$$F = \frac{(SSE_w - SSE_{DC} - SSE_{LDC})/K}{(SSE_{DC} + SSE_{LDC})/(n_{DC} + n_{LDC} - 2K)} - F(K, n_{DC} + n_{LDC} - 2K)$$

where K = number of parameters (including the intercept); n = number of observations; SSE = sum of square of errors; W = world-wide sample; DC = subsample for DCs; LDC = subsample for LDCs. For models 1, 3 and 5 the ratio F (8310) is 0.68. The two sets of observations can be considered to come from the same structure at the 0.05 level of significance if $F < 1.94$, given the degrees of freedom of our subsamples. A similar result is obtained for models 2, 4 and 6.

Appendix

Table A-6.1   Correlation matrices

	R&DMNC	**MAN**	**FA**	**KLPAR**	**ACQ**	**RESRV**	**REQ**
Worldwide sample							
R&DMNC							
MAN	0.357						
FA	0.127	0.350					
KLPAR	−0.150	0.126	−0.033				
ACQ	−0.117	−0.068	−0.099	0.121			
RESRV	0.076	−0.076	0.131	−0.082	−0.065		
REQ	0.061	−0.004	0.087	−0.046	−0.171	0.361	
GNPCAP	−0.145	−0.018	−0.067	0.045	0.237	−0.326	−0.636
Sample for DCs							
R&DMNC							
MAN	0.345						
FA	0.162	0.357					
KLPAR	−0.141	0.152	−0.349				
ACQ	−0.075	−0.079	−0.077	0.114			
RESRV	−0.060	−0.113	0.134	−0.068	0.082		
REQ	0.015	−0.012	0.045	−0.026	−0.102	0.110	
GNPCAP	−0.086	−0.057	0.003	−0.019	0.159	0.144	−0.647
Sample for LDCs							
R&DMNC							
MAN	0.526						
FA	−0.082	0.304					
KLPAR	−0.199	−0.276	−0.154				
ACQ	−0.194	−0.031	−0.122	0.070			
RESRV	0.143	0.071	−0.055	0.102	−0.056		
REQ	−0.106	0.030	0.077	0.087	−0.108	−0.049	
GNPCAP	0.065	0.098	−0.130	0.124	0.134	0.487	−0.475

Sources: GNPCAP was taken from *International Finance Statistics, Supplement on Output Statistics*, Supplement Series No. 8, Washington DC: IMF, 1984; RESRV comes from *International Finance Statistics, Supplement on International Reserves*, Supplement Series No. 6, Washington DC: IMF, 1983; The variable REQ was constructed from the *1977 Benchmark Survey of US Foreign Direct Investment*, US Department of Commerce, 1981. All the remaining variables are constructed from the IUI 1978 *Survey of Swedish Multinational Corporations*.

7
MNCs and Structural Adjustment in Latin America: Lessons from the Debt Crisis

7.1 Introduction

In the backwash of the debt financing of the 1970s and the world-wide recession of the early 1980s, many developing countries, particularly in Latin America, ran into serious debt-servicing difficulties. To cope with this debt crisis, radical policy changes were introduced. These 'structural adjustment programmes' generally included deregulation and privatization of the economies, and opening them to external markets and competition.[1] The shift from inward to outward orientation has involved shifting production from domestic to export markets. In this study, we examine the extent to which a number of heavily-indebted Latin American countries have redirected their sales of manufactured goods to world markets and the role of multinational corporations in this shift. We are particularly interested in investigating whether affiliates of multinational firms are better equipped to redirect their sales than local firms in developing countries.[2]

It is not difficult to think of reasons why MNCs should find it easier to switch markets than other firms. MNCs have internal markets already set up to supplement external markets. This could give them opportunities to switch their sales of finished products or components from local to overseas markets. MNCs also presumably have greater access than local firms to market information, distribution channels and international marketing skills, all of which facilitate access to export markets.

There are a number of possible measures of 'export performance' by countries and groups of firms that one could use. One is the rate of growth of exports. Another might be the growth of exports to devel-

81

oped country markets, the more competitive part of world markets and those in which the exporters would be sure to earn convertible currency. Still another would take account of the industries in which exports were originally concentrated and measure the degree to which the countries' or firms' export growth exceeded or fell short of what it would have been if it had simply kept up with the world growth of exports in each industry.

A somewhat different way of judging export performance would be to examine the proportion of output exported, or the propensity to export, assuming that one of the tasks of adjustment is that of shifting sales from domestic to export markets. An ambiguity in changes in the propensity to export is that a rise could be achieved by increasing exports from increasing production, by moving sales from local to export markets without changing production, or simply by reducing domestic sales or even reducing both export and domestic sales, but the latter more rapidly. Clearly, the last would be the least desirable form of adjustment from the point of view of the host country.

The chapter is organized as follows. The next section examines the export growth of five heavily-indebted Latin American countries for which data on US multinationals' trade is available, and compares them with a less-heavily-indebted group of Asian countries for which we also have MNC data. We take 1977–82 to represent the period before the debt crisis and periods after 1982 to represent the debt crisis era. The third section investigates similar measures of export performance for US affiliates in these countries during the same periods. Changes in export propensities of US affiliates and their host economies are discussed in the fourth and fifth sections, respectively. The sixth section looks at US affiliates' export performance by industry group, and the seventh section concludes the study.

7.2   The export performance of countries

The manufactured exports of all developing market economies as a group were increasing rapidly in nominal terms, expressed in US dollars, in the five years before the debt crisis (see Table 7.1). The countries that were not later labelled as being heavily indebted raised their manufactured exports (in $US) by over 16 per cent per annum between 1977 and 1982, while the heavily-indebted countries increased their exports by about 15 per cent per annum. After 1982, the rate of increase was only 2.5 per cent per year for the more

Table 7.1 Average annual growth rates of manufactured exports from developing countries, various periods, 1977–88, percentages

	Nominal values			**Purchasing power over developed country manufactured exports**		
	1977–82	**1982–6**	**1982–8**	**1977–82**	**1982–6**	**1982–8**
Total developing market economies	13.2	8.5	14.8	6.7	5.0	8.5
Latin America	10.4	6.8	11.9	4.0	3.4	5.8
Asia, except Middle East	15.5	10.7	17.2	8.8	7.2	10.8
Five heavily-indebted Latin American countries	15.2	2.4	11.6	8.5	–0.9	5.5
Brazil	15.0	3.2	9.5	8.3	–0.2	3.5
Chile	6.1	3.5	12.7	0.0	0.1	6.5
Colombia	10.8	0.8	7.6	4.4	–2.4	1.7
Mexico	12.3	11.2	21.4	5.8	7.7	14.8
Venezuela	33.5	–28.8	–15.5	25.7	–31.1	–20.2
Chile, Colombia, Mexico	10.5	9.0	18.9	4.0	5.4	12.4
Seven less-indebted Asian countries[a]	16.5	11.2	17.7	9.7	7.6	11.3

Notes: [a] Hong Kong, India, Malaysia, Singapore, South Korea, Taiwan and Thailand.
Source: Lipsey *et al.* (1991), table A7.1.

indebted group up to the end of 1986, but then rose rapidly to almost 12 per cent for the period up to the end of 1988. For the less-indebted countries, the annual rate of increase between 1982 and 1988 reached almost 18 per cent.

A somewhat different picture of the two periods is given by the second set of three columns in Table 7.1, which shows the same export growth in terms of the purchasing power over manufactured products exported by developed countries to developing countries. In these terms, the less-indebted countries are seen to have enjoyed not only substantial real export growth in manufactures between 1977 and 1982, but even faster growth in 1982–8 than before: a rise in the growth rate of over 15 per cent. The heavily-indebted countries are shown to have had slower real manufactures export growth in the 1977–82 period than had the less-indebted countries, and declines in real manufactured exports from 1982 to 1986. In the three restructuring countries – Chile, Colombia and Mexico – real export growth from 1982 to 1988, especially after 1986, outran that of the less-indebted countries.

7.3 The export performance of manufacturing affiliates of US firms

The export performance of US affiliates in the same countries and in two geographical areas during the same periods is described in Table 7.2. In the heavily-indebted Latin American countries, these affiliates expanded their exports more rapidly than their host countries in most periods, but the data are ambiguous for 1982–8. In real terms, their export growth was somewhat higher in 1982–8 than before the debt crisis. This acceleration can be explained largely by affiliates in Mexico, but it probably extended to Chile as well; in Brazil there was a deceleration of export growth by US affiliates after 1982. That

Table 7.2   Average annual growth rates of exports by US majority-owned manufacturing affiliates in developing countries, various years, 1977–88

	Nominal values			Purchasing power over developed country manufactured exports		
	1977–82	1982–6	1982–8	1977–82	1982–6	1982–8
Total developing market economies	15.3	7.4	11.6	8.6	3.9	5.4
Latin America	14.9	8.4	12.4	8.2	4.9	6.3
Asia, except Middle East	15.2–15.6	7.0–8.2	11.1–11.5	8.5–8.9	3.5–4.7	5.0–5.4
Five heavily-indebted Latin American countries	15.7–16.4	14.2–14.6	16.1–16.7	9.0–9.6	9.0–9.6	9.7–10.3
Brazil	16.2	7.0	10.0	9.4	3.6	4.0
Chile	8.4–26.6	n.a.	22.0–38.8	2.2–19.2	n.a.	15.3–31.2
Colombia	9.0	−2.6	10.6	2.7	−5.7	4.6
Mexico	16.0	26.8	25.4	9.2	22.7	18.5
Venezuela	n.a.	n.a.	n.a.	n.a.	n.a.	n.a.
Seven less-indebted Asian countries[a]	15.6–16.3	8.3–9.6	12.4–13.1	8.9–9.6	4.8–6.0	6.3–6.9

Notes: [a]   Hong Kong, India, Malaysia, Singapore, South Korea, Taiwan and Thailand.
Source: Blomström and Lipsey (1993), table A.2.

slowdown in growth was also evident for affiliates in Latin America as a whole.

In the less-indebted group of Asian developing countries, the rate of export growth in real terms by US affiliates was lower after 1982 than before. Although the individual country data (not shown here) are somewhat skimpy, the comparisons with aggregate export growth in these countries suggest that the US multinationals' affiliates kept up with their countries' export growth before 1982, but lagged after that, and this was also the case for US affiliates in the developing Asian countries as a group. In other words, although US affiliates in Asia did well in terms of exports during the 1980s, locally-owned Asian firms and other multinationals in the region did better.

An important difference between the two groups of developing countries is that while US firms are the major multinationals in Latin America, and therefore among the heavily-indebted countries, this is not the case among the Asian countries listed. In these, Japanese firms play more of a role than do US firms. Thus the US affiliates are a good approximation of multinationals in general in Latin America, while in the Asian countries a large part of exports by multinationals were made by Japanese firms and are not included in our data.[3]

7.4   The export propensities of affiliates of US multinationals

There has been a long-term trend towards greater export orientation among the foreign affiliates of US firms. It has been present in affiliates in both developed and developing countries, but the export propensity of affiliates in developing countries was in 1977 less than 60 per cent of that in developed countries, and in 1982 still only about 60 per cent as large (Table 7.3). After 1982, however, the export propensities of LDC affiliates leapt, rising by almost 50 per cent to over 80 per cent of that of affiliates in developed countries in 1986, and almost 90 per cent in 1987 and 1988. This sudden, dramatic shift was centred in the heavily-indebted countries, suggesting the possibility that the debt crisis might have had some role in the transformation.

US affiliates in the Asian countries, especially those not heavily indebted, have had high export propensities throughout the period since 1977. There is only a little difference in export behaviour between the first year and later years, on average, although there are some substantial shifts in individual countries. To the extent that there

Table 7.3   Export propensities (exports as a percentage of total sales) of US majority-owned manufacturing affiliates, various years, 1977–88

	1977	1982	1986	1987	1988
Total developed market economies	33.1	36.6	39.3	39.1	39.1
Total developing market economies	18.1	22.0	32.5	34.7	34.5
Latin America	9.7	11.9	20.0	21.1	22.2
Asia, except Middle East	57.0	59.6–60.6	66.8	66.3	64.8–73.9
Five heavily-indebted Latin American countries	7.9	9.6–10.0	20.0–20.8	21.5	21.8
Brazil	8.9	12.4	16.9	16.4	18.7
Chile	16.1	12.5–27.2	27.8[a]	32.1	50.7
Colombia	3.9	3.3	4.1	5.7	5.5
Mexico	10.4	10.8	34.5	38.8	33.9
Venezuela	0.4	n.a.	1.4	1.1	0.7
Seven less-indebted Asian countries[b]	66.1–68.2	67.5–71.9	72.7–74.0	72.0	61.5–74.1

Notes: [a] 1985;
[b] Hong Kong, India, Malaysia, Singapore, South Korea, Taiwan and Thailand.
Source: Blomström and Lipsey (1993), tables A.2 and A.3.

was any change, it was a reduction in export propensities. However, all except those in India had export propensities above 50 per cent in every year.

Among affiliates in the heavily-indebted countries, the course of events was very different. They were far less export-orientated than those in the less-indebted group in 1977. After 1982, however, those in almost every heavily-indebted country moved strongly towards exporting. By 1988, the average export propensity in the heavily-indebted countries was more than twice that of 1977. An indication that indebtedness, rather than geographical location, was a determinant of this shift is the fact that affiliates in the one heavily-indebted Asian country for which we have data (but not shown here), The Philippines, shifted towards exporting almost as much as did the Latin American affiliates.

How was this shift in the orientation of sales carried out? In the long run, such a shift could conceivably be accomplished by increases in production largely or entirely dedicated to export markets, without any reduction in local sales. In the short run, a large expansion in exports would presumably have to be at the expense of local buyers unless the producers had excess capacity. Between 1982 and 1986, the increasing export propensities of US manufacturing affiliates in developing countries as a group, and particularly in Latin America and in heavily-indebted countries, were more the result of decreasing sales, and particularly decreasing local sales, than of increasing exports (see Table 7.4). While the exports of US affiliates in Latin America increased by $1.8 billion (or 38 per cent) between 1982 and 1986, their local sales decreased by almost $9 billion, or 25 per cent, over the same period. Among the heavily-indebted countries, the decrease in affiliates' local sales ($8.3–8.6 billion) was almost four times the increase in exports ($2.2–2.5 billion). In developing Asia, in the same years, both exports and domestic sales grew, but export growth was much larger, coming from increased production rather than from declining domestic consumption.

However, by 1988, the picture had changed considerably. Total sales of affiliates were higher than in 1982 in Latin America as a whole and in heavily-indebted countries as a group, and in all but one of the individual countries. There were still decreases in local sales in both groups of countries and for affiliates in two of the five heavily-indebted countries, but these were far outweighed by increases in exports. Thus, by 1988, most of the growth of exports by US affiliates was coming from increased production rather than from decreased local sales.

The reversal after 1986 can be seen more clearly in the data for 1986–8, when the growth of affiliate local sales in Latin America, in the heavily-indebted countries as a group, and in the three restructuring countries (Chile, Colombia and Mexico) outpaced export growth by large margins. In contrast, affiliates in the less-indebted Asian countries continued to increase exports more than local sales.

7.5 Export propensities of countries

We would like to compare affiliate behaviour with that of domestic firms across regional and indebted groupings. However, we do not have regional production data and are limited to some

Table 7.4 Change in total sales, local sales and exports, various periods, 1982–8, in US majority-owned manufacturing affiliates in developing countries (US$ million)

	1982–6			1982–8			1986–8		
	Sales	Local sales	Exports	Sales	Local sales	Exports	Sales	Local sales	Exports
Total developing market economies	–5250	–8917	3667	11482	1129	10353	16732	10046	6686
Latin America	–7029	–8819	1790	3206	–1567	4773	10235	7252	2983
Asia, except Middle East	1979	–154––242	1737–2133	8085	2436–2996	5119–5649	6106	2294–3020	3086–3812
Five heavily-indebted Latin American countries	–6090	–8608––8264	2174–2518	3934	–1004––904	4838–4938	10024	7360–7604	2420–2664
Brazil	–669	–1323	654	2938	1310	1628	3607	2633	974
Chile	–4	–176–12	–16–172	293	–2–54	239–295	297	–14–230	67–311
Colombia	–530	–524	–6	146	96	50	676	620	56
Mexico	–1782	–3402	1620	2275	–671	2946	4057	2731	1326
Venezuela	–3105	–3127––3083	–22–22	–1718	–1737––1693	–25–19	1387	1390	–3
Chile, Colombia, Mexico	–2316	–4158––3858	1542–1842	2714	–577––521	3235–3291	5030	3337–3581	1449–1693
Seven less-indebted Asian countries[a]	2558	152–639	1919–2406	7907	2018–2678	5224–5916	5349	1717–2166	3183–3632

Note: [a] Hong Kong, India, Malaysia, Singapore, South Korea, Taiwan and Thailand.
Source: See Table 7.3.

comparisons between affiliates and their host countries for individual countries.

The production data we do have (gross output at producers' prices) are, for at least some of the countries, incomplete, and incomplete to a changing extent over time. The countries' export propensities derived using these output figures as denominators are almost certainly overstated, both because the output estimates are incomplete in coverage – often omitting small plants – and because most are in producers' prices, or even factor cost, while exports add costs of transportation to the border and other costs incurred by intermediaries such as wholesalers.

The national export propensities for manufactures estimated from these data (see Table 7.5) show clearly the much higher export orientation of the less-indebted Asian countries' manufacturing industries, compared with those of Latin America. However, the average export propensity of manufacturing in heavily-indebted countries, starting from a much lower level than those of the less-indebted group, more than doubled between 1982 and 1986. The greatest increase, by far, was for Mexico.[4] It resulted not only from an almost 100 per cent rise in export values in US dollars, but even more from the incredibly sharp fall in the dollar value of production, which must have been far greater than any decline in physical output.

The export propensities rose also for the other countries in this group between 1982 and 1986, except that for Venezuela. Thus, while export propensities in heavily-indebted countries were still relatively low in 1986, some force had apparently encouraged a shift from domestic sales to exporting.

Although these country export propensities for Latin America appear almost as high as, or even higher than, those for US affiliates (Table 7.3), more often than not that comparison is inconclusive because the denominators in the country ratios (Table 7.5) are seriously understated. However, it does appear from the comparisons of changes that the US affiliates raised their export propensities more between 1982 and 1986 than the countries did, and in particular more than non-affiliates did.

In Asia, on the other hand, the countries' export propensities, apart from the two entrepôt countries, Hong Kong and Singapore, are almost all lower than those of US affiliates, despite the overstatement of the country ratios. Since the country ratios in Asia were rising and the affiliate export propensities falling, the two sets of ratios were coming closer over time.

Table 7.5   Export propensities in manufacturing (exports as a percentage of value of output) in eleven developing countries, various years, 1977–88

	UN trade tapes			Shortcut method		
	1977	**1982**	**1986**	**1986**	**1987**	**1988**
Four heavily-indebted Latin American countries[b]	8.8	11.3	18.9	19.0	n.a.	n.a.
Chile	28.0	23.5	26.2	25.5	n.a.	n.a.
Colombia	6.1	5.5	5.8	5.8	n.a.	n.a.
Mexico	7.4[a]	9.6	34.9	35.5	51.8	50.6
Venezuela	7.1	14.8	4.3	4.0	n.a.	n.a.
Seven less-indebted Asian countries						
Hong Kong	65.7	60.3	64.7	114.3[d]	125.8[d]	n.a.
India	9.9	6.1	n.a.	n.a.	n.a.	n.a.
Malaysia	56.9	48.0	54.6	49.8	54.0	n.a.
Singapore[e]	89.9	110.5	105.7	104.7	111.0	122.9
South Korea	30.6	32.9	33.5	33.8	n.a.	n.a.
Taiwan	33.2	36.7	41.7	40.7	41.8	43.9
Thailand	n.a.	12.4	25.7	25.9	n.a.	n.a.
Total, five less-indebted countries[c]	**42.1**	**44.0**	**45.6**			
Total, four less-indebted countries[d]			**53.4**	**61.8**	**65.2**	**n.a.**

Note: [a] Maquiladora exports to USA estimated from US data. Corresponding 1982 ratio is 7.7%.
[b]   Chile, Colombia, Mexico and Venezuela. The 1982 ratio corresponding to 1977 is 10.1%.
[c]   Hong Kong, Malaysia, Singapore, South Korea and Taiwan.
[d]   Hong Kong, Malaysia, Singapore and Taiwan.
[e]   The propensities over 100% in the shortcut calculations reflect the fact that the published data are on a general trade basis, including re-exports. The data from the UN tapes are domestic on the special trade basis, including only domestic exports. The high ratios for Singapore are more of a puzzle, but probably reflect the large entrepôt trade also.
Source: Blomström and Lipsey (1993), tables A.1 and A.5.

Another way of examining the role of the US affiliates is through their shares in exports of manufactures. Within Latin America, and within the heavily-indebted countries as a group, they increased their share substantially between 1977 and 1986, but lost ground in the next

Table 7.6   Sales outside the host country by US majority-owned manufacturing affiliates as a percentage of the value of manufactured exports, twelve developing countries, various years, 1977–88

	UN trade tapes			Shortcut method		
	1977	**1982**	**1986**	**1986**	**1987**	**1988**
Total developing market economies	7.4	8.1	7.7	6.9	6.2	6.0
Latin America	13.6	16.6	17.6	16.0	14.7	15.4
Asia, except Middle East	6.7	6.6–6.7	5.7–6.0	5.1–5.3	4.7	4.3–4.4
Five heavily-indebted Latin American countries	11.8[b]	11.4–11.8	17.7–18.5	16.9–17.6	14.8	14.4
Brazil	15.2	16.0	18.6	16.9	14.3	15.1
Chile	1.9	2.1–4.6	1.2–10.7	1.3–11.0	5.3	7.7
Colombia	7.2	6.6	5.7	5.8	7.9	7.8
Mexico	14.2[a]	13.4	22.7	22.3	18.1	16.0
Venezuela	1.0	0.1–1.1	2.2	2.3	2.3	1.4
Chile, Colombia, Mexico	9.9[c]	10.5–11.0	18.0–19.6	17.8–19.4	15.9	14.4
Seven less-indebted Asian countries	6.5–6.7	6.3–6.7	5.9–6.0	5.3–5.4	4.9	4.4–4.6
Hong Kong	8.2	6.7	4.6	2.6	2.4	1.9
India	0.4	0.2–1.0	0.4	0.3	0.2	1.0–4.2
Malaysia	9.6	18.8	19.7–21.2	21.6–23.2	21.0	18.4
Singapore	19.8	14.9	18.9	19.0	17.3	13.8
South Korea	1.5	1.1	1.1	1.0	0.9	0.9
Taiwan	6.2	4.2	3.4	3.5	2.7	2.9
Thailand	0.6–6.1	1.0–9.8	6.9	6.8	6.9	6.0

Notes: [a]   Corresponding 1982 ratio is 16.8.
[b]   Corresponding 1982 ratio is 12.1–12.5.
[c]   Corresponding 1982 ratio is 12.2–12.8.
Source: Blomström and Lipsey (1993), tables A.1 and A.2.

two years (see Table 7.6). In the Asian countries and the less-indebted countries as a group, in contrast, the shares of US affiliates in exports were declining most of the time. The decline was slight outside of Hong Kong and Taiwan, and may have been offset by increasing Japanese shares, but there was a substantial decrease in those two host countries. Only in Malaysia, among this group of countries, were US firms' shares of country exports increasing.

It seems, then, that the strong export performance of US affiliates relative to local firms after 1982 was not a world-wide phenomenon, but was concentrated in the heavily-indebted countries. And that export performance of US affiliates consisted more in the degree to which they shifted the direction of their sales towards exports, than in the rate of growth of their exports.

7.6   Export performance by industry group

Since the US affiliates in Latin America are active in a very different set of industries from those in South-East Asia, their export performance could to some extent reflect the world-wide fortunes of their industries rather than the debt circumstances or macroeconomic policies of their host countries. (It should be added, however, that the industry distribution of US firms' investment and production may itself be a reflection of the openness or import-substitution orientation of the host countries.) The 1982 distributions of US affiliates' exports from the two regions are shown in Table 7.7. For the affiliates in Asian countries, mainly less indebted, three-quarters of exports were in electrical machinery, and the greater part of the rest was in non-electrical machinery, both relatively fast-growing sectors in world trade. Exports by affiliates in Latin American countries were much more evenly distributed across the seven industry groups.

The growth rates of US affiliate exports in the two areas, by industry, shown in Table 7.8, point up the fact that foods and metals, which accounted for 23 per cent of exports by Latin American affiliates but for less than 4 per cent of Asian affiliates' exports in 1982, were slow-

Table 7.7   Industry distribution of sales outside the host country by US manufacturing affiliates in Latin America and developing Asia, 1982

	Latin America (%)	**Developing Asia, except Middle East** (%)
Foods	15.0	1.1–2.4
Chemicals	21.7	3.2
Metals	7.6	0.9
Non-electrical machinery	13.0	9.2–10.2
Electrical machinery	13.0	74.8
Transport equipment	14.3	3.9
Other manufacturing	15.5	5.4

Source: Blomström and Lipsey (1993), tables A.2 and A6.

growing industries for US affiliates in developing countries world-wide before 1982. Machinery and transport equipment, fast-growing industries, were 40 per cent of Latin American affiliates' exports and 88–89 per cent of exports by Asian affiliates. The sharpest contrast between the two areas was in chemicals, in which export growth accelerated for Asian affiliates, while in Latin America the industry switched from being the fastest-growing in exports in 1977–82, to a declining exporter after 1982.

It would appear that the Latin American affiliates would have done considerably better in exporting, on average, if they had been in the same industries as the Asian affiliates. Within industries, their exports did not seem to grow particularly slowly in 1977–82 relative to Asian

Table 7.8 Average annual growth rates of exports by US majority-owned manufacturing affiliates in developing countries, by region and industry, various years, 1977–88

	Nominal values			Purchasing power over developed country manufactured exports (%)		
	1977–82	1982–6	1982–8	1977–82	1982–6	1982–8
All developing countries						
Foods	4.2	0.9	9.8	−1.8	−2.4	3.8
Chemicals	22.8	−4.4	2.2	15.7	7.5	−3.4
Metals	5.6	−6.0	10.4	−0.5	−9.1	4.3
Non-electrical machinery	22.0	11.7	17.8	14.9	8.1	11.3
Electrical machinery	16.7	6.3	9.5	9.9	2.9	3.5
Transport equipment	17.3	31.3	25.0	10.5	27.0	18.1
Other manufacturing	11.6	2.0	8.7	5.1	−1.3	2.7
Latin America						
Foods	7.9	−3.6	7.9	1.6	−6.7	2.0
Chemicals	28.4	−10.3	−4.5	20.9	−13.2	−9.7
Metals	5.0	−5.7	11.8	−1.1	−8.7	5.6
Non-electrical machinery	19.5	3.1	12.1	12.6	−0.2	6.0
Electrical machinery	12.2	14.9	13.9	5.7	11.2	7.7
Transport equipment	12.0	38.4–39.3	30.7	5.4	33.9–−34.8	23.5
Other manufacturing	18.0	−6.4–−0.1	5.0	11.2	−9.5–−3.3	−0.7
Asia, except Middle East						
Foods	n.a.	n.a.	n.a.	n.a.	n.a.	n.a.
Chemicals	6.3	19.9–20.5	23.9	0.2	16.0–16.6	17.1
Metals	−5.1	n.a.	n.a.	−10.6	n.a.	n.a.
Non-electrical machinery	26.3–28.7	18.0–23.4	20.5–24.5	18.9–21.2	14.2–19.4	13.9–17.7
Electrical machinery	17.2–17.5	4.9	8.6	10.4–10.7	1.5	2.6
Transport equipment	n.a.	−1.4–3.9	−0.4	n.a.	−4.6–0.6	n.a.
Other manufacturing	−0.5	n.a.	n.a.	−6.3	n.a.	n.a.

Source: Blomström and Lipsey (1993), table A.6.

or all developing-country affiliates; they did better than developing-country affiliates in general in three out of seven industries. Even in 1982–6, they had faster export growth in two industries.

While the growth rates of affiliate exports were not distinctively different between Latin America and Asia or developing countries in general, there was one respect in which there were clear regional differences. Export propensities of affiliates in Latin America were lower than those in Asia or developing countries in general in almost every industry in every period (see Table 7.9). To some extent, that difference may have reflected the fact that Latin American markets were larger than Asian markets, but it may also reflect a difference in policies towards trade: a more inward orientation in Latin America. However, there was a distinct shift towards export orientation by

Table 7.9 Export propensities (exports as a percentage of sales) of US majority-owned manufacturing affiliates in developing countries, by region and industry, 1977–86

	1977	1982	1986	1987	1988
All developing countries					
Food	15.1	11.1	15.3	16.0	18.4
Chemicals	7.2	11.7	11.2	11.1	12.1
Metals	27.2	20.0	22.8	28.8	34.3
Non-electrical machinery	20.6	29.6	20.4	42.9	45.2
Electrical machinery	53.7	64.4	71.0	71.5	74.6
Transport equipment	7.5	11.1	35.5	42.9	33.7
Other manufacturing	12.2	13.1	18.9	18.8	20.1
Latin America					
Food	12.4	10.5	12.5	10.9	16.3
Chemicals	5.5	11.2	9.0	8.2	8.5
Metals	19.4	14.4	16.6	20.3	27.5
Non-electrical machinery	13.2	18.4	21.9	22.6	26.0
Electrical machinery	17.2	22.8	34.4	33.9	43.0
Transport equipment	7.3	8.9	34.9–35.8	44.7	37.3
Other manufacturing	7.1	9.5	10.5–13.6	13.6	12.9
Asia, except Middle East					
Food	29.2–38.0	7.4–16.6	28.8	34.9	24.7
Chemicals	15.3	12.0	19.5–19.9	21.7	23.7
Metals	66.3	29.9	33.2–46.2	56.3–72.7	41.7–85.2
Non-electrical machinery	70.8	69.3–76.3	76.8–83.5	80.5–81.7	73.6–81.4
Electrical machinery	86.8–87.8	87.8	91.6	90.9	87.0
Transport equipment	n.a.	>39.1	>42.8	n.a.	n.a.
Other manufacturing	41.8–56.7	31.8–57.6	19.9–48.2	24.8–56.0	18.9–39.5

Source: Blomström and Lipsey (1993), tables A.6 and A.7.

Latin American affiliates in all industries from 1977 to 1988. Some of the shift began in 1977–82, but it accelerated after 1982 in all industries except chemicals. Affiliates in Asia were also becoming increasingly export-orientated after 1982 in most of the industries for which we can make calculations, but in some cases they had little room to increase the share of production they sold abroad because it was already high.

The greater initial inward orientation of Latin American affiliates may have given them more scope than Asian affiliates had for switching sales from domestic to foreign markets after 1982. However, data for Asian affiliates are too heavily suppressed to permit many comparisons. The largest absolute increase in exports by Latin American affiliates, in the transport equipment industry, was accompanied by a similar, but even larger, decline in domestic sales between 1982 and 1986, and therefore by a drop in total sales. But by 1988, total sales were well above the 1982 level and only half the export increase was a switch out of local sales (see Table 7.10). The next-largest export increase, in electrical machinery, came more out of increased production; and in non-electrical machinery, by 1988, local sales had risen even more than exports. In foods, chemicals, metals and other manufacturing, exports and domestic production stagnated or, more often declined, between 1982 and 1986, so that we cannot say there was a shift of output from domestic to export markets. By 1988, exports had recovered dramatically, mainly via a shift from local to export markets, except in chemicals. The data are poor for Asian affiliates because there is so much suppression in the source, but there is little indication of any major shifting of sales among markets. The growth of exports was accompanied either by a growth in domestic sales, or by declines in domestic sales that were too small to account for much export growth.

7.7 Conclusions

The distinctive feature of the export performance of US multinationals' affiliates in heavily-indebted Latin American countries after the debt crisis began was their sharp shift from selling in host country markets to exporting. One aspect of this shift was the faster growth of their exports than of the exports of their host countries. Another was the sharp rise in their export propensities between 1982 and 1986, larger than for the host countries, although the host countries too were

Table 7.10 Changes in total sales, local sales and exports, US majority-owned affiliates in developing countries, by region and industry, 1982–6 and 1982–8 (US$ million)

	1982–6			1982–8		
	Sales	**Local sales**	**Exports**	**Sales**	**Local sales**	**Exports**
All developing countries						
Foods	−1 903	−1 933	30	471	−176	647
Chemicals	−1 425	−1 210	−215	1 196	1 013	183
Metals	−941	−810	−131	158	−323	481
Non-electrical machinery	586	−96	682	3 096	1 055	2 041
Electrical machinery	1 249	−171	1 420	3 881	170	3 711
Transport equipment	−593	−2 376	1 783	2 060	−482	2 542
Other manufacturing	−2 225	−2 321	96	620	−129	749
Latin America						
Food	−1 853	−1 757	−96	95	−313	408
Chemicals	−1 770	−1 411	−359	−11	233	−244
Metals	−783	−709	−74	47	−290	337
Non-electrical machinery	−170	−249	79	1 335	735	600
Electrical machinery	412	−41	453	422	−301	723
Transport equipment	−510	−2 523--−2 299	1 789--1 852	1 414	−1 260	2 674
Other manufacturing	−2 354	−2 352--−2 184	−170--−2	−95	−345	250
Asia, except Middle East						
Foods	−108	−263--37	75--155	148	−39--41	107--187
Chemicals	425	27--224	201--209	1 314	819	495
Metals	n.a.	n.a.	−17--15	≤141	n.a.	n.a.
Non-electrical machinery	739	65--112	627--674	1 727	281--326	1 304--1 446
Electrical machinery	808	−127	935	3 329	473	2 856
Transport equipment	n.a.	n.a.	−13	n.a.	n.a.	23--27
Other manufacturing	n.a.	n.a.	204--261	n.a.	n.a.	n.a.

Source: Blomström and Lipsey (1993), tables A.6 and A.7.

shifting their sales to export markets. In both these measures, the behaviour of affiliates in the heavily-indebted Latin American countries differed distinctly from those in the less-indebted Asian developing countries, so that it cannot be explained as a general characteristic of the affiliates or of developing countries in general. Much of the shift in markets by US affiliates involved more reductions in host country domestic sales than increases in exports, and the affiliates' shares in exports did not rise substantially during this period. The implication is that the affiliates were quicker than domestic firms to reduce their local sales, and they achieved much of their gains in export propensities that way. It would not be surprising that multinationals reacted this way if debt problems caused host countries to restrict the conversion of local currency income to US dollars, since there would be little incentive for US firms to accumulate depreciating local currencies.

Thus the flexibility of the multinationals' affiliates – compared with other firms in their host countries – in the face of the debt crisis was shown by their ability to increase rapidly exports from debt-ridden countries, their ability to change the orientation of these affiliates from domestic sales towards exports, but also by their ability to withdraw from domestic markets when they became less attractive or more risky.

Another lesson from this period is that events take time to unfold. The story of the responses to the debt crisis in 1988 looked very different from that of 1986. Over the longer term, but not the shorter one, the export growth of the three Latin American countries undergoing 'structural adjustment' outran even that of the Asian developing countries. And over the longer term, but not the shorter one, most of the gains in affiliate exports came from rising production rather than falling host country consumption.

The results of this study also suggest that multinationals carry a potential to export from production facilities that were largely set up to serve local markets in host countries (that is, those in Latin America), and that these firms are better equipped to convert import-substituting industries to exporting than are local firms. Future research should investigate whether the firms' responses could be explained by changes in their host countries' exchange rates and in trade, balance of payments, and investment policies.

Notes

1. For a discussion of the Latin American development model that led to the debt crisis, see Blomström and Meller (1991).
2. For a more general discussion of the role of trade in the structural adjustment required by the Latin American debt crisis, see Edwards and Savastano (1988).
3. Blomström (1990), and Blomström and Lipsey (1993), table A.3.
4. See Lopez (1991) for a detailed study of the Mexican structural adjustment process.

Part II
Host Country Strategies

8
Multinational Corporations and Spillovers

8.1 Introduction

The operations of multinational corporations continue to stir strong emotions, both in the home countries and abroad. In the major home countries, the debate on foreign direct investment has ranged from worries that outward FDI may substitute for domestic investment and erode technology leadership, to the argument that firms must invest abroad in order to stay competitive in an increasingly international environment. The attitudes towards MNCs have also been mixed in the host countries, although the proponents of FDI seem to have gained the upper hand since the late 1980s. Most host countries have liberalized their FDI regulations since the early 1980s – many are now actively trying to encourage foreign firms to invest – and the benefits of inward FDI on capital formation, employment, exports and technology are generally considered to dominate the costs of foreign ownership of local factors of production.

The most important reason why countries try to attract foreign investment is perhaps the prospect of acquiring modern technology, interpreted broadly to include both product, process and distribution technology, as well as management and marketing skills. By inviting MNCs to invest within their national boundaries, host countries hope to gain access to technologies and skills they do not yet possess. Foreign investment can result in benefits for host countries even if the MNCs decide to carry out their foreign operations in wholly-owned affiliates, since technology is to some extent a public good. These benefits take the form of various types of externality, and are often referred to as 'productivity spillovers'. For example, local firms may be able to improve their productivity as a result of forward or backward linkages with MNC affiliates; they may imitate MNC technologies; or they may hire workers trained by MNCs. The increase in competition that occurs as a result of foreign entry may also be considered a benefit, in particular if it forces local firms to introduce new technology and work harder. Another group of potential host country benefits that have contributed to the more positive attitudes towards FDI can be categorized as 'market access spillovers'. MNCs often possess strong competitive advantages in entering world markets, such as experience and knowledge of international marketing, established international distribution networks, and lobbying power in their home countries. As a result of their own export operations, MNCs may pave the way for local firms to enter the same export markets, either because they create transport infrastructure or because they disseminate information about foreign markets that can also be used by local firms.

Similar positive externalities from MNC operations may take place in the home countries as well, although the term 'spillover' has rarely been used in the home country debate. One reason may be that it is sometimes difficult to define exactly what is a spillover for the home country. For example, it is clear that foreign investment typically allows the MNC to grow larger than would otherwise be the case, which brings opportunities to benefit from economies of scale, both for the MNC itself and its local suppliers. Hence, productivity in the home country may increase as a result of FDI, but to what extent is this a spillover? What happens within the MNC can hardly be characterized as a spillover, but the effects on its suppliers may be regarded as productivity spillovers if the suppliers become more competitive as a result of the FDI. However, there are some more obvious home country spillovers as well. Most MNCs have concentrated their research and development (R&D) operations in their home country. It has often been suggested that there are important externalities from R&D, and it is possible that international operations that generate more research activities in the home country also enhance these productivity spillovers. Firms may also wish to establish affiliates in 'foreign centres of excellence' in order to draw on the existing stock of technical knowledge and learn from innovations made by local firms. Moreover, there may be market access spillovers on non-multinational home country firms: the distribution networks and the knowledge of foreign markets that are built up through FDI can perhaps benefit the entire home economy.

The purpose of this chapter is to examine and discuss the evidence on externalities from the activities of MNCs. The main focus will be on productivity and market access spillovers from MNCs to local firms in host countries – this is the area where existing research efforts have been strongest – but we shall also discuss spillover effects on the home countries of MNCs.

8.2   Spillovers from MNC activities: a conceptual discussion

What are productivity spillovers?

When companies establish affiliates abroad, they differ from existing firms in the host country for two reasons. One is that they bring with them some amount of the proprietary technology that constitutes their firm-specific advantage, and allows them to compete successfully with other MNCs and local firms that presumably have superior knowledge of local markets, consumer preferences and business practices. In industries with rapidly changing technologies (and, more generally, in developing host countries) the competitive assets of MNCs are likely to be related to new products and processes. In mature industries, MNCs may base their competitiveness more on marketing skills or organizational advantages, such as the ability to specialize across international borders, in order to exploit the local comparative advantages of various host countries. Another reason is that the entry and presence of MNC affiliates disturbs the existing equilibrium in the market and forces local firms to take action to protect their market shares and profits. Both these changes are likely to cause various types of spillover that lead to productivity increases in local firms.

Generally, productivity spillovers are said to take place when the entry or presence of MNC affiliates lead to productivity or efficiency benefits in the host country's local firms, and the MNCs are not able to internalize the full value of these benefits. The simplest example of such a spillover is the case where a local firm improves its productivity by copying some technology used by MNC affiliates operating in the local market. Another kind of productivity spillover occurs if the entry of an affiliate leads to more severe competition in the host economy, so that local firms are forced to use existing technology and resources more efficiently. A third type of spillover effect takes place if the competition forces local firms to search for new, and more efficient, technologies. These effects may take place either in the foreign affiliate's own industry, or in other industries among the affiliate's suppliers or customers.

The first reason to suspect that productivity spillovers may be important is that the technologies used by multinationals are not always available in the market. Abstracting from the fact that several means of extracting technology rents may occur simultaneously in reality, we can assume that the MNC has three alternative ways to exploit its technological advantages internationally. The MNC can produce for export in the home country; it can sell its technology to foreigners; or it can establish an affiliate abroad and control foreign production directly.

However, markets for technology are often imperfect, which makes the transaction costs for sales of technology to outsiders high. The reason may be that the relevant technologies are not easily codifiable in the form of patents and blueprints, or that it is difficult to evaluate the technology and agree about prices and licensing costs that are acceptable to both parties (see, for example, Buckley and Casson, 1976; and Teece, 1981). MNCs therefore often prefer direct investment over licensing, and the preference for FDI may be particularly strong when the newest and most profitable technologies (or those that are very close to the MNCs' principal lines of business) are exploited. Thus, local firms' only chance to gain access to the technology may sometimes lie in reverse engineering or the hiring of former MNC employees with special skills, or through some other type of spillover. This reason for the importance of spillovers may be most valid for the more developed host countries and industries, because the technical skills required to imitate the newest and most profitable technologies are typically very high.[1]

The bias towards the internal use of technology may be present even when there are no explicit imperfections in the market for technology. Some technologies are simply more valuable when internalized in foreign affiliates of the MNCs that developed them than when used by outsiders – the technology in question may have been developed for the specific purposes of the MNC; the operationalization of the technology may require an organization whose members have some specific skills; or the adaptation of the technology to a new environment may be significantly less costly when done by the MNC that developed the technology. In these cases, it may be unprofitable for local firms to acquire the technologies in the open market, unless there are some simultaneous spillovers of skills to facilitate the adoption of the new technology. It should, of course, be noted that spillovers may be important even where local firms are able to acquire MNC technologies through licensing and other market transactions. In fact, when local industry is dynamic and innovative, it is not unusual to observe 'virtuous cycles' of cross-licensing and spillovers between local firms and affiliates of foreign MNCs (see Cantwell, 1994).

Another general reason why spillovers may be significant is that direct contact with users appears to be a principal factor explaining technology diffusion. Before a new process or product innovation becomes widespread in the market, potential adopters have limited information about the costs and benefits of the innovation and may therefore associate it with a high degree of risk. As the potential adopters come in contact with existing users (for example, MNC affiliates), information about the technology is diffused, the uncertainty regarding the pros and cons of the innovation is reduced, and the likelihood of imitation or adoption increases. In this way, the entry of foreign affiliates may demonstrate the existence and profitability of new products and processes, and encourage local firms to adopt some of them: these diffusion processes may even be repeated every time innovations are transferred from the MNC parent to the affiliate. This is an argument for spillovers even when access to new technology is not restricted by proprietary factors, because information about foreign technology is generally more expensive for local firms than for MNC affiliates. In addition, it can be assumed that 'contagion' effects are more important for less-developed host countries, where indigenous skills and information are in shorter supply.[2]

A third reason to expect positive external effects from FDI is related to the typical features of MNCs – scale economies, high initial capital requirements, intensive advertising and, not least, advanced technology. These are also industry characteristics that signal high barriers to entry, high concentration, and perhaps some inefficiency that follows from low levels of competition. Entry by new domestic firms into such industries in potential host countries is likely to be difficult; MNCs, on the other hand, are both likely to enter just those industries and be well-equipped to overcome the entry barriers. They can coordinate their international operations and concentrate specific processes to few locations if scale economies are important entry barriers. If the barriers are made up of high capital costs, MNCs may have larger own funds than local firms, or access to cheaper financing on international markets. Barriers related to product differentiation and technology, finally, are not likely to stop a multinational, since these features often characterize the MNCs themselves.

The entry of MNCs into this kind of monopolistic industry is likely to increase the level of competition and force existing firms to become more efficient. Foreign entry may, of course, also lead to a fall in the number of firms in the industry if the least efficient local companies are forced out of business. This raises the fear that foreign MNCs may outcompete all local firms and establish monopolies that are even worse than the domestic oligopolies they replace: in addition to restricting competition, there is a risk that MNC monopolies may also repatriate profits and avoid taxation through transfer pricing. The actual outcome is likely to vary between industries, depending on the ability of domestic firms to respond to the foreign challenges. However, it is often argued that the level of competition is likely to become fiercer, because the MNC affiliates' strategies typically stir up the established patterns of 'gentlemanly competition'. Hence, Caves (1971, p. 15) asserted that 'whatever the market structure that results from the influence of direct investment, it can be argued that entry by a foreign subsidiary is likely to produce more active rivalrous behaviour and improvement in market performance than would a domestic entry at the same initial scale'. Another point to note is that this increase in competition may be more effective in inducing technological change and productivity improvements than profit incentives, since 'threats of deterioration or actual deterioration from some previous state are more powerful attention-focussing devices than are vague possibilities for improvements' (Rosenberg, 1976, p. 124).

Productivity spillovers in home countries

Although the existing literature on FDI has not discussed the home country effects of foreign investments in terms of productivity spillovers, it is still clear that some of the potential benefits from FDI to the home economy can be interpreted along these lines. In particular, outward FDI focusing on foreign industry clusters with leading technologies may be a way to get access to valuable foreign technology. However, in the home country context, it is often more difficult to identify productivity spillovers. One reason is that most leading MNCs are large, globalized firms with hundreds of foreign production affiliates and a highly developed international division of labour within the MNCs. If further FDI creates a potential for spillovers, it is not obvious that these will be realized in the formal home country of the MNC. Instead, the spillovers may benefit or hurt firms in the vicinity of some of the MNC's other foreign affiliates. Another reason concerns the definition of productivity spillovers. As noted earlier, FDI opens up opportunities to benefit from economies of scale, since it allows the MNC to grow larger than would be possible if its production was restricted to a single country. The resulting reduction in average costs may sometimes generate productivity spillovers. For example, there are spillovers if the MNC produces intermediate goods that become available at a lower cost to all home country firms as a result of FDI, and if this cost reduction raises the international competitiveness of home country firms. Similarly, spillovers are present in a situation where MNC suppliers are able to move down their average cost curve and become more competitive in other trans-actions as a result of their sales to the MNCs. However, the direct con-sequences of FDI – such as the achievement of economies of scale in the MNC's own operations – are not spillovers, nor are there any spillovers if the MNCs are able to internalize the gains from produc-tivity improvements elsewhere, for example by forcing suppliers to lower their prices. As we shall discuss in more detail later, the prob-lems in distinguishing between direct effects and externalities come up again in attempts to observe or measure the extent of home country spillovers.

Other possible spillover effects in the home countries stem from the structural changes that take place as domestic firms become (more) multinational. As MNCs expand their foreign operations, there is often a shift in the structure of their production in the home country: instead of producing finished goods for export to foreign (and domes-tic) customers, MNCs are likely to specialize in production and exports of intermediates to their foreign affiliates. Various types of spillover effects are possible as a consequence of this specialization. For example, if the home country's labour force is well educated and wages are relatively higher in the home country than in the host coun-tries, the structural shift is likely to bring an increasing emphasis on home country production in advanced industries with high labour productivity – simple production processes requiring much unskilled labour may be moved to foreign affiliates. Positive productivity spillovers may occur if the specialization allows home country firms to move down their learning curves and become more competitive in 'high-tech' industries, or if it motivates fixed investments that can serve other purposes than those directly related to the MNCs' foreign investment. An example of the latter could be the establishment of advanced training institutes or specialized business service or techni-cal consulting firms which would not have a sufficient market if indus-try did not specialize as a result of FDI. These types of effect are often discussed under the heading 'agglomeration', although many of the externalities in question can also be labelled 'spillovers'.

On the other hand, if the foreign investments are made in countries where skilled labour is more abundant than in the home country, one consequence could be a reduction of the technology intensity of home country production, and negative productivity spillovers. This would occur if the MNC decided to move R&D and other advanced production stages to its foreign affiliate, because of the larger supply of labour skills. However, it is unlikely that this kind of technological erosion occurs very commonly. Instead, FDI in more developed host countries is often part of a strategy to acquire modern technology and to upgrade the home country's technical capacity and skills. This strategy has arguably been followed by many MNCs based in the newly industrialized Asian economies investing in Western Europe and the USA (see Tolentino, 1993).

In this context, it should be noted that R&D is one of the production stages that MNCs typically have chosen to concentrate to the home country. The production of R&D is generally considered to be one of the activities with the largest potential externalities, and the increase in home country R&D that is made possible by FDI may thus be connected with large positive productivity spillovers. These effects may occur as a consequence of demonstration effects and linkages between MNCs and their local suppliers and subcontractors, but it is equally likely that they arise as a result of labour mobility: the training of R&D personnel by MNCs may benefit local firms if former MNC employees take employment in other home country firms. Empirical evidence suggests that this is an area where most home countries generally stand to benefit from the operations of their MNCs: although the foreign affiliates of MNCs have increased their R&D efforts, the great majority of R&D is still undertaken in the home countries.

What are market access spillovers?

To enter a foreign market and to become a successful exporter, a company must not only be a competent manufacturer, but it will also need to manage the international marketing, distribution and servicing of its products – tasks that are typically connected with high fixed costs. Few local firms, particularly those in developing countries, have the skills and resources to take on all these challenges on their own (see further in Keesing and Lall, 1992). A MNC parent or affiliate is likely to be in a better position to establish export operations, since it can benefit from the existing international network of the entire corporation. Contacts with other parts of the corporation provide both knowledge of international market conditions and access to foreign marketing and distribution networks. Moreover, MNCs are often larger than local firms and may be able to afford the high fixed costs for the development of transport, communications and financial services that are needed to support export activities.

The export operations of MNCs may influence local firms (in the home as well as host countries) in various ways. It is necessary to distinguish between the direct and indirect effects of MNC exports in this context. The direct effects occur when local firms are employed as suppliers and subcontractors to MNCs. Although the local suppliers of MNCs do not always export under their own name, they too benefit from access to foreign markets. This may allow them to expand output and achieve economies of scale, but it is not clear whether these productivity gains should be categorized as spillovers, as discussed in the previous section: the MNCs may be able to internalize any cost reductions in supplier firms by negotiating lower prices. However, it is also likely that the linkages with export-orientated MNCs provide knowledge about product and process technologies and foreign market conditions – for example, foreign preferences regarding design, packaging and product quality – and if this information can be used profitably in the supplier companies' other operations, there are undeniable spillovers. If the knowledge gained as a supplier to MNCs helps a company to establish its own direct exports to a foreign market, we have an example of market access spillovers. MNCs in retail and wholesale trade have been particularly important in providing international marketing channels for local firms, and the role of Japanese trading companies for East Asian exports was noted by the early 1970s (Hone, 1974). The subsequent export success of many independent local firms from the region implies that market access spillovers may have taken place. A more recent example is the Swedish furniture retailer IKEA, whose export success has opened up a large foreign market for its subcontractors in Sweden (and elsewhere): it will be interesting to see whether any of these firms are able to establish their own export operations in the future.

In addition to the market access spillovers that require some type of linkage between MNCs and local firms, there may also be several indirect effects that benefit local export performance. In the simplest case, local firms may learn how to succeed in foreign markets simply by copying MNCs, although more tangible externalities are usually needed. For example, MNCs may have affiliated firms in the prospective export market who can lobby for trade liberalization, and local firms may benefit from any reduction in trade barriers that is achieved. There may be spare capacity in the distribution or marketing facilities created by MNCs, which local firms may use at, or slightly above, marginal cost. The MNCs may also train their local staff in export management, and these skills may spill over to local firms if MNCs' employees change jobs. Other channels for the diffusion of information on foreign market conditions are trade associations and other industry organizations, of which MNCs are often prominent members. Market access spillovers are potentially important in both the host and the home countries, although the effects may be most significant where the indigenous resources are weakest – that is, in developing countries. It should also be noted that while we discuss productivity spillovers and market access spillovers as separate concepts, they are likely to be very hard to distinguish in practice. Breaking into a new market does not only require information about marketing and entry modes, but also efficient production, and spillovers from FDI may have an influence on both of these.

Identifying spillovers from MNC activities

The earliest discussions of productivity spillovers in the theoretical literature on foreign direct investment date back to the early 1960s, and refer to the effects of FDI on the host countries of multinationals. The first author to include productivity spillovers (or external effects) systematically among the possible consequences of FDI was MacDougall (1960), who analyzed the general welfare effects of foreign investment. Other early contributions were provided by Corden (1967), who looked at the effects of FDI on optimum tariff policy, and Caves (1971), who examined the industrial pattern and welfare effects of FDI.

The common aim of these studies was to identify the various costs and benefits of FDI, and productivity spillovers were discussed together with several other indirect effects that influence the welfare assessment, such as those arising from the impact of FDI on government revenue, tax policies, terms of trade and the balance of payments. The fact that spillovers were taken into account was generally motivated by empirical evidence from case studies rather than by comprehensive theoretical arguments – the detailed theoretical models analyzing spillovers did not appear until the late 1970s.[3] Yet the early analyses made clear that MNCs may improve *allocative efficiency* by entering into industries with high entry barriers and reducing monopolistic distortions, and induce higher *technical efficiency* if the increased competitive pressure or some demonstration effect spurs local firms to more efficient use of existing resources. They also proposed that the presence may lead to increases in the rate of *tech-*

nology transfer and diffusion. More specifically, case studies showed that foreign MNCs may:

(i)   contribute to efficiency by breaking supply bottlenecks (but that the effect may become less important as the technology of the host country advances);
(ii)   introduce new expertise by demonstrating new technologies and training workers who later take employment in local firms;
(iii) either break down monopolies and stimulate competition and efficiency, or create a more monopolistic industry structure, depending on the strength and responses of the local firms;
(iv)   transfer techniques for inventory and quality control and standardization to their local suppliers and distribution channels; and
(v)   force local firms to increase their managerial efforts, or to adopt some of the marketing techniques used by MNCs, either on the local market or internationally.

Although this diverse list gives some clues about the broad range of various spillover effects, it says little about how common or how important they are in general. This raises the question, 'How can we measure the significance and scope of spillovers?'

It is not difficult to picture an ideal study of productivity spillovers in host countries. To examine how the development of technology and productivity in individual local firms is related to the presence of foreign MNC in the local market, the study would require detailed micro data, both quantitative and qualitative. The study would have to cover several years, to take into account the fact that spillovers are not instantaneous. It should also include a large number of firms and industries, so that inter-industry spillovers could be observed, and it would be possible to draw statistically significant conclusions. With this kind of detailed information, it would also be possible to study productivity spillovers in the home countries of MNCs, and examine the presence of market access spillovers. However, to the best of our knowledge, no comprehensive analyses of this character have ever been made – one reason, of course, is the extreme data requirements. Additional empirical evidence on spillovers must therefore be drawn from two other sources.

First, in addition to the few case studies focusing directly on spillovers, there are a large number of detailed case studies discussing other aspects of FDI in different countries and industries which often contain valuable 'circumstantial evidence' of spillovers. For example, many analyses of the linkages between MNCs and their local suppliers and subcontractors have documented learning and technology transfers that may make up a basis for productivity spillovers or market access spillovers. These studies seldom reveal whether the MNCs are able to extract all the benefits that the new technologies or information generate among their supplier firms, so there is no clear proof of spillovers, but it is reasonable to assume that spillovers are positively related to the extent of linkages. Similarly, there is much written on the relationship between MNC entry and presence and market structure in host countries, and this is closely related to the possible effects of FDI on competition in the local markets. There are also studies of demonstration effects, technology diffusion and labour training in foreign MNCs that are relevant for our purposes.

Second, there are a few statistical studies examining the relationship between a foreign presence in a host country industry and productivity (or productivity growth) in the locally-owned share of the industry or in individual locally-owned firms. These studies typically estimate production functions for locally-owned firms, and include the foreign share of the industry as one of the explanatory variables. They then test whether a foreign presence has a significant positive impact on local productivity (or productivity growth) once other firm and industry characteristics have been acknowledged. There are no similar statistical studies of productivity spillovers in home countries, but there is one study employing statistical techniques to examine whether firms located near exporting MNCs are more likely than others to become exporters. Although the data used in these analyses are often limited to few variables, aggregated to industry level rather than plant level, and in several cases of a cross-section rather than time-series or panel character, they do provide some important evidence on the presence and pattern of spillover effects.

8.3 Empirical evidence on spillovers

It is difficult to get an overview of the empirical evidence on productivity and market access spillovers because there are only a few studies referring explicitly to spillovers, while there is concurrently an abundance of literature discussing MNCs and their impact on host and home countries in more general terms, as noted above. To provide an overview of the evidence, we have therefore structured the presentation as follows: we begin by examining the effects of FDI on host countries, and distinguish between spillover effects that are related to backward and forward linkages between MNCs and domestic firms; MNC training of local employees; effects of demonstration and competition from MNCs; and effects on industry structure from MNC operations. Linkages and labour training create opportunities for both productivity spillovers and market access spillovers, whereas the effects of competition and industry structure are more likely to concern productivity than export performance in locally-owned firms. In addition, we review the results of the available statistical studies of spillovers. Thereafter, we continue to the evidence from home countries.

Effects on host countries

Linkages between MNCs and local firms

Some of the productivity spillovers and market access spillovers from FDI operate via the linkages between the MNC's foreign affiliate and its local suppliers and customers. The spillovers occur when local firms benefit from the MNC affiliate's superior knowledge of product or process technologies or markets, without incurring a cost that exhausts the whole gain from the improvement.[4] Backward linkages arise from the MNC affiliate's relationships with suppliers, while forward linkages come from contacts with customers.

Backward linkages

Some of the 'complementary activities' that may create spillovers through backward linkages are identified in Lall (1980a). In summary, Lall notes that MNCs may contribute to raise the productivity and efficiency in other firms as they:

- help prospective suppliers (domestic as well as foreign) to set up production facilities;
- provide technical assistance or information to raise the quality of suppliers' products or to facilitate innovations;
- provide or assist in purchasing of raw materials and intermediaries;
- provide training and help in management and organization; and
- assist suppliers to diversify by finding additional customers.

In his empirical study, Lall (1980a) examines two Indian truck manufacturers (one MNC and one joint venture) and finds significant backward linkages of all five types mentioned above. In particular, he notes that the truck manufacturers had been active in the establishment of supplier firms: of the thirty-six sampled supplier firms, sixteen had been launched by the principals.[5] Behrman and Wallender (1976), who examine the operations of General Motors, ITT and Pfizer in several host countries, find similar linkages. They emphasize the ongoing character of the contacts and information flows between MNCs and their local suppliers. Evidence on the development of linkages is also provided by, for example, Watanabe (1983a, 1983b) and UNCTC (1981).[6]

In addition to demonstrating various types of linkage that create a potential for productivity spillovers and market access spillovers, these studies also suggest that the local content in MNC production is one of the determinants of the strength of linkages. Reuber *et al.* (1973), in a comprehensive survey of MNC affiliates in developing countries, note that over a third of the total value of goods and services purchased in 1970 by all affiliates included in their survey were provided by local firms. However, there were systematic differences in local purchases depending on the affiliates' market orientation, the parent's nationality, and the host country. Local-market-oriented affiliates purchased more from local firms than did export-oriented affiliates (perhaps because import licences are easier to obtain for exporters); European MNCs relied more on local firms than did US or Japanese firms (perhaps because they are generally older and have already built up local supplier networks); and affiliates in Latin America and India purchased more local inputs than did affiliates in the Far East (probably because of differences in local content requirements). In addition to these factors, it seems that the technical capability of potential local suppliers must be important to take into account.

Moreover, there is a tendency for the share of local inputs to increase over time, also for export-orientated affiliates. McAleese and McDonald (1978), who studied Irish manufacturing during the period 1952–74, show that local purchases of inputs increase as the MNC affiliates mature. Several factors contribute to the gradual development of linkages: further production processing stages are added over time, the autonomous growth of the manufacturing sector brings up new suppliers, and some MNCs take deliberate action to attract and develop local suppliers.[7] Hence it is possible that spillovers also become more common over time, as increasing numbers of local firms establish various types of contact with foreign MNCs.

In addition to the linkages and spillovers that result from cooperation between affiliates and local firms, it is also possible that there are effects which occur as suppliers are forced to meet the higher standards of quality, reliability and speed of delivery of the MNCs. For example, Brash (1966), in a study of the impact made by General Motors on its Australian local suppliers, emphasizes the importance of the MNC's stricter quality control, which also had an impact on the suppliers' other operations. Katz (1969, p. 154) reports that foreign MNCs operating in Argentina 'forced their domestic suppliers to adopt productive processes and techniques used by the suppliers of their main firms in their country of origin'. Similarly, Watanabe (1983a) notes complaints from small local producers in the Philippines about the large foreign firms' tough requirements on both product characteristics and prices: in developing countries, in particular, this alone may have an effect on what technologies are used, and perhaps also on the general competitive climate. However, there is very little additional evidence on such 'forced linkage effects'.

Some less optimistic conclusions on the effects of linkages are suggested by Aitken and Harrison (1991), who examined Venezuelan manufacturing in the period 1976–89, and conclude that the effect of foreign investment on the productivity of upstream local firms is generally negative. They assert that foreign firms divert demand for domestic inputs to imported inputs, which means that local supplier firms are not able to benefit from potential economies of scale. Their results differ from most other findings in this respect. One reason is that their study also includes local firms that have not been fortunate enough to establish linkages with foreign affiliates, and because they do not take into account the increase in local content that seems to take place over time. Yet their conclusions highlight the need for more research where the connection between spillovers and linkages is examined explicitly.

Forward linkages

There is much less evidence of forward than of backward linkages. Only a minority of the firms studied by Reuber *et al.* (1973) claimed to have contributed significantly to the development of local distributors and sales organizations. However, McAleese and McDonald (1978) report that forward linkages in the Irish economy grew in much the same way as did backward linkages. In particular, they assert that many MNCs commenced operations with heavy export orientation, but that the importance of the home market increased over time.

Blomström (1991) discusses forward linkages in finer detail, and emphasizes the growing technical complexity in many industries. On the one hand, this could mean that only MNCs can afford the necessary R&D to develop and manufacture modern products; and on the other, that the industrial application of, for example, computer-based automation and information technologies might require expertise from the manufacturers. This, he argues, would contribute to increasing the role of MNC–customer contacts, especially in the smaller countries. One of the few empirical works touching on this issue is the study by Aitken and Harrison (1991) noted above. They conclude that spillovers from forward linkages seem to be important in most industries – in fact, they argue that the downstream effects of foreign investment are generally more beneficial than the upstream effects.

Summarizing, there is much evidence of the existence and potential of backward linkages, and a suspicion about the growing importance of forward linkages as well. Some of the host country characteristics that may influence the extent of linkages – and thereby the extent of spillovers – are market size, local content regulations, and the size and technological capability of local firms. Moreover, linkages are likely to increase over time, as the skill level of local entrepreneurs grows, new suppliers are identified, and local content increases. This constitutes circumstantial evidence for spillovers, but it must also be mentioned that there are hardly any studies where the connection between linkages and spillovers is explicit.

Training of local employees in MNC affiliates

The transfer of technology from MNC parents to affiliates is not only embodied in machinery, equipment, patent rights and expatriate managers and technicians, but is also realized through the training of the affiliates' local employees. This training affects most levels of employees, from simple manufacturing operatives through supervisors to technically advanced professionals and top-level managers. Types of training range from on-the-job training to seminars and more formal schooling to overseas education, perhaps at the parent company, depending on the skills needed. Although higher positions are often initially reserved for expatriates, the local share typically increases over time. The various skills gained while working for an affiliate may spill over as the employees move to other firms, or set up their own businesses.

The evidence on spillovers from the MNC affiliates' training of local employees is far from complete, and comes mainly from developing-country studies. Considering that the public education systems in developing countries are relatively weaker, it is also possible that spillovers from training are relatively more important there. However, there is scattered evidence of effects in the industrialized countries, perhaps mainly regarding management skills. It is possible, for example, that the inter-firm mobility of managers has contributed to the spread of specific management practices from Japan to the USA and Europe, and, in earlier times, from the USA to Europe (Caves, 1996). Moreover, casual observation suggests that the mobility of employees from MNCs in the computer and software industries contributes to spillovers, both within the industry and elsewhere.

Studies in developing countries have recorded spillovers of both technical and management skills. For example, Gerschenberg (1987) examines MNCs and the training and spread of managerial skills in Kenya. From detailed career data for seventy-two top and middle-level managers in forty-one manufacturing firms, he concludes that MNCs offer more training of various sorts to their managers than private local firms do, although not more than joint ventures or public firms. Managers also move from MNCs to other firms and contribute to the diffusion of expertise. Of the managers in private local and public firms who had training from elsewhere, the majority had received it while working for MNCs – joint ventures, on the other hand, seemed to recruit mainly from public firms. Yet mobility seemed to be lower for managers employed by MNCs than for managers in local firms. This is not surprising remembering the common finding that MNCs pay more for their labour than do local firms, even taking skill levels into account: in fact, it is not unreasonable to hypothesize that the fear of a 'brain-drain' to local firms is one of the reasons behind the higher wages in MNCs. Katz (1987) points out that managers of locally-owned firms in Latin America often started their careers and were trained in MNC affiliates.[8]

Chen (1983), in a study of technology transfer to Hong Kong, chooses to emphasize training of operatives. In three out of four sampled industries, the MNCs' incidence of undertaking training and their training expenditures were significantly (several times) higher than those for local firms. Consequently, he concludes that 'the major contribution of foreign firms in Hong Kong manufacturing is not so much the production of new techniques and products, but the training of workers at various levels' (p. 61).

Another factor in the dissemination of technology and human capital skills is related to the R&D efforts undertaken by the MNC affiliates. Here, we shall only hint at some of the results in a very extensive research field. First, MNCs do undertake R&D in their host countries, although it is strongly concentrated to the home countries. The affiliates' research efforts could be important, and should be compared with the R&D efforts of local firms, rather than with the parents' total R&D. Comparing these, Fairchild and Sosin (1986) conclude that foreign firms in Latin America exhibit more internal local R&D activity than is normally assumed, and that their total expenditure on research is very similar to that of domestic firms. In addition, they have access to the aggregate expertise base of the parent and related affiliates, and sometimes also to the parent's R&D facilities. The affiliates' R&D may therefore be more efficient than that of local firms. Not much is known, however, about what type of R&D is done in affiliates – traditionally, much has been adaptation of products and processes – and even less is known about the mobility of R&D personnel or the effects on the host country's technological capability.[9]

Judging from the aggregate evidence on spillovers from the training of MNC personnel, there seems to be a definite accumulation of human capital skills in the MNCs' employee stock. Some of these skills can be appropriated by local firms when employees move to new jobs, but how much is an open question. The fact that most studies deal with the spread of management skills suggests that they are less firm-specific than are technical skills, and can more easily be used in other contexts: the empirical evidence, however, is too limited for any more definite conclusions.

Demonstration effects and effects of competition

There are a few case studies where pure demonstration effects of FDI on local firms in the host countries of MNCs have been discussed. Riedel (1975) claims that horizontal demonstration effects from the operations of MNCs were an important force behind the development of the manufacturing export sector in Hong Kong in the 1960s. Swan (1973) suggests that multinationals are important not only for the diffusion of the specific technologies they use, but more generally because they strengthen international communication channels, which makes demonstration across international borders possible. Tilton (1971), in a study of the semiconductor industry, points to the importance of new MNCs in introducing US innovations into European countries. Lake (1979), also examining the semiconductor industry, argues that affiliates of US MNCs have been more active than local firms in the diffusion of new technology in Great Britain. Mansfield and Romeo (1980) show that the technologies transferred to affiliates are younger than those sold to outsiders, and that there are cases where the affiliates' technology imports have induced local competitors to imitate their behaviour.

These case studies suggest that demonstration may be an important channel for spillovers in both productivity and market access. However, there have been too few studies to reveal how important the simple demonstration effects are, nor do we know whether they are more important in some countries or industries than in others. One reason is that pure demonstration effects often take place unconsciously: it is seldom documented how and where a firm first learns about a new technology or product that is subsequently adopted. Another reason is that demonstration effects are often intimately related to competition. Summarizing a comparison of MNC and local technologies, Jenkins (1990, p. 213) notes that 'over time, where foreign and local firms are in competition with each other, producing similar products, on the same scale and for the same market, there is a tendency for local firms to adopt similar production techniques to those of the MNCs. Indeed this is part of a general survival strategy, whereby in order to compete successfully with the MNCs local capital attempts to imitate the behaviour of the MNCs'.

Some case studies at both firm and industry level are also available to describe the combined effects on local firms of demonstration and competition from MNCs. For example, Langdon (1981), in a study of FDI in the Kenyan soap industry, reports that the entry of foreign MNCs also introduced mechanized production, and local firms found themselves unable to sell handmade soap in the urban markets. Instead, they were forced to introduce mechanized techniques to stay in business. Similarly, foreign entry into the Kenyan footwear industry led to increased competition and changes in the production techniques of local firms (Jenkins, 1990). In the Brazilian textile industry, the establishment of an affiliate by a foreign firm brought in synthetic fibres: the consequent stagnation of demand for cotton textiles led to the disappearance of some local firms, and forced others to seek joint ventures with foreign firms in order to get access to competitive technology (Evans, 1979).

Some authors have hypothesized that the most important influences of MNCs on local firms operate through the interaction of demonstration and competition (Blomström, 1986a), and several reasons to expect important effects from competition were noted in the conceptual discussion: most important, MNCs are likely to enter into industries where potential local challengers are discouraged by high barriers to entry and where competition between existing local firms may therefore be limited.

In practice, it is difficult to distinguish between effects of demonstration and competition when it comes to imitation or adoption of new technologies, and the most valuable information from case studies may therefore be related to how local firms respond to increased competition in the short run, before imitation takes place. The immediate local reaction may be merely to enforce stricter or more cost-conscious management and motivate employees to work harder, in order to reduce slack or improve X-efficiency. It is possible that this seemingly simple response might make a more substantial contribution to productivity than improvements in resource allocation (see Leibenstein, 1966, 1980). Bergsman (1974), on the basis of a study of industry in six developing countries, argues that X-efficiency is several times as important as allocative efficiency in increasing incomes in these countries. Also Pack (1974), in a study of LDC manufacturing industries, and Page (1980), referring to evidence for three manufacturing industries in Ghana, suggest that factors related to X-efficiency – mainly management and capacity utilization – are more important than changes in resource allocation (via changes in relative factor prices) to improve performance (see also White, 1976).

The potential productivity improvements from these types of reaction are probably larger in the less-developed countries than elsewhere, simply because the initial inefficiencies are often larger. On the other hand, local firms in the less-developed countries may be too weak to mount a competitive response to foreign entry, whereas the locals in industrialized host countries can often be expected to reply competitively. Various defensive corporate agreements, such as amalgamations among local firms or cooperative ventures with other foreign firms, may improve the local firms' competitiveness, even in developing countries (Lall, 1979c; and Evans, 1977), but there are no direct cross-country comparisons available, and there are not enough case studies for more comprehensive conclusions. Exactly what the reaction is – and how important the spillover benefits are – is likely to depend on the initial conditions in the market, and how much of an impact MNC entry makes on concentration and competition.

Effects on industry structure

The uncertainty regarding the generality of competition effects motivates an examination of some studies of FDI and industry structure in host countries. A central problem here is whether MNC entry and presence explain industry structure, or whether industry structure determines if MNCs will enter or not. This is an important question, since we have argued that one of the reasons to expect spillovers is the improvement in efficiency and resource allocation that may follow from MNC entry into monopolistic host country industries. Another problem is that there is some confusion regarding effects that are endemic to MNCs and those that are only speeded up by MNC presence. Few authors have been able to make a proper distinction between these two effects, but it may not be a crucial issue in the present context. What matters is the impact made by MNCs, and not the question of whether it is caused by foreign ownership or some other of the MNCs' characteristics. Yet another (perhaps more important) complication is that there is no simple relationship between competition and efficiency, on the one hand, and concentration on the other. This will warrant some further comments later.

Moving to the empirical findings, it is clear that the overwhelming majority of studies are able to establish a positive correlation between foreign entry and presence and seller concentration in host country industries (see, for example, Dunning, 1993; and Caves, 1996, for surveys). However, the causal links are more difficult to establish. One finding is that the correlation disappears once other determinants of concentration are taken into account, and that MNCs do not cause concentration but are drawn to concentrated industries (Fishwick, 1982; and Globerman, 1979b). Knickerbocker (1976) shows that entries by MNCs into the US market in the 1960s led to a lower concentration, and that the same pattern was evident also for Canada, Italy, France and West Germany. Commenting on these and other studies, Caves (1996, p. 89) concludes that the 'correlations do not themselves prove that any direct causal relationships exist between foreign investment and concentration'. It should, however, be noted that most of the studies look at effects of MNC entry, and it is possible that the concentration-reducing impact does not hold for already-established affiliates, who may instead be interested in building barriers to entry.

Regarding the studies of less-developed countries, most authors have not been able to – or have not even tried to – determine whether the high degrees of concentration in the industries where foreign affiliates are present have been caused by MNCs, or whether MNCs have just been attracted to these industries by good profit opportunities. Two (seemingly contradictory) exceptions are Evans (1977), who claims that MNCs tended to reduce concentration in the oligopolistic Brazilian pharmaceutical industry, and Newfarmer (1979), who argues for the opposite effect – caused by interlocking directorates, collusion, cross-subsidization, and other 'oligopolistic tactics' – in the Brazilian electrical equipment industry.

Lall (1978b) hypothesizes that it is plausible that MNCs speed up the natural concentration process in LDCs, or that the weakness of local competitors allows MNCs to achieve a higher degree of market dominance than in developed countries. Lall (1979c) proceeds to argue that the level of concentration probably falls in the short run following MNC entry, as the affiliate adds to the number of firms in the industry, but that this may be reversed in the long run. The MNCs may buy out local firms or force them out of business, their success may force local firms to fusions and amalgamations, or they may be more skilled as lobbyists than others, thus adding to entry barriers and protection. Looking at the effects of MNCs on concentration in forty-six Malaysian industries, he asserts that the presence of foreign firms, on balance, increased concentration. This was brought about both by the MNCs' impact on general industry characteristics – such as higher initial capital requirements, capital intensity, and advertising intensity – and by some apparently independent effect of foreign presence, perhaps related to 'predatory' conduct, changes in technology and marketing practices, or gains of policy concessions from the government. Similar results were reported for Mexico in Blomström (1986b). Thus the evidence seems to suggest that there is a larger risk that MNCs crowd out local firms in LDCs than in developed countries.

The assumption implicit in much of the discussion above is that competition improves efficiency and welfare, but there are cases where this is not necessarily the case. First, economies of scale are important determinants of industrial productivity. To the extent that foreign entry increases concentration in relatively small national industries, resource allocation and efficiency may well improve with the increase in average firm size. Whether this effect is stronger than that from the presumably reduced competition depends on market characteristics and trade policy. For example, a fall in the number of competitors from thirty to twenty may not necessarily harm the competitive environment, but a reduction from three to two certainly will. Similarly, increased concentration is likely to have more harmful effects in protected industries than in import-competing or export-orientated industries.[10]

In fact, free trade and imports may well be good substitutes for large numbers of domestic competitors: Scandinavian, and particularly Swedish, industrial policies have for a long time built on this assertion (Hjalmarsson, 1991), although the competition between the few remaining large firms has also been important (Porter, 1990; and Sölvell *et al.*, 1991). The conclusion by Chen (1983, p. 90) from his study of Hong Kong manufacturing, where all industries are either export-orientated or import-competing, is consistent with these arguments: 'There are indications that the presence of foreign investment in an industry may have the effect of eliminating wasteful competition . . . [without introducing] damaging monopolistic elements into the industry.'

Second, focusing more closely on technology, there is the classic 'Schumpeterian dilemma' of weighing the static allocative efficiency of competitive markets against the supposed dynamic efficiency of monopolistic and oligopolistic firms. The rate of technical progress can perhaps be higher in concentrated markets, since firms there have internally generated profits to use for R&D, and are generally larger and more able to enjoy economies of scale in R&D. It is also possible that market structure has some impact on what the R&D efforts aim to achieve.

In fact, empirical studies seem to show that market structure affects both the rate and type of technical progress. Looking at the overall rate of technical change, Kamien and Schwartz (1982) summarize a survey of research in industrialized countries by concluding that neither perfect competition nor perfect monopoly, but rather mildly oligopolistic markets, are most conducive to technical progress. Moreover, Katz (1984) and Teitel (1984) in studies of Latin America, and Lall (1980) for India, show that technical change in industries with limited competition largely aims to overcome supply bottlenecks – for example, by substituting imported raw materials and components – while change in more competitive industries is characterized by cost-reducing and quality-improving innovations. In these cases, however, limited competition is intimately tied to import-substitution rather than concentration, although there is a certain overlap.

Summarizing the evidence on the relationship between MNC entry and presence and industry structure, it seems that MNCs enter mainly into industries where barriers to entry and concentration are relatively high, and add initially to the number of firms in the market. In the long run, MNCs may contribute to some increase in concentration, but efficiency may still benefit, particularly if protection does not also guarantee an easy life for the MNC affiliate. Most of the evidence, however, is related to MNC entry rather than to MNC presence – the dynamic aspects of MNCs and competition in host country markets are not well researched. Moreover, much of the evidence refers to effects in developed countries, and it is not possible to disregard the risk that MNC entry into developing countries replaces local production and forces local firms out of business, rather than forcing them to become more efficient (see, further, Frischtak and Newfarmer, 1994).

Statistical testing of spillovers

Although there is plenty of empirical evidence of spillovers from the studies reviewed above, there are only few direct analyses and tests of the existence and significance of spillovers in a more general setting, presumably because of measurement problems and lack of suitable data.[11] In addition, most of the studies that are available focus on intra-industry effects. An early exception is Katz (1969), who notes that the inflow of foreign capital into the Argentinian manufacturing sector in the 1950s had a significant impact on the technologies used by local firms. He asserts that the technical progress did not only take place in the MNCs' own industries, but also in other sectors, because the foreign affiliates forced domestic firms to modernize 'by imposing on them minimum standards of quality, delivery dates, prices, etc. in their supplies of parts and raw materials' (Katz, 1969, p. 154).

The earliest statistical analyses of intra-industry spillovers include studies for Australia by Caves (1974), for Canada by Globerman (1979a), and for Mexico by Blomström and Persson (1983).[12] These authors examine the existence of spillovers by testing whether foreign presence – expressed in terms of the foreign share of each industry's employment or value added – has any impact on labour productivity in local firms in a production function framework. Foreign presence is simply included among other firm and industry characteristics as an explanatory variable in a multiple regression. All three studies conclude that spillovers are significant at this aggregate level, although they cannot say anything about how spillovers take place.

Some more recent studies also present results that are consistent with these early analyses. Chapter 9 in this volume asks whether the spillovers in the Mexican manufacturing sector were large enough to help Mexican firms converge toward US productivity levels during the period 1965–82. The answer is affirmative: foreign presence seems to have a significant positive impact on the rates of growth of local productivity. Nadiri (1991b), in a study of the impact of US direct investment in plant and equipment on the manufacturing sectors in France, Germany, Japan and Great Britain between 1968 and 1988, comes to similar conclusions. Increases in the capital stock owned by US multinationals seem to stimulate new domestic investment in plant and equipment, and it appears that there is also a positive impact of FDI on the growth of total factor productivity in the host countries' manufacturing sectors.

There are also some studies suggesting that the effects of foreign presence are not always beneficial for local firms. For example, Haddad and Harrison (1991, 1993), in a test of the spillover hypothesis for Moroccan manufacturing during the period 1985–9, conclude that spillovers do not take place in all industrial sectors. Like Blomström (1986a), they find that foreign presence lowers the average dispersion of a sector's productivity, but they also observe that the effect is more significant in sectors with simpler technology. This is interpreted to mean that foreign presence forces local firms to become more productive in sectors where best-practice technology lies within their capability, but that there are no significant transfers of modern technology. Furthermore, they find no significant effects of foreign presence on the rate of productivity growth of local firms, and interpret this as additional support to the conclusion that technology spillovers do not occur.

Aitken and Harrison (1991) use plant-level data for Venezuelan manufacturing between 1976 and 1989 to test the impact of foreign presence on total factor productivity growth. They conclude that domestic firms exhibited higher productivity in sectors with a larger foreign share, but argue that it may be wrong to conclude that spillovers have taken place if MNC affiliates systematically locate in the more productive sectors. In addition, they are also able to perform some more detailed tests of regional differences in spillovers. Examining the geographical dispersion of foreign investment, they suggest that the positive impact of FDI accrued mainly to the domestic firms located close to the MNC affiliates. However, effects seem to vary between industries. Aitken and Harrison (1991) is also one of the few studies, apart from Katz (1969), where inter-industry spillovers from foreign investment are discussed explicitly. As noted earlier, they assert that forward linkages generally brought positive spillover effects, but that backward linkages appeared to be less beneficial because of the foreign firms' high import propensities (although there were differences between industrial sectors).

Cantwell (1989), who investigates the responses of local firms to the increase in competition caused by the entry of US multinationals into European markets between 1955 and 1975, also argues that positive technology spillovers did not occur in all industries. His analysis differs notably from the other studies discussed in this section – he does not focus on productivity, but rather on changes in the market shares of foreign and local firms – but his conclusions are interesting. He asserts that 'the technological capacity of indigenous firms . . . was the major factor in determining the success of the European corporate response' (p. 86) to the US challenge, and that the size of the national market was an additional determinant. More specifically, Cantwell suggests that the entry of US affiliates provided a highly beneficial competitive spur in the industries where local firms had some traditional technological strength, whereas local firms in other industries – especially in countries where markets were too small to allow both kinds of firm to operate on an efficient scale – were forced out of business or pushed to market segments that were ignored by the foreign MNCs.

Recently, some authors have also explicitly discussed the apparent contradictions between the earlier statistical spillover studies. In line with Cantwell (1989), Chapter 10 of this volume argues that spillovers should perhaps not be expected in all kinds of industry. In particular, foreign MNCs may sometimes operate in 'enclaves', where neither products nor technologies have much in common with those of local firms. In such circumstances there may be little scope for learning, and spillovers may not materialize. Conversely, when foreign affiliates and local firms are in more direct competition with each other, spillovers are more likely. Examining data for Mexican manufacturing, we find no signs of spillovers in industries where the foreign affiliates have much higher productivity and larger market shares than local firms; in industries without these enclave characteristics, on the other hand, there appears to be a positive relation between foreign presence and local productivity. Chapter 11 of this volume presents similar findings for the Uruguayan manufacturing sector.

Another possible explanation for the divergent findings from the existing statistical tests is proposed in Chapter 12 of this volume, which focuses on effects of competition in Mexican manufacturing. The earlier studies tested the hypothesis that productivity spillovers are strictly proportional to foreign presence, but Chapter 12 here argues that this is not always the case. Spillovers from competition, in particular, are not determined by foreign presence alone, but rather by simultaneous interactions between foreign and local firms. Hence, it is possible that the spillovers are larger in cases where a few foreign MNC stir up a previously protected market than in a situation where foreign affiliates hold large market shares, but refrain from competing hard with local firms. In fact, sometimes a large foreign presence may even be a sign of a weak local industry, where local firms have not been able to absorb any productivity spillovers at all and have therefore been forced to yield market shares to the foreign MNCs.

These recent analyses point to the significance of local conditions in host countries as determinants of the magnitude and scope of spillovers. A high level of local competence and a competitive environment both contribute to raise the absorptive capacity of the host country. In addition to explaining some of the differences between countries and industries when it comes to productivity benefits from FDI, they also highlight a possible role for economic policy in host countries. So far, foreign MNCs have typically been controlled through various types of performance and technology transfer requirements, but it appears that policies supporting a more competitive environment are useful alternatives for countries aiming to maximize the productivity benefits of FDI.[13]

In one of the few available statistical analyses of market access spillovers, Aitken *et al.* (1994) hypothesize that one firm's export activities may reduce the costs for foreign market access of other potential exporters located nearby. Testing a logit specification for over 2000 Mexican manufacturing plants during the period 1986–90, they find that locating near an exporting MNC raises the probability of exporting for an individual firm, but that there is no corresponding effect from locating near locally-owned exporters. Hence, Aitken *et al.* (1994, p. 25) conclude that 'Foreign-owned enterprises are a natural conduit for information about foreign markets and technology, and a natural channel through which domestic firms can distribute their goods. To the extent that foreign investors directly or indirectly provide information and distribution services, their activities enhance the export prospects of local firms.' Although their study cannot say anything about what the channels for market access spillovers are, they are able to demonstrate that the effects are significant at the national level. Similarly, Kokko *et al.* (1997) argue that the presence of export-orientated foreign MNCs in the Uruguayan manufacturing sector has a positive impact on the exports of local firms. Clearly, more research is called for in this area.

Effects on home countries

The existing literature on the home country effects of FDI has seldom referred explicitly to spillovers, although some of the consequences that have been identified in case studies can probably be classified as such, as noted in the conceptual discussion. In particular, it is likely that the linkages between MNCs and their suppliers in the home countries yield similar effects as linkages in the host countries. For example, productivity spillovers could occur if the MNCs have to adapt their products to local conditions abroad and if that adaptation implies that the suppliers in the home country also have to change their production processes in order to meet the new requirements. As noted earlier, it is also possible that some productivity spillovers may occur as a result of 'reverse technology transfer'. MNCs establishing affiliates in foreign 'centres of excellence' may benefit from spillovers and learn about new technologies that are transferred back to the home country (see Braunerhjelm and Svensson, 1996; Cantwell, 1989; Cantwell and Hodson, 1991; Kogut and Chang, 1991; and Zander, 1994 for a discussion). One of the few quantitative studies of these kinds of spillover is Globerman *et al.* (2000), who examined Swedish patent data and claim that the pattern of Swedish outward investment is a significant determinant of the knowledge and technology flows to Sweden. This type of learning is, of course, most likely when the foreign investment is located in advanced industrial economies, such as Germany, Japan or the USA.

Similarly, market access spillovers to local suppliers in the home countries are possible, and probably more likely in cases where the MNCs are involved in vertically integrated operations that require trade in intermediates between different parts of the corporation. It is also possible that home country firms without formal linkages to the MNCs can benefit from market access spillovers. A positive effect of production abroad on home country exports may result if production of one part of a parent company's range of products familiarizes a market with the parent company's (or the home country's) name and reputation. For example, Swedish products are highly regarded for their quality in Latin America, partly because Swedish MNCs have been producing there for decades. However, we are not aware of any detailed studies that can be used to examine the incidence of this kind of spillover.

The effects of labour training taking place within the multinationals may also be comparable to those in host countries – the skills embodied in MNC managers who work or receive parts of their training in foreign affiliates may in particular be transferable to other firms in the home countries. For example, a manager of a foreign subsidiary may return to the home country for a new position in a local firm which has no international experience, and use his or her knowledge of the foreign country to open up an export market for the new employer. Another potential source for productivity spillovers in the home country is the MNCs' research and development activities. The research skills embodied in scientific personnel are often of a general character that can be used in many circumstances, and the training provided by MNCs may therefore easily spill over to local firms. However, we are again plagued by a lack of detailed case studies, and it is not possible to make any conclusive statements about the significance of these effects.

The structural effects of FDI, on the other hand, may differ in both magnitude and character from those in host countries. These effects are likely to be particularly significant for some of the smaller home countries such as the Netherlands, Sweden and Switzerland, where the 'own' MNCs are much more important for the national economy than foreign MNCs are in most host countries. Although empirical studies have generally observed complementarity between overseas production and home country exports (see Blomström and Kokko, 1994 for a survey of the literature), we know that the home country's export structure changes as a result of foreign investment. Instead of shipping finished products to foreign consumers, MNC parents turn to shipping intermediate products to their foreign affiliates. Moreover, exports from the MNC's suppliers of raw materials and intermediates in the home country may increase as a result of foreign investment.

Both positive and negative productivity spillovers may be related to these structural effects of FDI.

For example, in the case of Sweden, we know the country's MNCs concentrate their home production in two areas: R&D and intermediate products (Blomström and Kokko, 1994). This is presumably an optimal location choice for the firms, but the net effects for Sweden as a home country are not equally obvious.

Starting with the research activities, there seems to be an agreement that R&D spillovers are both prevalent and important (Griliches, 1992). Moreover, R&D spillovers are often considered to be a major source of endogenous growth in various recent growth models (see, for example, Romer, 1990). Thus the increasing R&D activities at home that normally follow a firm's investment abroad can be expected to result in positive spillovers in the home country. The effects on the home country of a specialization in intermediate products have, however, caused some worry. For example, Andersson (1993) argues that there are differences between markets for simple intermediates, and markets for more advanced and differentiated finished goods. The first type are competitive and leave no room for profits, whereas the latter type are often oligopolistic and characterized by higher profits, faster product development, and more room for increases in real wages. Thus Andersson (1993) argues that the specialization in production of intermediates that follows from FDI may be connected to slower economic development, perhaps because of negative spillovers. There are no detailed empirical studies addressing this issue at an aggregate level, but case studies on resource-based MNCs suggest that this type of international specialization occurs at the firm level (Vertinski and Raizada, 1994).

8.4 Concluding remarks

The evidence on spillovers from foreign direct investment in host countries suggests that such effects exist and that they may be substantial, both within and between industries, but there is no strong evidence on their exact nature and magnitude. However, recent research suggests that host country spillovers vary systematically between countries and industries, and that the positive effects of FDI are likely to increase with the level of local capability and competition.

The effects of outward FDI on the home country have generally been believed to be positive, but the recent debate has revealed some concern about the consequences of the international division of labour taking place within MNCs. The spillovers to the home country – positive or negative – are perhaps not evenly distributed across all the different activities taking place within large MNCs, but concentrated in certain areas. The significance and character of home-country spillovers may therefore vary, depending on what activities the MNCs retain in their home country and how internationalized the firms are. However, this is a sparsely researched area, and it is impossible to draw any welfare conclusions from the existing results. Moreover, in most cases, we do not know what the alternative to increasing multinationalization would have been.

Notes

1. Some empirical evidence in support of this argument is provided by Mansfield and Romeo (1980), who study the dissemination of twenty-six US technologies and conclude that transfers to affiliates tend to be of a later vintage than technologies sold to outsiders. The average age of their sample of technologies at the time of their first transfer to affiliates in developed countries was 5.8 years (9.8 years for affiliates in developing countries), whereas the corresponding figure for outside licensing and joint ventures was 13.1 years. Behrman and Wallender (1976) and McFetridge (1987) also find that the transfer lags tend to be shorter for intra-firm transfers.

2. Mansfield and Romeo (1980) also present indirect evidence for this argument. They claim that the export of technologies from parents to US affiliates abroad speeded up the emergence of competing products or processes in the host countries by an average of 2.5 years in about a third of the cases studied. In addition, they report that more than half of the managers of a sample of British firms believed that they had introduced some products and processes earlier as a consequence of transfers of technology to US affiliates operating in the United Kingdom. More evidence will be presented later, in the survey of empirical studies of spillovers.

3. For theoretical studies, see, for example, Findlay (1978); Koizumi and Kopecky (1977); Das (1987); and Wang and Blomström (1992). Some other early empirical studies are Balasubramanyam (1973); Brash (1966); Deane (1970); Dunning (1958); Forsyth (1972); Gabriel (1967); Rosenbluth (1970); and Safarian (1966).

4. However, the existence of linkages does not prove that there are spillovers, but the two are probably closely related. Even if the MNC affiliate charges for the support it provides to their local suppliers and distributors, it is not always able to extract the full value of the resulting productivity increases.

5. The domestic content in Lall's two cases was extremely high – probably over 90 per cent – and both firms had extensive supplier networks, with 500 and 339 independent suppliers, respectively. It should be noted that

these characteristics already distinguish the Indian experience from others, since an extreme import substitution policy made India a virtually closed economy until the mid-1980s. Hill (1982), who examines the Philippines' appliance and motor-cycle industries, argues that inter-firm linkages are often significantly weaker than in the Indian case. More liberal import policies reduce local content, the smaller size of most markets makes much production economically non-viable, and the assembler character of many principal firms makes them incapable of offering technical assistance to suppliers. Similarly, Lindsey (1984) argues that the positive impact of MNCs on the Philippines' economy has been very limited.

6.   Lall (1978) reviews numerous other studies of linkages between MNCs and local firms, and Halbach (1989) summarizes a detailed study of subcontracting and linkages in several South-East Asian industries.

7.   This last point is noted in numerous other studies. Dunning (1958), in one of the earliest contributions, maintains that foreign firms are generally engaged in the training of local suppliers. In addition to the comprehensive evidence on local content, Reuber *et al.* (1973) argue that MNCs actively support the establishment of independent local suppliers. Lim and Pang (1982) also underscore this in their study of the Singapore electronics industry: they point specifically to the role of MNCs in suggesting entrepreneurial possibilities and assisting in the establishment of supplier firms, and their 'willingness to bear the initial costs of encouraging and patronizing local suppliers, who in the long run would be cost-competitive' (p. 591). What distinguishes their study is, first, that it is concerned with export-orientated TNCs, whereas most others look at import-competing industries; and second, that they show how the development of linkages in Singapore was relatively rapid during the late 1970s. Most other studies seem to suggest a much slower process.

8.   Wasow and Hill (1986) provide similar evidence for the dissemination of management skills in the Philippines' insurance industry. Similarly, Yoshihara (1988) underlines the importance of training in foreign companies (and overseas education) for Chinese-owned firms in South-East Asia. Behrman and Wallender (1976) recognize spillovers of both managerial and technical skills. In particular, they note that several of the MNC affiliates' subcontractors had been established by former employees. Hill (1982) also identifies similar cases in the Philippines' appliance and motor-cycle industries, but argues that they were insignificant. Nevertheless, twelve out of twenty assembler firms had some subcontractors that were established by former employees.

9.   For some recent evidence, see Cantwell (1995); Patel and Pavitt (1994); and Zander (1994).

10. The Peruvian automotive industry in the late 1960s and early 1970s (like many other industries in countries with extreme import-substitution policies) provides a striking example of the fact that low concentration does not necessarily equal high efficiency. At that time, '13 firms, each with some foreign ownership, were assembling 18 brands and over 25 models of automotive vehicles, mostly passenger cars. Facing a limited

local market, none of these firms was able to use more than 30 per cent of its installed capacity' (UNCTC, 1981, p. 19).

11.   It should also be noted in this context that both intra-industry and inter-industry R&D spillovers have been identified and estimated, mainly for developed countries, but without explicit reference to MNCs and FDI. See, for example, Bernstein (1988, 1989) and Nadiri (1991a). The fact that this kind of spillover seems to take place offers some indirect support to the hypothesis that there are technology spillovers between MNC affiliates and local firms. The conclusion that technological innovations (proxied by R&D measures) in some domestic firms have positive effects on the productivity of other domestic firms is analogous to the situation where technological innovations (proxied by the size of the technology gap or the amount of technology imports) in foreign affiliates have positive effects on the productivity of local firms.

12.   See also Blomström (1989). Moreover, Chen (1983) presents a detailed discussion and some statistical evidence of spillovers in the major manufacturing industries in Hong Kong, although he does not examine the whole manufacturing sector. More specifically, he shows that foreign firms have been more active than local firms in importing new technologies to Hong Kong, and that the rates of technology diffusion have been higher in the industries where foreign firms hold larger market shares.

13.   For example, Chapter 13 and 14 show that the technology imports of foreign affiliates are partly determined by the competition in the host country market.

9
Multinational Corporations and Productivity Convergence in Mexico

9.1 Introduction

Since the 1960s the developing countries have had very different experiences regarding income and productivity growth, and the extent to which they have converged on developed countries. Some, such as the Asian newly-industrialized countries (NICs), clearly are in a process of rapid convergence, whereas others, such as most countries in Africa, show no sign of convergence. This indicates that the realization of the potentiality for productivity catch-up simply because of backwardness depends strongly on another set of causes, some of which are internal and others external to the countries themselves (see Abramovitz, 1986).

Among the external factors that might influence a country's productivity, multinational firms deserve special attention. In recent times, MNCs have become an important agent in the production of technology. Such firms now produce, own and control most of the world's advanced technologies. They also play a central role in the international diffusion of new technology (see Blomström, 1991). Over four-fifths of the stock of foreign direct investment originates from only half a dozen countries – the USA, Great Britain, Japan, Germany, Switzerland and the Netherlands – where most of the new technology is produced and from where it is spread to the rest of the world. However, despite the enormous amount of controversy over the transfer of technology by multinationals, in both their home and host countries, there are no studies dealing with the roles of these firms in productivity convergence among countries.

In this chapter we examine the impact of the operations of foreign-owned multinational firms on the growth of productivity of Mexican manufacturing industries. We investigate both the extent to which the penetration of a sector by foreign-owned firms affects the prod-

134

uctivity of local firms in that sector, and whether there is any evidence of convergence between this industry's productivity level and that of the USA. Thus we concentrate on intra-industry influences, and primarily on the external effects or 'spillovers' of foreign direct investment.

Earlier studies of such technology spillovers – focusing on Australia (Caves, 1974); Canada (Globerman, 1979a); Mexico (Blomström, 1989; and Kokko, 1992); Morocco (Haddad and Harrison, 1993); and Venezuela (Aitken and Harrison, 1991) – generally found some support for the spillover benefit hypothesis, although it was weaker in the cases of Morocco and Venezuela. Because of great methodological difficulties in investigating these effects and a relative paucity of data, none of these studies was able to analyze in any depth the nature of spillover efficiency. Furthermore, none of them tried to evaluate the importance of such spillovers for productivity growth in the host country.

This chapter has two major sections: the first looks at the productivity spillovers between domestic and foreign firms in Mexico, and the second, at Mexico's international catch-up. There is also a brief summary section at the end.

9.2 Convergence between foreign and local firms in Mexico

Multinationals, technology transfer, and convergence

The convergence hypothesis asserts that when the productivity level of one (or several) country(ies) is substantially superior to that of a number of other economies, largely as a result of differences in their productive techniques, those laggard countries that are not too far behind the leaders will be in a position to embark on a catch-up process. This process will continue as long as the economies that are approaching the leader's performance continue to be able to learn from the leader. But as the distance between the two groups narrows, the stock of knowledge not absorbed by the laggards will grow smaller and approach exhaustion. The catch-up process usually terminates at that point, unless some supplementary and unrelated influence fortuitously comes into play. Meanwhile, those countries that are so far behind the leaders that it is impractical for them to profit substantially from the leaders' knowledge will generally not be able to participate in the convergence process at all, and many such economies will find themselves falling even further behind.

The most important influence underlying this hypothesis is the transfer of technology that constantly takes place among economies. Technology may be transferred from one place to another through a variety of channels, but since the Second World War, multinational corporations have become a powerful institution for the spread of new technology. Multinational firms not only establish subsidiaries abroad, but they also transfer technology through a number of other arrangements, including licensing, franchising, management contracts, marketing contracts and technical service contracts.

Subsidiary production, or what we might call foreign direct investment (FDI), is still the dominant mode through which multinational firms exploit their intangible assets in foreign markets, and there are several ways in which such investment may facilitate the diffusion of technology from advanced to developing countries. One is simply that the multinationals set up operations in developing countries that are beyond the technological capabilities of the host country's firms. Even if there were no leakage of the technology to local firms, there would still be a geographical diffusion of technology, but with no change in its ownership.

Technology transfer through foreign direct investment can also result in indirect productivity gains for the host developing countries, through the realization of external economies. Generally these benefits are referred to as *spillovers*, which indicates the importance of the way in which the influence is transmitted. These spillovers may occur in several ways. The most important channel is presumed to be via competition (see Blomström, 1986a). Existing inefficient local firms may be forced by the competition of foreigners to make themselves more productive by investing in physical or human capital, or importing new technology.

Another source of gain to the host economy is the training of labour and management provided by the multinationals, which may then become available to the economy in general. Since such resources are in a short supply in developing countries, this type of spillover efficiency is expected to be more important there.

A third potential source of spillover efficiency benefits is through the impact made by the foreign subsidiaries in the host economy on their local suppliers, by insisting that they meet standards of quality control, delivery dates, prices and so on. This aspect should be particularly important to countries such as Mexico, where legislation requires domestic content during the period studied here.

Although all these influences would cause positive long-run effects on the host country's productivity, there are, also several offsetting forces at work. First, technology transfer within multinationals is far from free (see Teece, 1976). It involves a substantial commitment of real resources and a sequence of overlapping stages of activity. This slows down the technology transfer process and makes multinationals unwilling to share information. Second, the technology that is used by the MNCs may be unsuitable for local firms in developing countries. Kokko (1992) shows, for example, that there may be no spillovers if the technological gap between foreign and local firms is too large. Both of these positions suggest little technology spillover between the MNCs and the local firms in the country. Third, Lall (1980b) argues that imports of technology through foreign investment may work as an important first injection to local technological development, but that too much reliance on foreign technology may retard the basic design and development activity in the host country, thus causing negative long-run effects on productivity.

To determine whether the presence of MNCs acts as a catalyst or a hindrance to productivity growth in Mexico, we begin by investigating productivity convergence among foreign and local firms in Mexican manufacturing industries. For this purpose we use unpublished data from the Mexican Census of Manufactures 1970 and 1975 (see Appendix for a description of the data). These are the only two years for which data by ownership are available. Though the period is unfortunately short, the results are none the less quite strong. We first investigate trends within twenty broad manufacturing industries and then perform a regression analysis.[1]

Aggregate trends

It is clear from Table 9.1 that, in 1970, foreign firms displayed higher labour productivity than did Mexican firms (also see Table A-9.1 in the Appendix for data on the extent of multinational activity by industry). The productivity of foreign firms, measured both by value-added and gross output, was, on average, more than twice that of local firms. The labour productivity level of MNCs exceeded that of locally-owned firms in every industry. Among Mexican firms, labour productivity was significantly higher in state-owned than in privately-owned firms, although the state companies were not as efficient as the affiliates of the multinationals.

To a large extent, the differences in labour productivity are related to differences in the firms' capital intensity. This can be seen from

Table 9.1　Comparison of labour productivity levels between foreign and domestic firms in Mexico, 1970[a]

Industry[b]		Productivity level by segment as a fraction of the overall productivity level of the industry							
		Value added per employee				Gross output per employee			
		MNC	Locally-owned		Total domestic[c]	MNC	Locally-owned		Total domestic[c]
			State	Private			State	Private	
20	Food	2.19	0.78	0.85	0.84	2.12	0.79	0.86	0.85
21	Tobacco	1.17	–	0.16	0.16	1.16	–	0.19	0.19
22	Textile mill products	1.43	0.62	0.96	0.94	1.38	0.60	0.97	0.95
23	Apparel	2.48	1.75	0.95	0.96	2.31	1.92	0.95	0.96
24	Lumber and wood	2.41	1.42	0.92	0.95	2.58	1.13	0.93	0.94
25	Furniture	1.41	1.85	0.94	0.97	1.10	1.93	0.95	0.99
26	Paper	1.33	1.51	0.87	0.91	1.52	1.22	0.83	0.86
27	Printing and publishing	2.00	0.99	0.95	0.95	1.72	0.86	0.97	0.97
28	Chemicals	1.28	0.94	0.75	0.77	1.17	1.20	0.82	0.86
29	Petroleum and coal	2.04	1.63	0.54	0.74	1.87	1.60	0.60	0.78
30	Rubber and plastics	2.50	–	0.65	0.65	2.36	–	0.68	0.68
31	Leather	1.87	1.36	0.98	0.98	1.70	3.36	0.98	0.98
32	Stone, clay and glass	1.74	0.88	0.90	0.90	1.84	0.81	0.89	0.88
33	Primary metals	1.13	1.13	0.79	0.92	1.16	1.11	0.78	0.91
34	Fabricated metals	1.51	3.70	0.87	0.89	1.42	4.22	0.89	0.91
35	Non-electrical equipment	1.47	1.54	0.75	0.76	1.59	2.21	0.68	0.69
36	Electric equipment	1.49	–	0.74	0.74	1.47	–	0.75	0.75
37	Transport equipment	1.37	1.07	0.62	0.75	1.53	1.06	0.47	0.65
38	Instruments	1.54	–	0.75	0.75	1.68	–	0.69	0.69
39	Misc. manufacturing	1.45	–	0.90	0.90	1.25	–	0.95	0.95
Total manufacturing		**1.88**	**1.33**	**0.75**	**0.79**	**1.85**	**1.53**	**0.75**	**0.80**

Notes:　[a]　Basic data are from worksheets provided by the Dirección de Estadística de la Secretaría de Industria y Commercio in Mexico. See Appendix for details.
[b]　Industries are classified by the US SIC code and include all 4 digit SICs in each industry. See the Appendix for detailed Mexican industry codes included in each US SIC code.
[c]　The total domestic sector is defined as the sum of state-owned and privately-owned firms, a separation that is available only for 1970.

Table 9.2, which shows the firms' capital–labour ratio as a fraction of the overall capital–labour ratio of the industry. The capital intensity was 2.5 times higher in foreign firms than in the privately-owned Mexican firms but, interestingly, about the same as in the state-owned firms. The greater efficiency of multinationals relative to both state-owned and privately-owned firms in Mexico still holds for total factor productivity (TFP), defined as a ratio of output to a weighted sum of labour and capital inputs (see notes in Table 9.3 for the definition).[2] As Table 9.3 indicates, the foreign firms' TFP measured by gross output was 34 per cent higher than that of local firms on average, with the difference being highest in tobacco (150 per cent higher),

Table 9.2 Comparison of capital-intensity levels between foreign and domestic firms in Mexico, 1970[a]

Industry[b]	Capital–labour ratio by segment as a fraction of the overall capital–labour ratio of the industry			
	MNC	Locally-owned		Total
		State	Private	domestic[c]
20 Food	2.06	2.32	0.75	0.86
21 Tobacco	1.13	–	0.37	0.37
22 Textile mill products	1.48	0.58	0.95	0.94
23 Apparel	2.48	1.62	0.95	0.96
24 Lumber and wood	4.67	1.24	0.84	0.87
25 Furniture	1.14	1.50	0.97	0.99
26 Paper	1.61	2.95	0.69	0.83
27 Printing and publishing	2.33	1.44	0.92	0.94
28 Chemicals	1.28	1.33	0.70	0.76
29 Petroleum and coal	1.01	1.36	0.92	1.00
30 Rubber and plastics	1.95	–	0.78	0.78
31 Leather	2.45	1.59	0.96	0.96
32 Stone, clay and glass	1.75	0.65	0.90	0.89
33 Primary metals	1.10	0.92	0.96	0.94
34 Fabricated metals	1.66	3.52	0.84	0.86
35 Non-electrical equipment	1.65	3.69	0.63	0.66
36 Electrical equipment	1.43	–	0.77	0.77
37 Transport equipment	1.31	1.25	0.60	0.79
38 Instruments	2.25	–	0.43	0.43
39 Misc. manufacturing	1.62	–	0.87	0.87
Total manufacturing	**1.85**	**1.85**	**0.73**	**0.80**

Notes: [a] Basic data are from worksheets provided by the Dirección de Estadística de la Secretaría de Industria y Comercio in Mexico. See Appendix for details. The 1970 capital stock figures are based on *capital invertido*.
[b] Industries are classified by the US SIC code and include all 4-digit SICs in each industry. See the Appendix for detailed Mexican industry codes included in each US SIC code.
[c] The total domestic sector is defined as the sum of state-owned and privately-owned firms, a separation that is available only for 1970.

petroleum (138 per cent), rubber (89 per cent), and transport equipment (78 per cent). In lumber and wood products, chemicals and miscellaneous manufacturing, the local firms' TFP exceeded that of the multinationals.

Table 9.3　Comparison of TFP levels between foreign and domestic firms in Mexico, 1970a

Industry[b]		Ratio of TFP level by segment to overall industry TFP							
		Value-added index				Gross output index			
		MNC	Locally-owned		Total domestic[c]	MNC	Locally-owned		Total domestic[c]
			State	Private			State	Private	
20	Food	1.29	0.42	1.02	0.93	1.25	0.42	1.03	0.94
21	Tobacco	1.05	–	0.35	0.35	1.05	–	0.42	0.42
22	Textile mill products	1.14	0.80	0.98	0.98	1.10	0.77	0.99	0.98
23	Apparel	1.37	1.31	0.97	0.98	1.28	1.43	0.98	0.98
24	Lumber and wood	0.82	1.26	1.00	1.02	0.87	1.00	1.01	1.01
25	Furniture	1.31	1.45	0.95	0.98	1.03	1.52	0.97	1.00
26	Paper	0.98	0.71	1.06	1.01	1.12	0.57	1.02	0.95
27	Printing and publishing	1.20	0.81	0.99	0.98	1.04	0.70	1.01	1.00
28	Chemicals	1.08	0.77	0.93	0.90	0.99	0.99	1.01	1.01
29	Petroleum and coal	2.03	1.28	0.58	0.74	1.86	1.25	0.64	0.78
30	Rubber and plastics	1.57	–	0.75	0.75	1.49	–	0.79	0.79
31	Leather	1.10	1.05	1.00	1.00	1.00	2.61	1.00	1.00
32	Stone, clay and glass	1.22	1.09	0.95	0.95	1.29	1.01	0.94	0.94
33	Primary metals	1.07	1.20	0.81	0.96	1.09	1.17	0.80	0.94
34	Fabricated metals	1.11	1.56	0.95	0.97	1.04	1.78	0.97	0.99
35	Non-electrical equipment	1.07	0.61	0.95	0.94	1.16	0.87	0.86	0.86
36	Electrical equipment	1.20	–	0.85	0.85	1.18	–	0.86	0.86
37	Transport equipment	1.16	0.93	0.81	0.85	1.30	0.92	0.61	0.73
38	Instruments	0.92	–	1.09	1.09	1.00	–	0.99	0.99
39	Misc. manufacturing	1.11	–	0.97	0.97	0.96	–	1.01	1.01
Total manufacturing		**1.24**	**0.87**	**0.90**	**0.90**	**1.22**	**1.01**	**0.90**	**0.91**

Notes:　[a]　Data are from worksheets provided by the Dirección de Estadística de la Secretaría de Industria y Comercio in Mexico. The 1970 capital stock figures are based on *capital invertido*. The TFP is measured as a ratio of industry output (Y) to a weighted average of employment (L) and capital stock (K): TFP = $Y/[\alpha L + (1-\alpha)K]$, where α is the industry's wage share.
[b]　Industries are classified by US SIC code and include all 4-digit SICs in each industry. See Appendix for detailed Mexican industry codes included in each US SIC code.
[c]　The total domestic sector is defined as the sum of state-owned and privately-owned firms, a separation that is available only for 1970.

The data in Table 9.4 indicate that Mexican firms caught up with the multinationals over time. Between 1970 and 1975, the multinationals' productivity lead in terms of labour productivity diminished in the manufacturing sector as a whole, as well as in three-quarters of the individual manufacturing industries. There was also a tendency towards convergence in total factor productivity over the same period, but these figures should be interpreted with great caution, since the capital stock figures for 1970 and 1975 are not directly comparable (see Appendix).[3]

In sum, we find that there are rather large productivity differences between foreign and local firms in Mexico, but that the foreign firms'

Table 9.4   Productivity convergence between foreign and domestic firms in Mexico, 1970 and 1975[a]

Industry[b]		Ratio of productivity levels between domestic and foreign firms						
		All 4-digit industries					4-digit industries with MNCs	
		Value-added per employee	Gross output per employee		TFP		Gross output per employee	
		1970	1970	1975	1970	1975	1970	1975
20	Food	0.39	0.40	0.50	0.75	0.54	0.48	0.59
21	Tobacco	0.14	0.16	–	0.40	–	0.16	–
22	Textile mill products	0.66	0.69	0.65	0.89	0.87	0.79	0.64
23	Apparel	0.39	0.42	0.71	0.77	1.36	0.42	0.72
24	Lumber and wood	0.39	0.37	0.44	1.16	1.19	0.36	0.44
25	Furniture	0.69	0.90	0.53	0.97	0.71	0.91	0.53
26	Paper	0.68	0.56	1.02	0.85	0.79	0.56	1.02
27	Printing and publishing	0.48	0.56	0.76	0.96	0.86	0.56	0.76
28	Chemicals	0.60	0.73	0.69	1.02	0.84	0.75	0.70
29	Petroleum and coal	0.36	0.42	0.59	0.42	0.69	0.53	0.64
30	Rubber and plastics	0.26	0.29	0.46	0.53	0.93	0.29	0.46
31	Leather	0.52	0.58	0.72	1.00	1.16	0.59	0.73
32	Stone, clay and glass	0.52	0.48	0.57	0.72	0.84	0.52	0.62
33	Primary metals	0.81	0.78	0.79	0.87	0.75	0.78	0.79
34	Fabricated metals	0.59	0.64	0.68	0.95	1.00	0.64	0.68
35	Non-electrical equipment	0.52	0.44	1.04	0.74	1.09	0.44	1.06
36	Electrical equipment	0.49	0.51	1.13	0.73	1.23	0.51	1.13
37	Transport equipment	0.55	0.42	0.36	0.57	0.45	0.43	0.36
38	Instruments	0.49	0.41	0.54	0.99	1.36	0.49	0.57
39	Misc. manufacturing	0.62	0.76	0.66	1.06	1.01	0.76	0.68
Total manufacturing		**0.42**	**0.43**	**0.61**	**0.75**	**0.79**	**0.47**	**0.64**

Notes: [a]   Data are from worksheets provided by the Dirección de Estadística de la Secretaría de Industria y Comercio in Mexico. The TFP figures are based on gross output in each year, but for 1970 the capital stock figures are based on *capital invertido*, and for 1975 on *activos fijos brutos*. Since the two concepts differ, comparisons based on the TFP figures in columns 4 and 5 of the table should be interpreted with caution. See Appendix for details.
[b]   Industries are classified by US SIC code. The results in the first five columns are based on all 4-digit SICs in each industry. The results in the last two columns are based on only the 4-digit SICs in which MNCs are present in either 1970 or 1975. See Appendix for the detailed Mexican industry codes included in each US SIC code.

lead has been diminishing. To examine whether this productivity catch-up is related to the presence of multinationals and the existence of spillovers between foreign and local firms, we next relate the latter's productivity growth to the presence of foreign firms in various industries.

Regression analysis

We use two regression forms. In the first, the dependent variable is the rate of labour productivity growth of local firms within an industry, and, in the second, it is the rate of convergence in labour productivity levels between local and foreign firms within a sector. These variables are related to the degree of foreign ownership of the industry and the gap in labour productivity between local and foreign-owned firms in 1970, as well as two other explanatory variables.

As Table 9.5 shows, the results are consistent in the two regression forms. Both labour productivity growth in local firms and productivity convergence between local and foreign firms are faster in industries with a greater share of employment accounted for by multinationals.[4] The Mexican firms' productivity growth and the rate of catch-up to the MNCs are also higher in sectors where the initial disparity in productivity levels between local and foreign firms is greater, a result that accords well with the 'advantages of backwardness' thesis. Furthermore, in sectors with higher capital–labour ratios, the productivity growth of locally-owned firms and the rate of catch-up are lower. This suggests that spillover gains from the new technology of multinationals are easier to incorporate when the investment requirements are small. Finally, convergence seems to be faster in industries with slower output growth, but output growth does not affect the rate of local firms' productivity growth. This indicates that the competitive pressures from the presence of multinationals in an industry may be greater in relatively stagnant industries. In rapidly-growing sectors, inefficient local firms can continue to survive without improving their productivity, but in slow-growing industries, the inefficient local firms can be driven out by the multinationals.[5]

The results so far suggest that technology spillovers exist from foreign direct investment, with a resulting convergence in productivity between foreign and local firms in Mexico, but are these spillover benefits large enough to generate an international catch-up? We now turn to this question by looking at the extent to which the labour productivity levels of Mexico and the USA have converged.

9.3   International catch-up?

Aggregate trends

We begin by comparing the productivity levels of foreign and domestic firms in Mexico with those of the USA in 1970.[6] As Table 9.6 shows, foreign firms were very close to the USA in terms of both labour productivity and TFP, whereas local firms in Mexico were far behind. The

Table 9.5   Regression analysis of productivity catch-up between foreign and locally-owned firms in Mexico[a]

Independent variables	Dependent variables			
	LPGLOC	**LPGLOC**	**LPGLOC**	**CONVLF**
Constant	−0.048	0.147*	0.172**	0.219**
	(1.52)	(2.94)	(3.47)	(3.06)
FORSHARE	0.351**	0.245**	0.372**	0.734**
	(3.59)	(3.34)	(4.06)	(5.53)
LFLPGAP70		−0.318**	−0.313**	−0.446**
		(4.35)	(4.24)	(4.18)
OUTPGRTH			−0.188	−0.166**
			(0.89)	(5.41)
KL 1970			−0.482*	−0.709*
			(2.15)	(2.18)
R^2	0.42	0.72	0.79	0.80
Adj. R^2	0.38	0.69	0.73	0.75
Standard error σ	0.078	0.055	0.051	0.074
Sample size[b]	20	20	20	20

Notes: [a] Estimated coefficients are shown together with the absolute value of the t-statistic in parentheses.
Key:
LPGLOC   = Annual rate of growth of gross output per employee in locally-owned firms, 1970 to 1975
FORSHARE = Share of employment in foreign-owned firms in total industry employment, averaged between 1970 and 1975
LFLPGAP70 = Ratio of gross output per employee in local firms to gross output per employee in foreign firms, 1970
OUTPGRTH = Average annual rate of growth of industry output, 1970 to 1975
KL1970   = Industry capital–labour ratio in 1970
CONVLF   = Ratio of *LFLPGAP75* to *LFLPGAP70*.
[b] Basic data are from worksheets provided by the Dirección de Estadística de la Secretaría de Industria y Comercio in Mexico. Industries are classified by the 2-digit US SIC code and include all 4-digit SICs in each industry. See Appendix for details.
*   Significant at the 0.05 level (two-tailed test).
**   Significant at the 0.01 level (two-tailed test).

MNCs' labour productivity and TFP both averaged 93 per cent of that of the USA, and in several industries they even exceeded the US levels. Labour productivity in Mexican firms, on the other hand, averaged only 39 per cent of that of the US firms. The technology gap, as measured by TFP. was smaller, at 60 per cent, which reflects the con-

Table 9.6　Mexican productivity levels by segment and industry as a proportion of US productivity levels 1970, by industry[a]

Industry[b]		Value-added per employee			TFP		
		MNC	Domestic	Total	MNC	Domestic	Total
20	Food	0.94	0.36	0.43	1.05	0.64	0.71
21	Tobacco	0.45	0.06	0.39	0.46	0.15	0.43
22	Textile mill products	1.09	0.72	0.76	1.17	0.95	0.98
23	Apparel	1.65	0.64	0.67	0.65	0.51	0.51
24	Lumber and wood	0.69	0.27	0.29	0.50	0.43	0.43
25	Furniture	1.03	0.71	0.73	0.82	0.62	0.63
26	Paper	0.84	0.57	0.63	0.92	0.85	0.87
27	Printing and publishing	0.82	0.39	0.41	0.64	0.48	0.49
28	Chemicals	0.85	0.51	0.66	1.15	0.87	1.01
29	Petroleum and coal	0.48	0.17	0.24	1.15	0.42	0.57
30	Rubber and plastics	1.66	0.43	0.67	1.76	0.71	1.00
31	Leather	0.97	0.51	0.52	0.50	0.47	0.47
32	Stone, clay and glass	0.79	0.41	0.46	0.85	0.59	0.63
33	Primary metals	0.76	0.62	0.67	1.07	0.94	0.99
34	Fabricated metals	0.55	0.33	0.37	0.58	0.46	0.48
35	Non-electrical equipment	0.66	0.34	0.45	0.57	0.47	0.52
36	Electrical equipment	1.10	0.54	0.73	0.96	0.66	0.79
37	Transport equipment	0.73	0.40	0.53	0.78	0.55	0.65
38	Instruments	0.87	0.42	0.56	0.42	0.56	0.48
39	Misc. manufacturing	0.51	0.32	0.35	0.51	0.42	0.44
Total manufacturing		**0.93**	**0.39**	**0.49**	**0.93**	**0.60**	**0.69**

Notes:　[a]　Basic data are from worksheets provided by the Dirección de Estadística de la Secretaría de Industria y Comercio in Mexico. The US data for the GDP by industry in current US dollars and full-time and part-time employees are from NIPA tables. The 1970 Mexican value-added was converted to 1975 pesos on the basis of the Mexican GDP deflator and then to 1975 US dollars on the basis of the 1975 exchange rate. The 1970 US value-added was converted from 1982 dollars to 1975 dollars using the US GDP deflator. The TFP index is based on value-added. The Mexican 1970 capital stock figures are based on *capital invertido*; the US capital stock figures are from Musgrave (1986) and are based on current US dollar values (the nearest equivalent). Since the two concepts differ, the last three columns should be interpreted with caution. The productivity ratios are relative to the productivity levels of the whole US industry.
[b]　Industries are classified by US SIC code and include all 4-digit SICs in each industry. See Appendix for the detailed Mexican industry codes included in each US SIC code.

siderably higher capital intensity of US production. The productivity levels for foreign and local firms taken together correspond rather well to those reported in Maddison and van Ark (1989).[7]

The finding that the foreign affiliates were so close to the USA in terms of productivity while local firms were lagging behind certainly suggests that multinational firms have contributed to a geographical diffusion of technology and acted as a bridge between more advanced and less advanced countries. But is this international diffusion of technology enough for an international catch-up? Table 9.7 presents the convergence in productivity between Mexico and the USA between 1970 and 1975. Overall, there seems to be no catch-up during the five-year period, but this varies among industries. The US productivity lead diminished in seven industries, while it increased in thirteen industries. The results for convergence are similar for the 2-digit industry sample, which includes only 4-digit Mexican industries with MNCs present, though, as expected, the Mexican productivity figures are higher. Since foreign participation varies among industries, it may very well be that foreign investment is related to international catch-up in one way or another. We shall return to this question later in our regression analysis.[8]

With data from the United Nations we were able to examine the convergence of labour productivity between Mexico and the USA between 1965 and 1984 (see Table 9.8).[9] During this longer period there was a clear convergence of productivity levels in all industries for which data are available. The biggest catch-up took place during the second half of the 1960s, but slowed down thereafter. Between 1970 and 1975 there was very little convergence, just as the census data in Table 9.7 show.

Regression analysis

Since the main purpose of this chapter is to analyze the role of MNCs in productivity convergence among countries, we shall, finally, by means of regression analysis, try to go deeper into that question by relating a sector's productivity catch-up to the degree of foreign ownership. As mentioned earlier, there are both direct and indirect effects on the total industry productivity of foreign direct investment. The direct effect is that an increase in the share of multinationals in an industry increases the productivity level of the whole industry, simply because MNCs have higher productivity than do local firms. The indirect effect, on the other hand, is the technological spillover between the multinationals and the local firms. Because of the lack of data for the pre-1970 and the post-1975 period, these two effects cannot be separated in the regression.

As before, we use two regression forms. In the first, the dependent variable is the rate of labour productivity growth of Mexican industries (local plus foreign firms), and in the second it is the rate of

Table 9.7   Convergence in productivity between Mexico and the USA: ratio of Mexican to US value-added per employee, 1970 and 1975[a]

Industries[b]	All 4-digit Mexican industries			4-digit Mexican industries with MNCs		
	1970	1975	Ratio	1970	1975	Ratio
20 Food	0.43	0.44	1.01	0.52	0.52	0.99
21 Tobacco	0.39	0.45	1.15	0.39	0.45	1.15
22 Textile mill products	0.76	0.79	1.04	0.85	0.87	1.02
23 Apparel	0.67	0.51	0.76	0.68	0.52	0.76
24 Lumber and wood	0.29	0.27	0.94	0.29	0.27	0.94
25 Furniture	0.73	0.59	0.81	0.73	0.59	0.81
26 Paper	0.63	0.57	0.90	0.63	0.57	0.90
27 Printing and publishing	0.41	0.44	1.06	0.41	0.44	1.06
28 Chemicals	0.66	0.60	0.90	0.68	0.61	0.89
29 Petroleum and coal	0.24	0.21	0.87	0.29	0.22	0.75
30 Rubber and plastics	0.67	0.64	0.96	0.67	0.64	0.96
31 Leather	0.52	0.43	0.82	0.53	0.43	0.82
32 Stone, clay and glass	0.46	0.50	1.10	0.49	0.54	1.10
33 Primary metals	0.67	0.66	0.98	0.67	0.66	0.98
34 Fabricated metals	0.37	0.46	1.24	0.37	0.46	1.24
35 Non-electrical equipment	0.45	0.51	1.14	0.45	0.52	1.15
36 Electrical equipment	0.73	0.55	0.75	0.73	0.55	0.75
37 Transport equipment	0.53	0.38	0.72	0.53	0.38	0.72
38 Instruments	0.56	0.46	0.81	0.64	0.48	0.75
39 Misc. manufacturing	0.35	0.35	0.99	0.36	0.36	1.00
Total manufacturing	**0.49**	**0.48**	**0.98**	**0.53**	**0.51**	**0.96**

Notes: [a] Basic data are from worksheets provided by the Dirección de Estadística de la Secretaría de Industria y Comercio in Mexico. The US data for GDP by industry is current US dollars and full-time and part-time employees are from NIPA tables. The 1970 Mexican value-added was converted to 1975 pesos on the basis of the Mexican GDP deflator, and the 1975 pesos were then converted to 1975 US dollars on the basis of the 1975 exchange rate. The 1970 US value-added was converted from 1982 dollars to 1975 dollars using the US GDP deflator.
[b] Industries are classified by US SIC code. The results in the columns 2, 3 and 4 are based on all 4-digit SICs in each industry. The results in columns 5, 6 and 7 are based on only the 4-digit SICs in which MNCs are present in either 1970 or 1975. See Appendix for the detailed Mexican industry codes included in each US SIC code.

Table 9.8   Convergence of labour productivity between Mexico and the USA: ratio of Mexico to US value-added per employee, 1965–84[a]

Industry		1965	1967	1970	1975	1977	1979	1982	1984
20	Food	0.42	0.50	0.51	0.52	0.62	0.56	0.47	0.51
21	Tobacco	0.35	0.54	0.55	0.92	1.00	1.04	0.87	0.75
22	Textile mill products	n.a.	n.a.	0.54	0.55	0.51	0.61	0.60	0.66
23	Apparel	n.a.	n.a.	n.a.	n.a.	n.a.	n.a.	n.a.	n.a.
24	Lumber and wood	0.47	0.54	0.55	0.51	0.64	0.91	1.10	1.11
25	Furniture	n.a.	n.a.	n.a.	n.a.	n.a.	n.a.	n.a.	n.a.
26	Paper	n.a.	0.56	0.67	0.68	0.60	0.61	0.61	0.68
27	Printing and publishing	n.a.	n.a.	n.a.	n.a.	n.a.	n.a.	n.a.	n.a.
28	Chemicals	0.43	0.55	0.69	0.52	0.51	0.51	0.50	0.60
29	Petroleum and coal	0.22	0.51	0.25	0.34	0.25	0.26	0.15	0.37
30	Rubber and plastics	1.10	1.40	1.71	1.34	1.14	1.32	1.32	1.85
31	Leather	n.a.	n.a.	n.a.	n.a.	n.a.	n.a.	n.a.	n.a.
32	Stone, clay and glass	0.56	0.64	0.68	0.78	0.73	0.75	0.91	0.79
33	Primary metals	0.55	0.58	0.68	0.64	0.58	0.62	0.64	0.83
34	Fabricated metals	n.a.	n.a.	0.51	0.45	0.45	0.51	0.53	0.61
35	Non-electrical equipment	n.a.	0.38	0.69	0.69	0.72	0.88	0.86	0.84
36	Electrical equipment	n.a.	n.a.	0.70	0.63	0.63	0.74	0.66	0.83
37	Transport equipment	n.a.	n.a.	n.a.	0.53	0.43	0.61	0.59	0.57
38	Instruments	n.a.	n.a.	n.a.	n.a.	n.a.	n.a.	n.a.	n.a.
39	Misc. manufacturing	n.a.	n.a.	n.a.	n.a.	n.a.	n.a.	n.a.	n.a.

Notes: [a]   Data for Mexican value-added and average number of employees are from United Nations. *Industrial Statistics Yearbook*, various years. The US data for GDP by industry in current US dollars and full-time and part-time employees are from NIPA tables. Before 1977, Mexico value-added is net of non-industrial menaces purchased from others. For Mexico, current pesos were first converted into 1975 pesos using the Mexican GDP deflator and then converted to 1975 dollars using the actual 1975 exchange rate. For the USA, the GDP in current dollars was converted into 1975 dollars using the US GDP deflator. Because of a discontinuity in the Mexican value-added series between 1976 and 1977, Mexican value-added after 1977 was adjusted as: $VA_t^* = VA_t(VA_{76} \cdot (GO_{77}/GO_{76})/VA_{77})$, where VA is value added and GO is gross output. See Appendix for the Mexican industries included in each US SIC code.

convergence in labour productivity levels between Mexican and US industries. These variables are related to the degree of foreign ownership of an industry in Mexico and the initial Mexican – US productivity gap. Both foreign ownership and the initial productivity gap are significantly related to productivity growth within Mexican industry and its speed of catch-up to the corresponding US productivity level (see Table 9.9). This holds for both the longer 1965–77 and 1965–84 periods, and the shorter 1970–5 period.[10] The capital–labour ratio is again significant and negative for productivity growth in Mexico, suggesting that catch-up with the USA is faster when the investment requirements are lower. Finally, output growth here is statistically insignificant.

9.4   Conclusion

Four principal findings emerge from this study. First, both labour productivity levels and TFP levels of locally-owned firms in Mexico have converged on those of foreign-owned firms. Second, both the rate of local firms' labour productivity growth and their rate of catch-up to the multinationals are positively related to the industry's degree of foreign ownership. Third, the gap in labour productivity between Mexican and US manufacturing diminished between the mid-1960s and the mid-1980s. Fourth, the rate of labour productivity growth of Mexican industries and its rate of convergence with the USA are higher in industries with a greater presence of multinationals. The results support the 'advantages of backwardness' thesis in two senses: first, between more advanced and more backward countries; and, second, between more modern and more backward segments of an industry.

The results also suggest that local firms in Mexico have gained productivity 'spillovers' from the presence of multinational firms in the Mexican economy. But there is also another possibility – namely, that competitive pressure from multinationals forces out inefficient local firms. This is consistent with the finding that convergence between local and foreign firms is faster when output growth is lower, though this finding might also be caused by the greater efficiency gains of local firms during periods of slack demand. With the data at hand we cannot distinguish between these two possibilities.

There is strong evidence that the presence of multinational firms acts as a catalyst to the productivity growth in Mexico, and that foreign direct investment speeds up the convergence process between Mexico and the USA. However, the available data do not allow us to say whether this is due to productivity spillovers or simply to the fact that MNCs are more productive than Mexican firms. Although we could not reject the spillover-benefit hypothesis, the productivity convergence between Mexico and the USA might also be because of, wholly or in part, the direct effect of foreign investment. This possibility is strengthened by the finding that the productivity levels of the foreign affiliates in Mexico were very close to those of corresponding industries in the USA, and that the Mexican firms were lagging far behind. Thus an increase in the share of multinationals within an industry will raise the level of productivity within the total Mexican industry, even

Table 9.9 Regression analysis of productivity catch-up between Mexican and US industries[a]

Independent variables	Dependent variables				
	LPG7075	**LPG6577**	**LPG6584**	**CONV6577**	**C0NV6584**
Constant	−0.069**	0.030*	0.257*	0.104**	0.106**
	(3.49)	(2.38)	(3.04)	(13.4)	(15.8)
FORSHARE	0.081*	0.078**	0.047**	0.039**	0.024*
	(2.22)	(4.21)	(3.79)	(3.43)	(2.44)
$MEXUSGAP_0$	−0.083*	−0.070**	−0.036*	−0.042**	−0.028*
	(2.65)	(3.49)	(2.42)	(3.14)	(2.38)
OUTPGRTH	−0.125				
	(1.48)				
KL1970	−0.234*				
	(2.46)				
R^2	0.46	0.72	0.62	0.64	0.49
Adj. R^2	0.31	0.66	0.56	0.58	0.40
Standard error σ	0.022	0.013	0.009	0.008	0.007
Sample size[b]	20	20	20	20	20

Notes: [a] Estimated coefficients are shown together with the absolute value of the t-statistic in parentheses.

LPG7075 = Annual rate of growth of value added per employee in Mexican industry, 1970 to 1975

FORSHARE = Share of employment in foreign-owned firms in total industry employment, averaged between 1970 and 1975

$MEXUSGAP_0$ = Ratio of value-added per employee in Mexican industry to value-added per employee in corresponding US industry at the beginning of the period

OUTPGRTH = Average annual rate of growth of industry output, 1970 to 1975

KL1970 = Industry capital–labour ratio, 1970

CONV6577 = Ratio of $MEXUSGAP_1$ to $MEXUSGAP_0$, where subscript 1 designates the end of the period.

[b] The variables *LPG6577, LPG6584, CONV6577* and *CONV6584* are computed from data in United Nations, *Industrial Statistics Yearbook*, various years. All other Mexican data are from worksheets provided by the Dirección de Estadística de la Secretaría de Industria y Comercio in Mexico. Industries are classified by the 2-digit US SIC code and include all 4-digit SICs in each industry. The US data are from NIPA tables. See Appendix for details.

* Significant at the 0.05 level (two-tailed test).

** Significant at the 0.01 level (two-tailed test).

if there is no productivity growth among local firms. Furthermore, the importance of this direct effect is strengthened by the fact that the largest catch-up effect was registered between 1965 and 1970, a time when Mexico received a large injection of foreign investment.[11]

Although we conclude that multinational firms have played an important role in Mexico's international catch-up, it may not be possible to generalize these results to all other countries. If the host country is too far behind, in the sense that it lacks the technical skills needed to respond to the foreign challenge, there may be no spillovers (for evidence, see Cantwell, 1989; and Kokko, 1992).[12] This is probably the case in most of the least-developed countries in the late 1990s. One might also ask whether there are any specific circumstances in Mexico that make Mexican firms benefit more from MNC technology than do firms in other countries. For example, there are extensive movements of labour and capital between Mexico and the USA that facilitate technology diffusion, and the dominance of the USA as a trade partner might be important.

Notes

1. Data on the proportion of output and employment accounted for by foreign firms in Mexican manufacturing industries are provided in Blomström (1989).
2. Unfortunately, data on capacity utilization are not available to allow for an adjustment for utilized capital input.
3. One would expect that productivity development would differ among industries depending on whether the sector produces non-tradables, exportables, or import substitutes. However, because Mexico during the 1970s was strongly inward-orientated, this is not a serious problem here (see Blomström, 1989). Most Mexican industries were highly protected from foreign competition at that time, which excluded them from the world market.
4. Results are almost identical for the share of industry output accounted for by MNCs, as well as the share of industry capital stock owned by MNCs. Indeed, the correlation among the employment share, output share and capital share each exceeds 0.95 (see Appendix Table A-9.1). It is also important to note that we have not included a measure of the extent of foreign licensing agreements by industry (such data are not available). Since this variable may be correlated with the share of industry output accounted for by MNCs, there may be an omitted variable bias in the results.
5. Regressions were also performed on the 4-digit industry level, with 219 observations. The coefficient estimates of the *FORSHARE* variable were consistently positive but generally less significant (typically at the 10 per cent level). The coefficient estimates of the other variables were quite similar to the 2-digit estimates but, again, the significance levels were generally lower. There are two possible reasons for the less robust results on the 4-digit level. First, the data are much 'noisier' at the more disaggregated level, since the number of firms in each industry group is substantially smaller. Second, there were major changes in 4-digit industry codes between 1970 and 1975, making the alignment of the 1970 and 1975 data at this level quite problematic.

6. As indicated in the notes of Table 9.6, the 1975 exchange rate was used to convert Mexican pesos to US dollars. See Maddison and van Ark (1989) for a discussion.

7. Comparative results are shown in Appendix Table A-9.2. Their approach relies mainly on the industrial censuses of each country, adjusted to a national accounts basis, using both national accounts and input–output data. The main advantage of this approach is the computation of industry-specific (their so-called industry of origin) price indices, which allow direct output comparisons between two countries on the industry level. As detailed in Maddison and van Ark (1989), these price indices are derived from production censuses by dividing the gross value of output by the corresponding quantities. Their approach is particularly advantageous, since it does not rely on general PPP conversion indices, which are based on expenditure data rather than on production data. Our ratio of Mexican to US value-added per employee in 1975 is about 25 per cent higher than that of Maddison and van Ark – 0.48 compared with 0.39. For most industries, the two sets of estimates are quite close. The exceptions are textiles and apparel and, particularly, rubber and plastics products, for which our estimated ratios are substantially higher than those of Maddison and van Ark.

8. Note that this period is atypical, since 1975 was a recession year in Mexico, but not in the USA.

9. Unlike the census data used earlier in this chapter, the UN data are based on samples of firms. Large firms are most probably over-represented in the sample data, since they show higher labour productivity than do the census data (compare the figures in Tables 9.7 and 9.8). An interesting question for future research is therefore whether only some parts of the Mexican industry (the 'modern' part) is converging, whereas others (the 'traditional' sector) are not. Such a pattern was suggested in Blomström (1986a) and will be examined further.

10. The fact that the results are slightly weaker for the 1965–84 period than for the 1965–77 period is probably because of the effects of the debt crisis on Mexico's productivity performance after 1982.

11. We know that the USA dominates foreign investment activities in Mexico. For example, the US Department of Commerce reports that, in 1977, US multinationals employed 302 000 people in Mexican manufacturing industries. The closest year for which Mexican data are available is 1975, and at that time all the foreign firms in manufacturing employed 312 549 people. Between 1966 and 1977, employment in US majority-owned affiliates in Mexico increased from 102 000 to 171 000 (there are no data on minority-owned affiliates for 1966).

12. This is presumably the reason for the weak support for the spillover-benefit hypothesis in Haddad and Harrison's (1991) study of Morocco, and in Aitken and Harrison's (1991) study of Venezuela. For example, in the Venezuelan study, they found spillovers only in 'low-tech' industries, such as food products, textiles and basic metals. These are industries in which we expect local firms' technologies to be relatively close to those of foreign affiliates.

Appendix: data sources and methods

Documentation for Mexican data on multinationals and domestic firms

Sources

The data on foreign and Mexican firms were provided by the Dirección de Estadística de la Secretaría de Industria y Comercio in Mexico and are from the Mexican Census of Manufactures, 1970 and 1975. The data are gathered at the plant level and cover the entire manufacturing industry, which is divided into 230 4-digit manufacturing industries. Because some information was missing, fifteen industries had to be discarded. In the regression analysis of productivity growth, at the 4-digit level, a further seventy industries had to be discarded because of a change in the classification system between 1970 and 1975. In particular, all 4-digit industries in 1970 that were divided into two or more industry classes in 1975 were excluded.

In the 1970 data, ownership is divided into three categories: foreign, state-owned, and privately-owned. In 1975, it is divided into two categories: foreign and Mexican. Companies whose shares are at least 15 per cent foreign-owned are classified as foreign. If the Mexican state owns more than 49 per cent of a plant, it is defined as being state-owned, even if foreigners own 15 per cent or more of its outstanding shares.

There are no comparable capital stock figures between 1970 and 1975. For 1970, we use *capital invertido*, which is the book value of net property, plant, and equipment, plus intangible capital. For 1975, we use *activos fijos brutos*, which is the gross value of property, plant, and equipment. Mexican deflators for GDP and gross fixed capital formation were derived from tables in United Nations, *National Accounts Statistics: Main Aggregates and Detailed Tables*, 1983.

Concordance scheme between US 2-digit SIC codes and 1970 Mexican 4-digit SIC codes

2-digit US SIC Code	All industries	Industries with MNCs	2-digit US SIC code	All industries	Industries with MNCs
20 Food and	2011	2011		2051	2058
kindred products	2012	2012		2052	2059
	2021	2021		2053	2061
	2022	2022		2054	2062
	2023	2023		2055	2071
	2024	2024		2056	2073

2-digit US SIC Code	All industries	Industries with MNCs	2-digit US SIC code	All industries	Industries with MNCs
	2025	2025		2057	2081
	2031	2032		2058	2082
	2032	2034		2059	2083
	2033	2041		2061	2084
	2034	2051		2062	2085
	2041	2055		2071	2091
	2073	2094		2072	2093
	2081	2095		2426	
	2082	2096		2427	
	2083	2097		2431	
	2084	2098		2432	
	2085	2099		2433	
	2091	2111		2434	
	2092	2113		2439	
	2093	2121			
	2094	2131	24 Lumber and	2511	2511
	2095	2132	wood products	2512	2512
	2096	2141		2521	2521
	2097			2522	2533
	2098			2531	2534
	2099			2533	
	2111			2534	
	2112				
	2113		25 Furniture	2612	2621
	2121		and fixtures	2621	3521
	2123			3521	
	2131				
	2132		26 Paper and	2711	2711
	2141		allied products	2712	2712
21 Tobacco	2211	2211		2721	2721
manufacturers	2212	2212		2722	2722
	2213	2213		2723	2723
22 Textile	2311	2311	27 Printing and	2811	2811
mill products	2312	2312	publishing	2812	2812
	2313	2313		2813	2813
	2315	2315		2814	2814
	2316	2316			
	2319	2319	28 Chemicals	3111	3111
	2321	2321	and allied	3112	3112
	2322	2322	products	3113	3113
	2323	2323		3121	3121
	2331	2334		3122	3122
	2333	2341		3131	3131
	2334	2343		3132	3132
	2341	2344		3141	3141
	2342	2346		3151	3151
	2343			3161	3161
	2344			3162	3162
	2345			3171	3171
	2346			3172	3191
23 Apparel and	2421	2421		3191	3194
other textiles	2422	2422		3192	3195
	2423	2424		3193	3196
	2424	2434		3194	3199
	2425			3195	
				3196	
				3199	

(continued)

2-digit US SIC Code	All industries	Industries with MNCs
29 Petroleum and coal products	3212	3213
	3221	3221
	3222	
30 Rubber and miscellaneous plastic products	3011	3011
	3012	3012
	3013	3013
	3181	3181
31 Leather and leather products	2411	2411
	2412	2413
	2413	2911
	2911	2912
	2912	
32 Stone, clay, and glass products	3311	3311
	3312	3312
	3321	3321
	3322	3323
	3323	3324
	3324	3329
	3329	3341
	3341	3342
	3342	3351
	3343	3352
	3351	3354
	3352	
	3353	
	3354	
33 Primary metal industries	3411	3411
	3412	3412
	3413	3413
	3421	3421
	3422	3422
	3423	3423
	3424	3424
34 Fabricated metal products	3511	3511
	3512	3512
	3513	3513
	3514	3514
	3517	3517
	3531	3531
	3541	3541
	3542	3542
	3543	3543
	3544	3544
	3545	3545
	3546	3546
	3547	3547
	3549	3549
	3987	3987

2-digit US SIC code	All industries	Industries with MNCs
35 Machinery, except electrical	3611	3611
	3621	3621
	3631	3632
	3632	3641
	3641	3651
	3651	3652
	3652	3653
	3653	3654
	3654	3655
	3655	3656
	3656	3659
	3659	
36 Electric and electronic equipment	3711	3711
	3721	3721
	3722	3722
	3723	3723
	3724	3724
	3731	3731
	3741	3741
	3742	3742
	3743	3743
	3749	3749
37 Transportation equipment	3811	3811
	3821	3821
	3831	3831
	3832	3832
	3834	3834
	3841	3841
	3842	3842
	3843	
38 Instruments and related products	3911	3911
	3912	3912
	3921	3921
	3922	3922
	3931	3931
	3984	
39 Misc. manufacturing industries	3941	3942
	3942	3951
	3951	3961
	3961	3971
	3971	3981
	3981	3982
	3982	3983
	3983	3986
	3985	3988
	3986	
	3988	

Documentation for Mexican industries included in UN data

ISIC	Industry name	Beginning of series
311/2	Preparation and preservation of meat	1965
	Condensed and evaporated milk and milk powder	1965
	Canned fruits and vegetables	1965
	Canned fish and shellfish	1965
	Wheat mills	1965
	Cornflour	1969?
	Tea and instant coffee	1969?
	Chewing gum	1965
	Biscuits and pastries	1965
	Yeast, baking powder, starch and similar products	1965
	Vegetable oils and margarine	1965
	Prepared foods for animals and fowl	1965
313	Malt	1969?
	Beer	1965
	Soft drinks	1975
	Carbonated water	1975
314	Cigarettes	1965
321	Spinning, weaving and finishing of cotton, artificial fibres and henequen	1967?
	Manufacture of yarns	1969?
	Manufacture of cashmere textiles, shawls and similar products	1969?
	Manufacture of wool	1973?
331	Manufacture of plywood, veneer and lamina	1965
341	Manufacture of pulp from fibre, paper and paperboard	1965
	Manufacture of articles of paperboard, including oil-impregnated board	1965
351	Manufacture of cellulosic fibres and other artificial fibres	1965?
	Manufacture of fertilizers	1965?
352	Manufacture of matches and candles	1965?
	Soap, detergents and other clearing compounds	1967
	Paints, varnishes and lacquers	1965
	Drugs and medicines	1975?
354	Manufacture of coke and other coal products	1965
	Regeneration of lubricating oils, including additives	1973
355	Manufacture of tyres and tubes	1965
362	Manufacture of sheet glass, glass fibres, safety glass and glass containers	1965?
369	Manufacture of hydraulic cement, brick, fireproof partitions and refractory mortar	1965?
	Manufacture of asbestos products	1973
371	Manufacture of iron and steel tubes and rods	1967
	Founding, casting and rolling of iron and steel	1965

(continued)

ISIC	Industry name	Beginning of series
372	Founding, refining, casting, extruding and drawing of copper and its alloys	1967
	Casting, extruding and drawing of aluminum and manufacture of aluminum solders	1965?
381	Manufacture of furniture and fixtures primarily of metal	1967?
	Manufacture of crown caps and other cast and enamelled metal products	1967?
	Manufacture of containers and other products from tinplate	1973
382	Manufacture and assembly of agricultural machinery and equipment	1965
	Manufacture and assembly of typing, computing and accounting machinery	1973
383	Manufacture of record players and receiving sets of radio and television	1969
	Manufacture of condensers and batteries	1967
	Manufacture and assembly of electrical apparatus and parts	1967
	Manufacture of other electronic equipment and apparatus	1975
384	Manufacture and assembly of motor vehicles, including tractors for trailers	1965
	Manufacture of bodies for motor vehicles	1965
	Manufacture of railroad equipment	1975

Note: ? indicates that the exact year of inclusion cannot be determined from the *UN Yearbook*. From 1975 to 1984, only 58 out of the 225 4-digit Mexican manufacturing industries are included in the UN tabulations.

Concordance scheme between US 2-digit SIC codes and UN 3-digit ISIC codes

US SIC		UN ISIC	
20	Food and kindred products	311/2	Food products
		313	Beverages
21	Tobacco manufactures	314	Tobacco
22	Textile mill products	321	Textiles
23	Apparel and other textiles	322	Wearing apparel
24	Lumber and wood products	331	Wood products
25	Furniture and fixtures	332	Furniture and fixtures
26	Paper and allied products	341	Paper and products
27	Printing and publishing	342	Printing and publishing
28	Chemicals and allied products	351	Industrial chemicals
		352	Other chemical products

US SIC		UN ISIC	
29	Petroleum and coal products	353	Petroleum refineries
		354	Petroleum, coal products
30	Rubber and miscellaneous plastics	355	Rubber products products
		356	Plastic products, n.e.c.
31	Leather and leather products	323	Leather and leather products
		324	Footwear
32	Stone, clay and glass products	361	Pottery, china, etc.
		362	Glass and products
		369	Non-metal products n.e.c.
33	Primary metal industries	371	Iron and steel
		372	Non-ferrous metals
34	Fabricated metal products	381	Metal products
35	Machinery, except electrical	382	Machinery, n.e.c.
36	Electric and electronic equipment	383	Electrical machinery
37	Transportation equipment	384	Transport equipment
38	Instruments and related products	385	Professional goods
39	Miscellaneous manufacturing	390	Other industries

US data

US data are as follows: (1) GDP is from Table 6.02 of the National Income and Product Accounts; (2) employment is from Table 6.06 of the National Income and Product Accounts; (3) capital stock figures are from John C. Musgrave, 'Fixed Reproducible Tangible Wealth in the United States: Revised Estimates', *Survey of Current Business*, January 1986, pp. 51–75; and (4) US deflators for GDP and gross fixed capital formation were derived from tables in *National Accounts, Main Aggregates*, vol. I, 1960–84, OECD, Department of Economics and Statistics.

Appendix

Table A-9.1   Activity of MNCs as a proportion of total industry activity, 1970 and 1975[a] (percent)

	Plants	1970			1975		
		Employment	Capital stock	Gross output	Employment	Capital stock	Gross output
20 Food and kindred products	0.2	11.6	23.9	24.6	6.8	7.6	12.8
21 Tobacco manufactures	49.2	83.2	93.8	96.8	3.2	0.3	0.3
22 Textile mill products	1.9	11.6	17.2	16.0	6.9	10.9	10.3
23 Apparel and other textiles	0.1	2.9	7.1	6.6	0.9	2.5	1.3
24 Lumber and wood products	0.2	3.4	15.8	8.8	5.3	20.0	11.3
25 Furniture and fixtures	0.5	5.9	6.8	6.5	2.0	3.2	3.8
26 Paper and allied products	4.4	21.7	34.9	32.9	16.0	10.7	15.7
27 Printing and publishing	0.4	4.6	10.6	7.9	7.9	9.7	10.1
28 Chemicals and allied products	11.9	45.5	58.4	53.2	43.0	50.8	52.2
29 Petroleum and coal products	8.6	20.1	20.3	37.6	28.1	32.4	39.9
30 Rubber and plastics products	0.8	19.0	37.0	44.9	16.3	36.0	29.9
31 Leather and leather products	0.2	2.6	6.5	4.5	2.4	5.4	3.4
32 Stone, clay and glass products	0.9	12.3	21.5	22.6	20.1	32.1	30.5
33 Primary metal industries	11.6	36.8	40.4	42.6	19.1	17.9	23.1
34 Fabricated metal products	0.9	17.6	29.4	25.0	16.9	27.9	22.9
35 Machinery, excluding electrical	3.1	34.2	56.3	54.4	13.5	14.5	13.1
36 Electric and electronic equipment	9.0	34.9	49.8	51.1	60.7	64.1	57.7
37 Transportation equipment	6.4	40.0	52.3	61.2	28.2	36.4	52.2
38 Instruments and related products	3.0	31.5	70.9	52.9	25.0	63.5	38.1
39 Misc. manufacturing	0.8	17.6	28.6	22.1	24.5	41.8	33.0
Total manufacturing	**0.9**	**19.2**	**35.4**	**35.4**	**18.3**	**25.5**	**27.1**

Note: [a]   Data are from worksheets provided by the Dirección de Estadística de la Secretaría de Industria y Comercio in Mexico. For 1970, the capital stock figures are based on *capital invertido*, and for 1975, they are based on *activos fijos brutos*.

Table A-9.2   Comparison of Maddison–van Ark and our estimates: ratio of
Mexican to US value-added per employee, 1975

	Blomström–Wolff[a]	Maddison–van Ark[b]
Food and food products (incl. beverages)	0.44	0.44
Tobacco manufactures	0.45	0.43
Textiles and apparel	0.65	0.37
Lumber and wood products	0.27	0.22
Chemical products	0.47	0.47
Rubber and plastics products	0.64	0.24
Leather and leather products	0.43	0.44
Stone, clay and glass products	0.50	0.40
Metal products	0.52	0.44
Machinery and transport equipment	0.45	0.36
Electric and electronic equipment	0.55	0.46
Other manufacturing	0.35	0.34
Total manufacturing	**0.48**	**0.39**

Sources: [a]   Table A-9.1.
[b]   Maddison and van Ark 1989, table 12 (geometric averages).

10
Technology, Market Characteristics and Spillovers

10.1 Introduction

There are numerous case studies to suggest that technology spillovers from foreign direct investment may provide important benefits for the host countries of multinational corporations (MNCs) (see Chapter 8). The technology and productivity of local firms may improve as foreign firms enter the market and demonstrate new technologies, provide technical assistance to their local suppliers and customers, and train workers and managers who may later be employed by local firms. The competitive pressure exerted by the foreign affiliates may also force the local firms to operate more efficiently and introduce new technologies earlier than would otherwise have been the case.

Studies of aggregate manufacturing in several countries – Caves (1974) on Australia; Globerman (1979a) on Canada; and Blomström and Persson (1983) on Mexico are the best known examples – have also found that a foreign presence has a positive impact on the productivity of local firms, and therefore concluded that spillovers are typically significant. However, there are cases where spillovers have apparently not taken place on a large scale, as suggested by studies of FDI in various European countries (Cantwell, 1989); in Moroccan manufacturing industries (Haddad and Harrison, 1991, 1993); and in Venezuelan manufacturing (Aitken and Harrison, 1991).

A possible reason for the apparently contradictory findings from the studies of these countries is that various host industry and host country characteristics may influence the incidence of spillovers. For example, the technology imports of MNC affiliates seem to be larger in countries and industries where the educational level of the local labour force is higher, where local competition is tougher, and where the host country imposes fewer formal requirements on the affiliates' operations (Chapter 14 in this volume; Kokko, 1992).

The affiliates' levels of technology or technology imports, in turn, probably have some impact on how large the spillovers to local firms will be.

Yet the available empirical evidence does not reveal how the spillovers we can observe are related to the level of technology in MNC affiliates, and it is not entirely obvious from a theoretical perspective what the relationship should be. In fact, two opposing arguments can be found in the literature on foreign investment and technology transfer. On the one hand, it is sometimes argued in discussions of the 'appropriateness' of MNC technology that MNC affiliates may be too advanced to leave any mark on local host country firms. The reason is that 'technical advances (and technologies) applicable to the factor-proportions of capital-rich developed countries are hardly of any use in improving techniques of low capital-intensity in less developed countries' (Lapan and Bardhan, 1973, p. 585). This suggests the hypothesis that spillovers are negatively related to the complexity of MNC technology or the size of the technology gap between affiliates and local firms. On the other hand, it is obvious that a certain technology gap is necessary for those spillovers that occur as local firms copy MNC technology or benefit from the MNCs' training of local employees, and it has been hypothesized that spillovers grow with the size of the technology gap (Findlay, 1978; Wang and Blomström, 1992).

The few empirical studies that more or less indirectly discuss the relationship between technology and spillovers reflect this confusion. In Chapter 9 we analyzed data for twenty 2-digit industries in Mexico in 1970 and 1975, and examined some factors influencing the rates of growth of gross output per employee in locally-owned Mexican firms, and the rates of convergence of gross output per employee between locally-owned firms and foreign affiliates. We found that both measures are positively related to the foreign share of industry employment and the initial labour productivity gap between locals and multinationals. This is consistent with the hypothesis that spillovers increase with the size of the technology gap. By contrast, Haddad and Harrison (1991, 1993), who study the effects of a foreign presence on the relative productivity of local firms in Moroccan manufacturing, imply that large technology gaps or advanced MNC technology inhibit spillovers. They find that a larger foreign presence leads to smaller deviations from best practice technologies in 'low tech' industries, but that there is no such effect in 'high tech' sectors, that are defined to include machinery, transport equipment, electronics, scientific instruments and chemicals. Their interpretation is that competition from foreign firms may push local firms towards best practice – for example, by forcing the least efficient firms out of business – but that there are no spillovers of advanced technology. Similarly, Cantwell (1989), seems to suggest that spillovers are most important in the industries where the technology gap is small. He examines the responses of local firms to the entry and presence of US multinationals in European markets 1955–75, and argues that the most positive impact on local technological capability can be seen in the industries where the local firms had a strong technological tradition and were able to challenge the invading US affiliates.

The purpose of this chapter is to investigate how spillovers observed in static cross-section analyses are related to various proxies for the complexity of MNC technology and the technology gap between locally-owned host country firms and MNC affiliates.[1] In the course of the study, we shall also find a reason to examine briefly the relationship between spillovers and the market shares of foreign firms. The next section describes the data set and the statistical model used for the empirical tests; Section 3 presents and discusses the regression results; and Section 4 concludes the chapter.

10.2   Data and variables

The data used here to examine the effects of technology differences on spillovers refer to the Mexican manufacturing industry in 1970, and are from unpublished worksheets provided by the Dirección de Estadísticas de la Secretaría de Industria y Comercio in Mexico, collected for the Mexican Census of Manufactures, 1971.[2] The information is gathered at the plant level and covers the entire manufacturing sector, which is divided into 230 4-digit industries with a further breakdown according to three ownership categories: domestic private, foreign, and state ownership. Plants with at least 15 per cent of shares owned by foreigners are defined as being 'foreign', and those where the Mexican state owns more than 49 per cent are defined as being state-owned, irrespective of the share of foreign ownership. The state-owned plants are excluded from the present sample, since they may operate under soft budget constraints, or have other goals (related, for example, to employment creation or geographical localization of operations) than profit maximization, as discussed in Blomström and Persson, 1983).

Because of missing information, fourteen of the 230 industries had to be omitted from the sample. For the remaining 216 industries, the data set includes information on employment, assets, value-added, industry concentration, payments of patents, and the division of employees between blue-collar and white-collar workers. For the 156 industries that hosted foreign MNC in 1970, the data on employment, assets and value-added are available separately for foreign and private local firms. For the other variables, information is only available for industry totals, without the breakdown according to ownership.

The statistical models used to examine spillovers in most earlier empirical studies of aggregate manufacturing (Caves, 1974; Globerman, 1979a; Blomström and Persson, 1983) have been based on linear estimations of the labour productivity of locally-owned firms as a function of the foreign firms' market share and various other industry characteristics, such as capital–labour ratios, labour quality, scale economies, and concentration. If foreign presence has been found to have a significant positive effect on local labour productivity (after the effects of other variables have been accounted for), it has been concluded that spillovers take place.[3] The main difference between the earlier models is that only Blomström and Persson (1983) use the capital-intensity of local firms as an exogenous variable. Hence they focus on spillovers that affect the efficiency in the use of given factor inputs, whereas Caves (1974) and Globerman (1979a) also capture the effect of foreign presence on the local firms' capital–labour ratios. We adopt the former model here, because it is likely to provide a more conservative estimate of the extent of spillovers. However, the data allow us to check the results by performing tests of the latter type as well.

Thus, we hypothesize here that the labour productivity of local firms can be estimated by the function:

$$VA/L^d = f(K/L^d, LQ, HERF, FOR) \tag{10.1}$$

where variables are defined as follows:

The dependent variable is VA/L^d, the average labour productivity in domestic firms, and it is measured as the ratio of value-added to total employment in locally-owned plants. The domestic firms' capital–labour ratio, K/L^d, is the ratio of total assets to total employment in locally-owned plants. The labour quality measure, LQ, is based on the ratio of white-collar workers to blue-collar workers

(W/B) in each industry's total employment.[4] However, we know *a priori* that foreign firms are likely to employ a higher proportion of white-collar workers, and since the W/B ratio refers to each industry as a whole, there is also a troublesome correlation between that and *FOR*, our measure of foreign presence. We have therefore constructed our labour quality proxy LQ as the sum '$a + e$' from the regression:

$$W/B = a + \beta\ FOR + e \tag{10.2}$$

In other words, LQ intends to reflect the share of W/B that is not explained by the degree of foreign presence in the industry.[5] The variable *HERF* is the Herfindahl index, and measures the level of concentration in each industry.[6] It is included to account for the expected effect of market structure on the value of output: more concentrated industries are supposedly better able to engage in monopoly pricing and should therefore display higher labour productivity, *ceteris paribus*. *FOR*, finally, is the ratio of the foreign plants' employment to total employment in each industry, and measures the degree of foreign presence: if spillovers take place, it is expected to have a significant positive effect on local labour productivity.[7]

In addition to the variables appearing in Equation (10.1), we will use three proxies for the technological characteristics of industries to divide the sample into 'high' and 'low' technology groups, and to construct interaction terms for the statistical tests. The first one is labelled *PAT*, and measures the average payments of patent fees per employee in each industry. *PAT* reflects the formal technology payments of all actors taken together (private local, foreign, and state-owned), but it is likely to be particularly highly correlated with those of foreign firms (although that information is not available separately for 1970): MNC affiliates account for most of the world's formal technology payments.[8] Hence, we treat *PAT* as a proxy for the technology level of the foreign affiliates in each industry, and the higher the patent payments, the more advanced are the affiliates' technologies assumed to be.[9]

The average capital intensity of the foreign affiliates, K/L^f, is another industry characteristic that may be positively related to the level of MNC technology. However, the simple correlation between *PAT* and K/L^f is only 0.11, and it is apparent that neither can measure technological complexity accurately. With perfect data, we would have preferred the *PAT* measure, but because of its possible shortcomings – MNC parents' technology pricing practices may not be cohesive, all technologies may not be patented, transfer pricing may occur, and so on – we have also included K/L^f as a proxy for technology.

Our third proxy, *PGAP*, reflects the labour productivity gap between local and foreign firms. It is defined as the ratio of value-added per employee in foreign plants to value-added per employee in private locally-owned plants. This is an indirect measure of the technology gap discussed by Findlay (1978), and Wang and Blomström (1992).

Table A-10.1 summarizes the variables, Table A-10.2 provides some descriptive statistics for the data set, and Table A-10.3 presents a correlation matrix (see pages 175 and 176, respectively).

To examine the effect of the size of the technology gap and the complexity of MNC technology on spillovers, we go on to make two types of test. First, we divide the sample into six subsamples characterized by 'high' or 'low' values for the variables *PAT*, K/L^f, and *PGAP*, estimate Equation (10.1) for each of these, and then compare coefficient estimates across each pair of subsamples. This allows the coefficients of all right-hand variables to vary across subsamples, and we are particularly interested to see if a foreign presence has an apparently similar effect on local productivity in industries with 'low' and 'high' technology (or 'small' and 'large' technology gaps). Comparisons of the broad functional relationships between subsamples are based on Chow tests, whereas statements comparing the coefficients of any specific variables are based on F-tests of the null hypothesis that there are no differences. Second, we include some interaction variables into Equation (10.1) to see whether the coincidence of advanced technology (or large technology gaps) and large foreign shares has any effect on the results.

10.3   Regression results

Regression equations (1.1) and (1.2) in Table 10.1 present the results of OLS estimations of Equation (10.1) for the entire sample of 216 industries, and for the 156 industries where foreign MNCs were present in 1970.[10] Equation (1.1) is included in Table 10.1 to allow a comparison with the tests in Blomström and Persson (1983), and the results here are very similar to theirs. Capital-intensity, labour quality, and foreign presence all have highly significant positive effects (in other words, spillovers, as we have defined them, are present), but the impact of producer concentration on local labour productivity is negligible. The main difference from the Blomström and Persson (1983) estimation is that we have no scale variable, but its absence does not seem to have any large effect on the coefficients of other variables: similarly, dropping the *HERF* variable leaves the results unchanged.[11]

Turning to equation (1.2) in Table 10.1, where only the 156 industries with foreign firms present are included, we see some small changes in estimated coefficients, and a fall in the significance levels for the impacts of labour quality and foreign presence. However, the spillover effect is still significant. There is also a decline in the explanatory power of the equation – both adjusted R^2 and the F-value fall – which may be caused by the smaller number of observations. The estimations discussed below include only industries where foreign firms were present in 1970, so equation (1.2) in Table 10.1 may serve as a point of reference.

Impact of industry characteristics on spillovers

Table 10.2 presents estimation results for six equations covering subsamples of industries grouped according to their levels of *PAT*, K/L^f, and *PGAP*, and for three equations where interaction terms have been added to the model.

The first two equations refer to groups defined according to the values of the variable *PAT*. The average payments for patents, trade marks and other fees per employee are lower than 600 pesos for the industries included in equation (2.1) in Table 10.2, and higher than 600

Table 10.1   Results of OLS estimations: labour productivity in private locally-owned manufacturing firms in Mexico, 1970

Equation	Constant	K/L^d	HERF	LQ	FOR	Adj. R^2	F	N
All industries								
(1.1)	0.265	0.464	−0.003	0.161	0.112	0.53	61.84	216
	(2.47)**	(11.77)***	(0.04)	(2.58)**	(3.49)***			
Industries with MNCs								
(1.2)	0.256	0.443	0.030	0.130	0.141	0.43	29.62	156
	(1.99)**	(8.47)***	(0.30)	(1.88)*	(2.38)**			

Notes: The dependent variable is VA/L^d. All variables are normalized by division with the sample means. Estimated coefficients are shown together with the absolute value of the t-statistic in parentheses. *, **, and *** denote significance at the 10, 5, and 1 per cent level of significance (two-tailed tests). For definitions of variables, see Table A-10.1 on page 175.

Table 10.2   Results of OLS estimations: labour productivity in private locally-owned manufacturing firms in Mexico, 1970, impact of industry characteristics

	Low PAT	High PAT	Low K/L^f	High K/L^f	Small PGAP	Large PGAP			
Equation	(2.1)	(2.2)	(2.3)	(2.4)	(2.5)	(2.6)	(2.7)	(2.8)	(2.9)
Constant	0.140	0.218	0.390	0.253	0.106	0.433	0.254	0.265	0.262
	(0.74)	(1.01)	(2.65)***	(1.09)	(0.72)	(3.38)***	(1.97)*	(1.99)**	(2.12)**
K/L^d	0.133	0.449	0.425	0.426	0.375	0.441	0.447	0.438	0.426
	(5.99)***	(5.36)***	(7.24)***	(3.54)***	(5.41)***	(9.99)***	(8.44)***	(7.94)***	(8.46)***
HERF	−0.059	0.155	−0.136	0.254	0.261	−0.343	0.023	0.030	0.024
	(0.15)	(0.98)	(1.20)	(1.26)	(2.05)**	(3.67)***	(0.22)	(0.29)	(0.25)
LQ	0.318	0.065	0.113	0.054	0.075	0.342	0.130	0.126	0.119
	(2.62)**	(0.70)	(1.41)	(0.66)	(1.13)	(4.38)***	(1.88)*	(1.77)*	(1.78)*
FOR	0.168	0.114	0.208	0.014	0.182	0.127	0.151	0.128	0.274
	(2.41)**	(0.85)	(3.34)***	(0.11)	(2.47)**	(2.32)**	(2.42)**	(1.72)*	(4.09)***
FOR*PAT	–	–	–	–	–	–	−0.006	–	–
							(0.51)		
FOR*K/L^f	–	–	–	–	–	–	–	0.014	–
								(0.28)	
FOR*PGAP	–	–	–	–	–	–	–	–	−0.104
									(3.75)***
Adj. R^2	0.41	0.40	0.46	0.22	0.43	0.74	0.42	0.42	0.47
F	17.85	10.55	30.40	4.46	27.36	37.12	23.64	23.57	28.56
N	97	59	107	49	105	51	156	156	156

Notes: The dependent variable is VA/L^d. All variables are normalized by division with the sample means. Estimated coefficients are shown together with the absolute value of the t-statistics in parentheses. *, ** and *** denote significance at the 10, 5, and 1 per cent levels of significance (two-tailed tests). For definitions of variables, see Table A-10.1 on page 175.

pesos for those in equation (2.2).[12] The results show that the estimated coefficient of *FOR* (that is, the spillover effect) is positive and significant at the 5 per cent level in the group with low average patent payments. The coefficient estimate in the group with high patent payments is comparable in size, but not significant. In isolation, this implies that spillovers generally do not occur in the industries with the most complex technologies. However, F-tests suggest that the null hypothesis of equal effects of *FOR* in both groups cannot be rejected. A possible explanation for this partly conflicting finding is that there is a large variance in the group with higher patent payments, and that we cannot, with a reasonable level of confidence, say much about whether spillovers will occur or not. Hence, high technology seems to make spillovers less likely, but there is no evidence to show that spillovers cannot occur in industries with complex technologies.

Equation (2.3) in Table 10.2, for industries where the average capital-intensity of foreign affiliates is below 200 000 pesos per employee, and equation (2.4), for industries with higher capital intensities in affiliates, provide a similar picture of spillovers. The spillover effect is positive and highly significant in the industries with less capital-intensive foreign affiliates, but not significant when affiliates are more capital-intensive. Yet the hypothesis that the coefficients of *FOR* are equal in the two subsamples cannot be rejected, judging by F-tests. In other words, spillovers seem less likely when foreign technologies are capital-intensive, but may nevertheless occur.[13]

The differences in the incidence of spillovers are smaller for the subsamples grouped according to the size of the productivity gap between affiliates and local firms. The coefficient of *FOR* is positive and significant both in equation (2.5) in Table 10.2, where the value-added per employee in foreign plants is at most twice as high as that in private locally-owned plants, and in equation (2.6), where affiliates are more than twice as productive as private locally-owned plants.[14] Productivity differences *per se* are apparently not serious obstacles for spillovers.[15]

Although the impact of *FOR* may be equal in all groups, there are some other significant differences between subsamples. A Chow test suggests that local labour productivity is not determined by similar factors in the two *PAT* groups. Labour quality has a significantly larger impact when patent payments are low, judging by an F-test. This is surprising, since it would be more reasonable to expect a strong impact of labour quality in industries with complex technologies that demand high labour skills. The most likely explanation is simply that *LQ* is an imperfect proxy for labour quality, but the data needed for more accurate measures are not available. Labour quality also has a larger positive coefficient when the labour productivity gap is larger, but it is impossible to draw any firm conclusions from this finding, for the same reason.

Another significant difference between the two *PGAP* groups is that the coefficient of the variable *HERF* is significant in both sub-samples, but with opposite signs. This is notable, since concentration did not have any significant impact in the full sample. More specifically, concentration seems to enhance local productivity when the gap between affiliates and local firms is small, but depress it when the gap is large. One possible explanation, suggested by Blomström (1986a), is that *HERF* reflects the existence of scale economies: local firms may benefit from scale economies when they are relatively productive compared to foreign affiliates, but not when they are lagging far behind the affiliates.

It is also possible that high levels of concentration and large technology gaps together signal situations where spillovers are less likely. In fact, the foreign affiliates in industries with these characteristics may operate in 'enclaves', in isolation from local firms. High levels of concentration and large productivity gaps may, for example, coincide in industries where the affiliates have been strong enough to take over the bulk of the market, and forced local firms into narrow niches where the products and technologies of MNCs are not profitable. In these cases, there is not much reason to expect any spillovers. In other industries, where MNCs are less dominant and where local firms are in more direct competition with affiliates, spillovers may well occur in spite of large technology gaps or advanced MNC technologies.

In equations (2.7) to (2.9) in Table 10.2, we have added some inter-action terms to the model used so far, in order to examine if the combination of advanced technology (or large technology gaps) and foreign domination inhibits spillovers. Equation (2.7) adds the term *FOR*PAT* to the estimation, but its coefficient is very small and not significantly different from zero. Comparing equations (2.7) and (1.2) (Table 10.2), it can also be seen that the interaction term does not have much effect on the estimated coefficients of other variables either. Hence, it seem reasonable to conclude that complex technology (as proxied by the variable *PAT*) does not impede spillovers even when it is accompanied by large foreign market shares. Equation (2.8), where the interaction term is defined as $FOR*K/L^f$, gives similar results.

Equation (2.9), by contrast, suggests that the simultaneous presence of large productivity gaps and large foreign shares has a notable impact on the outcome. The estimated coefficient of the interaction term *FOR*PGAP* is negative and highly significant. This appears to support the hypothesis that spillovers are smaller in industries with 'enclave' characteristics. Moreover, the coefficient of *FOR* is markedly larger in equation (2.9) than in the base case (that is, equation (1.2) in Table 10.1), which means that spillovers may be even more important than Blomström and Persson (1983) concluded in industries where affiliates and local firms are in direct competition with each other.

Before these results can be presented as conclusions, there is one more issue to consider. The statistical model used by Globerman (1979a) differs significantly from ours on one point, as noted earlier. The model we have estimated treats local capital intensity as given, and assumes that the spillovers we can measure are related to 'disembodied' technology. Globerman (1979a) uses K/L^f (instead of K/L^d) to control for industry differences in productivity and technology, which allows him also to capture the impact of a foreign presence on the average capital intensity of local firms (or on the average deviation between local and foreign firms' capital intensities). To make sure that this distinction does not have a serious effect on the findings from Table 10.2, it is necessary to comment on the results of 'Globerman-type' estimations of the equation:

$$VA/L^d = f(K/L^f, LQ, HERF, FOR) \qquad (10.3)$$

The estimation results are very similar to those presented in equations (2.1)–(2.9) (Table 10.2), and will therefore not be shown separately. The estimated spillover effects are not significantly different in the 'high' and 'low' technology groups, the interaction term *FOR*PGAP* has a significant negative impact on local productivity, but the other interaction terms are not significant. Hence the conclusion survives that advanced technology alone is probably not an obstacle to spillovers, but that large technology gaps and high foreign shares together may impede spillovers.

Finally, a brief look at which industries exhibit both high foreign shares and large productivity gaps might be useful, to confirm that it is reasonable to talk about 'enclaves' and 'dual markets'. Most of the industries with the highest values for the interaction term *FOR*PGAP* are such that superior marketing abilities and proprietary brand names and labels are likely to make up the competitive assets of foreign firms. Examples of the goods produced are perfumes and cosmetics, alcoholic beverages, cigars and cigarettes, chewing gum, instant coffee, prepared food products, clocks and watches, and photographic film. The monopolistic nature of these industries may mean that the products of foreign and local firms are not directly comparable, that foreign and local firms aim at different segments of the market, and that there may not be much scope for spillovers of production technology.[16]

Many of the other industries are such that the market leadership of the foreign affiliates is likely to be based on economies of scale. Examples here are office and computing machines, synthetic fibres, electric light bulbs and fluorescent tubes, some chemical industries, and primary metal industries. The affiliates operating here may have 'crowded out' the local firms so there is nobody to absorb the potential spillovers. It is also possible that the small local entrepreneurs in these industries may not be able to benefit much from learning about machines or management practices that are optimal for a plant that is ten, fifty or a hundred times larger than their own firm. Hence, it does not seem implausible to use the term 'enclave' for the industries where the combined impact of large productivity gaps and foreign domination is strongest, although the dual character of the markets can be caused by either highly differentiated products or scale economies.

10.4 Concluding comments

This chapter has examined technology spillovers in various groups of Mexican manufacturing industries in 1970, and has attempted to determine whether differences in the technology gap between local and foreign firms or differences in the level of technological complexity have any impact on the observed spillovers. A conclusion from the regression analysis is that factors related to technology *alone* do not seem to inhibit spillovers, but that large productivity gaps and large foreign market shares *together* appear to make up significant obstacles.

The industries where large productivity gaps and large foreign shares occur simultaneously seem to be characterized by differentiated products and/or significant economies of scale, which allow the foreign affiliates to crowd out local competitors from important segments of the market. As a result, the affiliates may operate in 'enclaves' – that is, isolated segments of the market where technologies, products and plant sizes are very different from those used by local firms. The large differences between foreign and local firms in these industries may explain why spillovers do not occur.

The finding that spillovers may differ across industries could explain some of the conflicting results from earlier studies of spillovers in aggregate manufacturing. Whether or not enclaves will occur is determined by various host country characteristics, such as history, market size, domestic technological capability, economic policies, and so on. These characteristics differ between host countries and make enclaves more common in some countries than others – the possibility of observing spillovers in aggregate manufacturing may vary accordingly.

The analysis also offers some obvious policy conclusions for host country governments that wish to encourage foreign investment in order to benefit from technology spillovers. Efforts to promote FDI should perhaps focus on industries where local technological capability is already relatively strong, or where product differentiation and scale economies are not so significant that foreign firms can easily take over the whole market.

Notes

1. It would be preferable to examine spillovers over time rather than in a static context, but the data used for the empirical analysis are only available for one year.
2. This is essentially the same database as that used by Blomström and Persson (1983). Estados Unidos Mexicanos (1973) summarizes much of the information, but the published data are not presented separately for local and foreign firms.
3. The models presented by Aitken and Harrison (1991) and Haddad and Harrison (1991, 1993) differ from the earlier studies on this point. They used plant-level data over several years, and examined the determinants of total factor productivity growth and deviations from best-practice technology. Because of a lack of suitable data, we are not able to replicate their tests.
4. Labour quality is often proxied by various wage measures, but these cannot be used here because of simultaneity problems: wages are

determined by labour productivity, which is what we are trying to explain.

5. Blomström and Persson (1983) constructed a similar labour quality proxy, but define it as only the error term e in the regression estimating W/B.

6. The Herfindahl index is calculated from plant-level data, and is defined as:

$$HERF = S \, (x_i/X)^2, \qquad i = 1, \ldots, n$$

where x_i is the employment of the n individual plants, and X is the total employment of the industry.

7. We also used a proxy for advertising expenditures in some estimations, but its effect was not significant, and it was dropped from the model. Similarly, a proxy for effective rates of protection was included in a subset of the sample, but this was dropped because the estimated effect was not significant, and because it was only available for ninety-three industries. Some additional explanatory variables have appeared in earlier studies. Blomström and Persson (1983) included proxies for economies of scale and average working time, but their effects were not significant: we were not able to replicate either of them because of lack of data. Globerman (1979a) used the average number of hours worked and proxies for plant-scale and product-scale economies to capture the same effects, and found a significant positive impact of plant-scale economies, but in most cases no significance for the other two variables.

8. Fairchild (1977) surveyed twenty-five pairs of manufacturing firms with direct US equity investment and 100 per cent Mexican ownership, respectively, operating in Monterrey, Mexico. Comparing the two types of firm, she concluded that four times as many US firms (or 'joint ventures') as local firms used US patents or licences in 1973. Since her sample of firms was closely matched in terms of the firms' age, assets, net sales and employment, and the goods produced, it is possible that the foreign affiliates' share of patent payments is even higher for our more heterogeneous sample.

9. We also used data on licence payments by US manufacturing industries in 1977 as an alternative for *PAT*. However, the US data were only available at the 2-digit level, and the Mexican 4-digit industries had to be aggregated into sixteen broad groups for the construction of the variable (see the Appendix to Chapter 9 for a concordance scheme between US 2-digit and Mexican 4-digit SIC codes). The results were similar to those for *PAT*, and are therefore not shown separately.

10. All results reported in the tables refer to linear estimations of the model. The estimations have also been made with logarithmic transformations of the variables: typically, adjusted R^2 increases, but the signs and significance levels of the coefficients remain unchanged. We retain the linear model throughout this chapter in order to be able to compare the results with earlier studies.

11. More detailed comparisons with the results in Blomström and Persson (1983) are not possible, since they normalized their variables in a different manner.

12. The cut-off points between 'high' and 'low' technology groups have been chosen on the basis of analyses of residuals from regression equation (1.2) in Table 10.1. The samples have been split approximately where changes in the pattern of residuals occur. The estimated coefficients in each pair of subsamples become more similar if lower cut-off points are chosen (since the subsamples themselves become more similar), whereas higher cut-off points do not change the results significantly (as long as the 'high' groups contain at least thirty observations).

13. Alternative proxies for technology levels, based on labour quality measures and the average labour productivity of foreign affiliates were also used for the grouping of industries, with results very similar to those presented in Table 10.2. The impact of *FOR* was consistently significant and positive in the 'low' technology group, but not significantly different from zero in the 'high' technology group; yet, F-tests failed to reject the null hypothesis that the coefficients of *FOR* were equal.

14. It should be noted that there is a possible selection bias in the grouping of industries according to *PGAP* if spillovers reduce the productivity gap. The industries with the smallest spillovers may automatically end up in the group with large *PGAP*s, whatever the reason for the lack of spillovers. However, it seems that the bias does not have a large impact on the results, since we also observe positive spillovers in that group.

15. It would also be interesting to examine if wholly- or majority-owned foreign affiliates and joint ventures have an identical impact on local technology and productivity, but the data do not distinguish between these two kinds of 'foreign' firms.

16. However, Caves (1971) suggests that marketing technology may also spill over, so that foreign presence has an impact even when production technologies are not comparable.

Appendix

Table A-10.1 Definitions of variables

Dependent variable

VA/Ld The ratio of value added to the total number of employees in private locally-owned manufacturing plants in each industry. Proxy for labour productivity.

Explanatory variables

K/Ld The ratio of total assets at book value to the total number of employees in private locally-owned plants in each industry. Proxy for capital intensity.

$HERF$ A Herfindahl index for each industry, including also foreign and state-owned plants. Measure of producer concentration.

W/B The ratio of white-collar workers to blue-collar workers in each industry, including also foreign and state-owned plants. Proxy for labour quality.

LQ The intercept and error term, '$a + e$', from the regression $W/B = a + \beta\ FOR + e$, to correct for the *a priori* known correlation between W/B and FOR. Proxy for labour quality.

FOR Share of each industry's total employment accounted for by foreign plants.

Selection criteria for grouping of observations

$PGAP$ Ratio of value added per employee in foreign plants to value added per employee in private locally-owned plants in each industry. Proxy for the technology gap.

PAT Ratio of the value of payments of patent fees and trade marks to total number of employees in each industry, including foreign and state-owned plants. Proxy for technological complexity.

K/L^f Ratio of total assets at book value to total number of employees in foreign plants in each industry. Proxy for capital intensity.

Table A-10.2   Descriptive statistics for 156 Mexican manufacturing industries with foreign plants, 1970

Variable	Unit	Mean	Standard deviation	Minimum	Maximum
VA/L^d	000s pesos	54.77	35.56	12.97	259.89
		(49.10)	(34.34)	(2.63)	(259.89)
K/L^d	000s pesos	112.57	92.06	14.54	568.63
		(98.47)	(91.28)	(4.55)	(568.63)
$HERF$		0.43	0.19	0.19	1.00
		(0.44)	(0.19)	(0.19)	(1.00)
W/B		0.33	0.23	0.06	1.63
		(0.29)	(0.21)	(0)	(1.63)
LQ		0.01	0.21	−0.35	1.39
PAT	000s pesos	1.84	6.03	0	51.14
		(1.36)	(5.19)	(0)	(51.14)
FOR		0.31	0.25	0	0.99
$PGAP$		2.03	1.62	0.41	10.19
K/L^f	000s pesos	196.98	207.80	0	2296.17

Notes: Figures within parentheses include also the sixty industries where foreign plants were not present in 1970. For definitions of variables, see Table A-10.1.

Table A-10.3   Simple correlation coefficients for exogenous variables, 156 Mexican manufacturing industries with foreign plants, 1970

K/L^d	1.00						
$HERF$	0.23	1.00					
	(0.19)						
LQ	0.11	−0.15	1.00				
	(0.19)	(0.11)					
FOR	0.34	0.48	−0.08	1.00			
	(0.38)	(0.23)	(0.00)				
PAT	0.19	0.04	0.13	0.28	1.00		
	(0.20)	(0.14)	(0.14)	(0.31)			
$PGAP$	−0.02	0.14	−0.04	0.13	0.53	1.00	
K/L^f	0.38	−0.01	0.22	0.05	0.11	0.28	1.00
	K/L^d	$HERF$	LQ	FOR	PAT	$PGAP$	K/L^f

Notes: Figures within parentheses include also the sixty industries where foreign firms were not present in 1970. For definitions of variables, see Table A-10.1.

11
Local Technological Capability and Productivity Spillovers from FDI in the Uruguayan Manufacturing Sector

11.1 Introduction

The predominant view in the literature on foreign direct investment is that various types of spillover may provide important benefits for the countries that host foreign multinational corporations. For example, numerous case studies have shown that the technology and productivity of local firms may improve as foreign firms enter the market and demonstrate new products and technologies, provide technical assistance to their local suppliers and customers, and train workers and managers who are later employed by local firms. There are also reports that the competitive pressure exerted by foreign affiliates has forced local firms to operate more efficiently and introduce new technologies earlier than would otherwise have been the case (see Chapter 8 for a review of the literature).

However, existing empirical studies differ in their estimates of the overall size and significance of spillovers. On the one hand, several studies of aggregate manufacturing suggest that spillovers are generally important. The earliest statistical tests – presented by Caves (1974), who examined Australian manufacturing in 1966; Globerman (1979a), with data for Canadian manufacturing 1972; and Blomström and Persson (1983), who studied Mexican manufacturing industries in 1970 – belong to this group. Although statistical models, variables and data quality differ between the studies, they all present evidence supporting the hypothesis that a foreign presence has a positive impact on the labour productivity of local firms in the affiliates' industries.[1] A more recent contribution to the group is our study in

Chapter 9, where we analyze Mexican manufacturing in the period 1970–5, and argue that spillovers have contributed to total factor productivity growth and led to a convergence of Mexican productivity towards US levels. Similarly, in an analysis of the effects of US direct investment on the manufacturing sectors of France, Germany, Japan and Great Britain, Nadiri (1991b) finds that increases in the capital stock owned by US firms appear to have significant positive effects on the host countries' productivity levels and productivity growth rates.

On the other hand, there are studies suggesting that spillovers are not important in general, or that they do not take place in all industries. For example, Haddad and Harrison (1993) examined data for Morocco during the period 1985–9, and concluded that there are no spillovers, since they were unable to find any evidence of a positive effect of foreign presence on multi-factor productivity growth in local firms. However, they note that competition from foreign firms appears to push local firms toward best-practice technologies in sectors with 'low' or moderately advanced technology. Aitken and Harrison (1991), using data for Venezuela between 1976 and 1989, conclude that there is no evidence of positive spillovers for a cross-section of manufacturing industries. Yet they find that large domestic firms located close to foreign firms tend to exhibit higher growth rates of multi-factor productivity, particularly in sectors such as food products, textiles and basic metals, where levels of technology are relatively low. Cantwell (1989) examines the responses of local firms to the emergence of US multinationals in the European markets 1955–75, and claims that the impact of FDI on domestic firms has not been beneficial in all industries. Technology spillovers have taken place mainly where local firms were initially relatively strong. Weaker local firms have either been forced out of business, or confined to limited segments of the market that are neglected by the foreign MNCs. Similarly, in the previous chapter we argued that spillovers are not automatic consequences of foreign investment, because they may not occur if foreign affiliates operate in 'enclaves' in isolation from local firms. On the basis of a cross-section study of Mexican manufacturing, we demonstrated that positive spillovers were less likely in industries where high foreign market shares and large productivity gaps between foreign and local firms coincide.

There is also a corresponding uncertainty regarding policy prescriptions for host countries that aim to maximize the benefits from foreign direct investment. Judging from the early results, soliciting foreign investment and subsidising foreign firms (for example, by offering tax holidays or import duty exemptions) may be rational from the point of view of the host country. Foreign direct investment appears to be an important channel for the transfer of modern technology to local firms, but the amount of FDI may be suboptimal in the absence of policy interventions because the spillover benefits are not internalized in the foreign firms' rates of return. The policy conclusions suggested by the latter studies are different. Haddad and Harrison (1993) conclude that their analysis does not support special treatment of foreign investors. A similar conclusion is implicit in Aitken and Harrison (1991), although the authors refrain from explicit policy recommendations (perhaps because of their slightly ambiguous results). Cantwell's (1989) analysis implies that general subsidies to foreign investment – and attempts to benefit from MNCs in the development of new industries – are not likely to pay off. Instead, governments (particularly in small countries) should concentrate their efforts in areas where their firms are already competitive. In a similar vein, our study in Chapter 10 suggests that FDI promotion should not focus on sectors where advanced technology, differentiated products and scale economies are likely to lead to the emergence of foreign enclaves.

In this study, we shall use detailed plant-level data for the Uruguayan manufacturing sector to examine more closely how the incidence of intra-industry spillovers is related to apparent technology differences between foreign and local firms. Our analysis is most closely related to those of Globerman (1979a), Blomström and Persson (1983), and our study in Chapter 10, but adds to their findings because we have access to plant data, which allows us to examine how the productivities of individual plants – rather than industry averages – are affected by a foreign presence. Moreover, Uruguay may represent a more typical case of FDI than do Mexico or Canada, where the proximity to the USA has meant that the flows of foreign investment are larger and the costs of technology transfer lower than for most other countries. Both these factors should make spillovers more likely and easier to observe. An indication of these underlying differences is that simple spillover tests for Uruguay do not show any firm signs of spillovers, as can be seen in Table 11.1 below.

The chapter proceeds as follows: Section 2 describes the data set and the statistical model used for the empirical tests; Section 3 presents and discusses the regression results; and Section 4 concludes.

11.2 Data and variables

The data used in the present study are taken from a plant-level survey of the Uruguayan manufacturing sector, 1988–90, collected by the Department of Economics at the University of the Republic of Uruguay, and from unpublished worksheets collected for the Uruguayan Economic Census of 1988 by the National Institute of Statistics in Montevideo. The full sample consists of all plants belonging to private, locally-owned manufacturing firms with more than 99 employees (some firms have more than one plant). The 289 plants in the sample accounted for 60 per cent of total output, 47 per cent of total employment, and 56 per cent of local sales of the Uruguayan manufacturing sector in 1988.

In the statistical tests presented in the next section, we have subtracted the plants operating in 4-digit industries without a foreign presence, because we need information on the size of the productivity gap between the local plant and the foreign affiliates in its industry. We were also forced to omit eight observations because of missing or uncertain data for some variables. Hence the sample used for the statistical tests consists of 159 plants. The following variables have been defined:

VA/L^d = A proxy for labour productivity in locally-owned plants, and is measured as the ratio of value-added to employment for each individual plant.

K/L^d = The ratio of the book value of fixed capital stock to employment for each locally-owned plant, and measures capital intensity.

RES = A rough proxy for each plants' capacity utilization. To construct this variable, we have used data on the capital intensity (K/L^d) and electricity consumption per employee in the locally-owned plants (KW/L^d). RES is defined as $\alpha + \varepsilon$ from the regression $KW/L^d = \alpha + \beta\ K/L^d + \varepsilon$, and is intended to measure the share of electricity consumption per employee that is not explained by capital intensity alone.

PAT^d = An estimate of the use of disembodied proprietary technology; measured as the payments for patents, trade marks and royalties per employee for each plant.

LQ = The share of management personnel in each plant's total employment, and a proxy for labour quality. The correlation between labour productivity and wages prevents us from using wage data to measure labour quality.

SIZE = The individual plant's opportunities to benefit from economies of scale. Defined as the plant's share of total sales in its 4-digit industry. This variable is highly correlated with measures of industry concentration, so it may also capture the degree of monopoly pricing in each industry.[2]

FOR = Our proxy for a foreign presence; it measures the foreign plants' share of the total output of the 4-digit industry to which the locally-owned plant belongs.

GAP = Measures the technology gap between locally-owned and foreign-owned firms. For the locally-owned plants that are less productive than the foreign affiliates, the variable is defined as the ratio of the average labour productivity of foreign-owned plants in the relevant four-digit industry to the locally-owned plant's own labour productivity. For locally-owned plants that exhibit higher labour productivity than their foreign-owned competitors, the variable *GAP* is the inverse of this ratio. Hence, *GAP* is equal to one if the locally-owned plant operates at the same labour productivity as its foreign-owned competitors, and increases with the difference in labour productivity. Values that are significantly higher than 1 are interpreted as signs of large differences in technology between the locally-owned plant and its foreign competitors. Large technology gaps may occur if foreign and local plants use different technologies (that is, they operate on separate production isoquants) or if they have chosen very different factor intensities (along the same isoquant), but it is also possible that a large gap indicates that they manufacture entirely different products despite being classified in the same 4-digit industry.

We shall proceed to make two types of test to examine the relationship between foreign presence and local productivity. Following earlier spillover studies, we begin by estimating the labour productivity of local plants as a function of plant- and industry-specific characteristics, including foreign presence, as in Equation (11.1) below:

$$VA/L^d = a + b_1 K/L^d + b_2 RES + b_3 PAT^d + b_4 LQ + b_5 SIZE$$
$$+ b_6 FOR + e \tag{11.1}$$

This equation incorporates the possible spillover effect of a foreign presence on local productivity; in line with earlier studies, we shall interpret a positive and significant coefficient for *FOR* as a sign that spillovers take place. The coefficients of our proxies for capital-intensity (K/L^d), capacity utilization (RES), use of proprietary technology (PAT^d), labour quality (LQ), and relative size $(SIZE)$ are all expected to be positive.

It should be noted that Equation (11.1) does not include any simultaneous effect of local productivity on foreign presence, although it has been argued in recent literature that such effects may well be important (see Cantwell, 1989; Chesnais, 1988; and Kokko, 1992). For example, the opportunity to benefit from spillovers of local technology may be an argument to locate a foreign affiliate in a market where existing firms are highly competitive. However, we have chosen a simple single-equation model, because this kind of 'strategic' foreign direct investment has not been significant in the case of Uruguay. Few Uruguayan firms operate with technologies that are advanced enough to be attractive to foreign investors, and most of the foreign firms that are significantly less productive than the leading local firms have been established in Uruguay for reasons other than access to local technology. The foreign firms exhibiting relatively low levels of labour productivity are typically active in mature industries such as slaughtering, dairy, wool, textiles and leather, where access to Uruguayan natural resources is the major investment motive, or in chemicals, where investors from Argentina and Brazil have been attracted by beneficial tax rules and bilateral trade agreements.

As a second step, we divide our full sample into two subsamples characterized by the size of the *GAP* variable, and estimate Equation (11.1) separately for locally-owned plants with small and large technology gaps. As noted above, the purpose is to examine whether the incidence of spillovers is related to the size of the technology gap. On the basis of earlier studies (Cantwell, 1989; Kokko, 1992), we expect to find stronger signs of spillovers in the subsample with smaller technology gaps. All results refer to OLS estimations of linear, additive versions of Equation (11.1).

11.3 Regression results

Regression equation (1.1) in Table 11.1 shows the results of the simplest spillover tests for our sample of 159 Uruguayan manufacturing plants. Capital intensity, capacity utilization and relative size, as expected all seem to have a positive impact on labour productivity. However, the estimated coefficient of the variable *FOR* is not significantly different from zero, which implies that a foreign presence does not have any substantial impact on local productivity: there are no signs of spillovers. Similarly, neither the use of proprietary technology nor labour quality, as proxied by the variables PAT^d and LQ, appear to have any significant effects. Yet, the model is relatively successful, in that it explains over 40 per cent of the variation in the dependent variable.

In equations (1.2) and (1.3) in Table 11.1 we have proceeded to divide the 159 industries into two subsamples characterized by the values for the variable *GAP*. Equation (1.2) covers seventy-nine locally-owned plants with small technology gaps, where labour productivity is not very different from that of the average foreign affiliate in their 4-digit industry, whereas equation (1.3) includes the eighty plants with the largest technology gaps.[3] The results suggest that there are significant differences between the two subsamples. Most important, the coefficient of *FOR* is positive and highly significant in the subsample with small technology gaps, but not significantly different from zero when the technology gap is large. In other words, there are strong signs of spillovers in the local plants facing small technology gaps, but not in the local plants that are far behind or far ahead of the average foreign affiliate in their industry.[4] Moreover, differences in labour quality and use of proprietary technology seem to be important determinants of productivity differences in the subsample with small gaps, but not in the subsample with large technology gaps.[5]

Small or moderate technology gaps seem to identify cases where foreign technologies are useful for local firms, and where the local firms possess the skills needed to apply or learn the foreign technologies. Large gaps, on the other hand, may signal that foreign technology is not relevant (because the product varieties manufactured by foreign firms are very different from local varieties), that local firms have nothing to learn from the foreign firms, or that local technological capability is so weak that foreign technologies cannot be used in local firms. In the previous chapter, we also suggested that the lack of spillovers in some industries may be explained by a dual industry structure or the presence of a foreign enclave. If this is the case, we would expect the industry distribution of the plants in the two subsamples to be very different. All local plants operating in industries

Table 11.1   Results of OLS estimations: labour productivity in private locally-owned manufacturing plants in Uruguay, 1990

Equation	159 plants (1.1)	Small GAP (1.2)	Large GAP (1.3)
Constant	−2.842	−2.299	−1.092
	(5.14)***	(2.04)**	(2.12)**
K/L^d	0.607	0.268	0.723
	(8.30)***	(2.29)**	(6.29)***
RES	2.683	2.236	1.210
	(5.30)***	(1.93)*	(2.89)***
PAT^d	0.035	0.158	−0.077
	(0.76)	(3.64)***	(1.07)
LQ	0.130	0.235	0.064
	(1.32)	(2.28)**	(0.45)
SIZE	0.289	0.395	0.189
	(4.94)***	(7.97)**	(1.86)*
FOR	0.098	0.275	−0.015
	(0.93)	(2.83)***	(0.09)
Adj. R^2	0.44	0.60	0.43
F	21.87	20.51	11.11
N	159	79	80

Notes: The dependent variable is VA/L^d. All variables are normalized by division with the sample means. Estimated coefficients are shown together with the absolute value of the t-statistics in parentheses. *, ** and *** denote significance at the 10, 5, and 1 per cent levels of significance (two-tailed tests).

with enclaves should be found in the large *GAP* group, and these enclave industries should not appear at all in the small *GAP* sample. Looking at the data, there are no strong signs of such a polarization. Plants from almost all industries appear in both subsamples, which indicates that it is not only industry characteristics, but also factors related to individual local firms, that determine whether spillovers will occur or not.

11.4 Concluding comments

In this study we have examined intra-industry spillovers from foreign direct investment in Uruguayan manufacturing plants in 1988, and attempted to determine whether differences in the technology gap between locally-owned plants and foreign plants have any impact on the observed spillovers.

Our regression analysis showed no signs of spillovers in simple tests covering the entire sample of 159 locally-owned manufacturing plants. However, looking separately at two subsamples of plants characterized by the size of the technology gap between the locally-owned plant and its foreign-owned competitors, we found significant differences in the impact of a foreign presence. Spillovers appeared to be positive and statistically significant in the subsample of plants with moderate technology gaps *vis-à-vis* foreign firms, but not in the group of local plants facing large technology gaps.

Referring back to the discussion regarding policy prescriptions in the introduction, these findings suggest that it is difficult to formulate general policies to maximize the spillover benefits from FDI for developing countries such as Uruguay. Measures to actively promote direct investment from abroad may not be sufficient to generate spillovers if the majority of local firms employ technologies that are very different from those used by foreigners. General policies to support local firms in industries with a foreign presence are likely to be inefficient for the same reason. Instead, selective support to local firms, aiming to improve their capability to identify and employ modern technologies, seems to be a necessary ingredient in a policy package to maximize the technological externalities from foreign direct investment.

Notes

1. Some related conclusions are provided by Katz (1969), for Argentine manufacturing. and Chen (1983), for Hong Kong, although their statistical tests are less comprehensive.
2. Direct measures of industry concentration (for example, C4, the share of the industry's sales accounted for by the four largest plants) cannot be used in the regression analysis, since these measures are highly correlated with foreign presence.
3. The cut-off value for *GAP* is 2.17 if both subsamples are to be of approximately the same size. The results are not sensitive to small changes in the cut-off values.

4. A Chow test allows us to reject (at the 5 per cent level of significance) the hypothesis that the two sets of observations in equations (1.2) and (1.3) in Table 11.1 are drawn from the same stochastic process.
5. There is a high simple correlation between the variables K/L^d and RES in the small GAP subsample, but this is not a major problem for the present purposes, since we are only trying to control for their combined effect on differences in labour productivity.

Appendix

Table A-11.1   Simple correlation coefficient

Whole sample (159 plants)

	K/L^d	RES	PAT^d	$SIZE$	LQ	FOR
K/L^d	1.00					
RES	0.00	1.00				
PAT^d	0.09	0.12	1.00			
$SIZE$	0.07	−0.01	0.04	1.00		
LQ	−0.09	−0.01	0.08	0.00	1.00	
FOR	−0.05	−0.10	−0.10	0.05	0.05	1.00
	K/L^d	RES	PAT^d	$SIZE$	LQ	FOR

Small *GAP* (79 plants)

	K/L^d	RES	PAT^d	$SIZE$	LQ	FOR
K/L^d	1.00					
RES	−0.79	1.00				
PAT^d	0.05	−0.04	1.00			
$SIZE$	0.11	−0.05	0.07	1.00		
LQ	0.00	−0.08	0.20	0.11	1.00	
FOR	0.04	0.03	−0.02	0.12	0.08	1.00
	K/L^d	RES	PAT^d	$SIZE$	LQ	FOR

Large *GAP* (80 plants)

	K/L^d	RES	PAT^d	$SIZE$	LQ	FOR
K/L^d	1.00					
RES	0.27	1.00				
PAT^d	0.15	0.27	1.00			
$SIZE$	0.04	0.03	−0.03	1.00		
LQ	−0.14	0.00	−0.01	−0.11	1.00	
FOR	−0.12	−0.20	−0.16	0.00	0.03	1.00
	K/L^d	RES	PAT^d	$SIZE$	LQ	FOR

12
Productivity Spillovers from Competition between Local Firms and Foreign Affiliates

12.1 Introduction

In the debate on the role of multinational corporations in international technology transfer, it has often been suggested that a large share of the host countries' benefits from foreign direct investment may come in the form of external effects or 'spillovers'. MNCs may, for example, introduce new technologies that are imitated by local producers, or train workers whose specific skills spill over when they set up their own firms or are hired by existing local firms. These benefits can be characterized as effects of *contagion and demonstration*. Other effects are related to *competition*, and occur when local firms are forced to become more productive – by introducing new technologies or increasing X-efficiency – in order to survive in markets where foreign affiliates are present.

To date, several empirical studies have attempted to test whether these types of externalities are significant enough to be observed at an aggregate level. The best-known contributions, by Caves (1974) for Australia, Globerman (1979a) for Canada, and Blomström and Persson (1983) for Mexico, all conclude that spillovers are likely to be important. However, the results of some more recent studies – for example, Aitken and Harrison (1991) for Colombia, and Haddad and Harrison (1993) for Morocco – suggest the opposite conclusion.

The contradictory findings are partly the result of differences in methodology and data availability, but it is also possible that there are systematic differences in spillovers across countries and industries. In our study of Mexican manufacturing (see Chapter 10), we argued that positive spillovers are less likely in industries with highly differentiated products and large economies of scale. Foreign and local firms may use entirely different technologies when products are differentiated, and economies of scale may allow the foreign affiliates to 'crowd out' local firms from their segments of the market. In both cases, MNC technologies may be irrelevant for local firms, so that the potential for spillovers is small.

Another possible explanation is that the empirical tests have not distinguished between effects of contagion and effects of competition. Existing studies, which typically measure spillovers as the impact of foreign presence on the level of local productivity or the rate of productivity growth, may have failed to capture some of the externalities. In fact, Wang and Blomström (1992) argue that spillovers from competition are not necessarily proportional to the presence of foreign firms, although demonstration and contagion effects are. Moreover, they assert that the former effect may dominate the latter, so that a large foreign presence may coincide with a small technology transfer, which arguably has been the case in many Latin-American countries.

In the present chapter, we shall use detailed data from Mexican manufacturing industries in 1970 to examine whether there are significant spillovers from competition that are not proportional to foreign presence.[1] The issue is important not only because it may help to explain why spillovers are not observed in all countries and industries, but also because it is relevant from a policy perspective. The empirical studies that have found positive externalities imply that host country policies aiming to maximize these benefits should focus on measures that increase the inflow of FDI. However, this is not an obvious conclusion if the amount of spillover is determined by other variables than just the extent of foreign presence.

The chapter is organized as follows: Section 2 looks briefly at some theoretical studies of endogenous spillovers; Section 3 presents the data, a statistical model, and the estimation method; Section 4 reports the results of endogeneity tests and regression analysis; and Section 5 concludes the chapter.

12.2   Endogenous spillovers in theoretical models

The available empirical studies of spillovers, and early theoretical models such as those by Findlay (1978), and Koizumi and Kopecky (1977), have assumed that spillovers are proportional to foreign presence, and independent of the behaviour of foreign affiliates and local firms. An important feature of newer models, however, is that the actions of both types of firm have an impact on spillovers.

These models, which draw on studies of international R&D competition (Cheng, 1984, 1987; Spencer and Brander, 1983); export rivalry (Brander and Spencer, 1985); foreign investment decisions (Horstmann and Markusen, 1987, 1989); and international transfers of product technology (Jensen and Thursby, 1986), analyze the problem in a strategic game-theoretic environment, where the competition between affiliates and local firms is of central importance.

An example is Wang and Blomström (1992), who argue that spillovers are largely endogenous outcomes of the interactions between foreign and local firms. They model a differential game involving an MNC affiliate and a local firm that are both able to influence spillovers, where each firm solves its individual dynamic optimization problems subject to the other firm's actions. The MNC's objective is to choose, for each time period, how much to invest in imports of new technology, and the local firm's objective is to decide how much to invest in learning to imitate MNC technology, given that both know the other party's decisions, and that:

(a)   a larger technology gap gives the MNC affiliate's products a 'quality advantage' that translates into higher profit because it can take out a higher price or capture a larger market share, whereas the profit of the local firm is negatively related to the size of the technology gap;

(b)   technology transfer is costly, and newer and more complex technologies are more expensive to transfer;

(c)   the technology gap between the firms grows as new technology is imported, but diminishes as a result of the local firm's learning efforts; and

(d)   some spillovers that are proportional to the size of the technology gap (or the affiliates market share) always take place irrespective of the local firm's active learning efforts.

The differential game is solved by defining the steady-state equilibrium conditions for each party's optimal control problem, subject to the other's decisions, and then finding the combination of technology import and learning decisions that fulfills the conditions for a unique, locally-stable, steady-state Nash equilibrium.

The most interesting conclusion of the Wang–Blomström model, from our perspective, is that the extent of spillovers is not determined by the degree of foreign presence alone. Instead, the results are related to the firms' investment decisions. The more the MNC invests in new technology, the higher the spillovers, *ceteris paribus*, because they are related to the size of the technology gap; the more a local firm invests in learning, the more of the potential spillovers it is able to absorb. In addition, there is a multiplicative second-order effect that is directly related to competition, since an improvement in local technology (for example, as a result of spillovers) reduces the technology gap, cuts into the affiliate's earnings, and forces it to import new technology (part of which may also spill over) in order to restore its profitability and market share.

Thus spillovers may be very significant in industries where the foreign share is relatively small, if only affiliates and local firms compete fiercely, and less important in industries where weak local competition allows the affiliates to capture large market shares. There are, in fact, some empirical observations that seem to be consistent with this type of model. For example, Cantwell (1989) argues that the effects of US direct investment on local technological capability in Western Europe 1955–75 were most beneficial in industries where local firms were relatively strong to begin with, because competition created continuing two-way exchanges between the firms, with 'reverse technology transfer' and intra-industry trade and production being a result.

If these effects are important in general, it seems clear that empirical studies focusing on the relationship between foreign presence and local productivity may yield misleading results. How, then, should an alternative statistical model look? Ideally, it would be based on pooled cross-section and time series data that would allow us to examine how changes in productivity and efficiency in both types of firm are related to foreign presence, the affiliates' technology imports, and local investment in learning. Unfortunately, such data are not available, and for our present purposes, we only have detailed information about Mexican manufacturing for one year. Instead of modelling the recursive mechanism described above, we must therefore settle for a less ambitious test based on data for that single year.

The statistical model we are going to use will contain two fundamental features. First, in line with earlier empirical studies, we shall assume that some externalities are proportional to a foreign presence, so that the foreign share of the industry should be included among the determinants of the labour productivity of local firms. Second, following Wang and Blomström (1992), we hypothesize that the productivities of foreign affiliates and local firms are jointly determined. Both affiliates and local firms should exhibit high X-efficiency in some industries (since both kinds of firm are forced to invest and work hard if one of them does) and low X-efficiency in others (since neither firm needs to worry about efficiency and productivity increases unless its rival does). In other words, we must construct a simultaneous model, where each firm's productivity is partly determined by its rival's productivity. Before that, however, we shall briefly look at the empirical data.

12.3   Data, model and method

The empirical data for this study are from unpublished worksheets provided by the Dirección de Estadísticas de la Secretaría de Industria y Comercio in Mexico, and refer to the operations of foreign and local firms in Mexican manufacturing industries in 1970. The information was collected at the plant level for the Mexican Census of Manufactures 1971, and covers the entire manufacturing sector, which is divided into 230 4-digit industries with a further breakdown according to three ownership categories: domestic private; foreign; and state ownership. Plants with at least 15 per cent of shares owned by foreigners are defined as 'foreign', and those where the Mexican state owns more than 49 per cent are defined as state-owned, irrespective of the share of foreign ownership. The state-owned plants are excluded from the present sample, since they may operate under soft budget constraints, or have other goals (related, for example, to employment creation or geographical localization of operations) than profit maximization, as discussed in Blomström and Persson (1983).

Fourteen of the 230 industries were discarded from the sample because of missing information, and another sixty industries were dropped because foreign firms were not present in 1970. For the remaining 156 industries, the data set includes the following variables, where superscripts d and f denote domestic and foreign firms, respectively:

VA/L^d and VA/L^f = Our proxies for labour productivity, and measure average value added per employee for locally-owned and foreign-owned firms in each industry.

K/L^d and K/L^f = The average capital-intensities of the two types of firm, defined as the ratio of total assets at book value to total employment.

FOR = The measure of foreign presence, calculated for each industry as the ratio of the foreign firms' employment to total employment.

LQ^f = The ratio of white-collar to blue-collar workers in each industry, which aims to measure the industry's average labour quality. We use it as the labour quality proxy for foreign firms.

LQ^d = The labour quality proxy for local firms, defined as the intercept and error term, '$a + e$', from the regression $LQ^f = a + \beta\ FOR + e$. It is included because the data on white-collar and blue-collar workers are not available for foreign and local firms separately, at the same time as there is an *a priori* known correlation between LQ^f and *FOR*, as discussed in Blomström and Persson (1983).[2]

TECH = Proxies the use of advanced technologies in each industry, and measures the average payments of licences, royalties and patent fees per employee for the whole industry.

HERF = The value of the Herfindahl index for each industry, including local, foreign and state-owned firms, and proxies the level of producer concentration.[3]

ADV = Measures each industry's average advertising expenditure per employee. Some descriptive statistics and correlations for the variables are given in the Appendix, Tables A-12.1 and A-12.2.

Given this information, we can now set up a simple simultaneous system which attempts to capture spillovers that are proportional to foreign presence as well as those caused by competition. The system is illustrated by Equations (12.1) and (12.2) below:

$$VA/L^d = a_0 + a_1 K/L^d + a_2 LQ^d + a_3 TECH + a_4 HERF$$
$$+ a_5 ADV + a_6 FOR + a_7 VA/L^f + e \tag{12.1}$$

$$VA/L^f = b_0 + b_1 K/L^f + b_2 LQ^f + b_3 TECH + b_4 HERF$$
$$+ b_5 ADV + b_6 VA/L^d + m \tag{12.2}$$

As in earlier spillover studies, Equation (12.1) suggests that the average value-added per employee of locally-owned firms in an industry, VA/L^d, is determined by their capital intensity, K/L^d, the skill level of their labour force, LQ^d, and their use of advanced technology, *TECH*. Because the dependent variable is in value terms, it is also likely to be influenced by the possibilities of engaging in monopoly or oligopoly pricing, and we assume that these possibilities are related to the level of producer concentration in the industry, *HERF*. Similarly, industries with high average advertising expenditures, *ADV*, may possess some asset (for example, a brand name or trade mark) that allows them to extract higher prices for their products. The employment share of foreign firms, *FOR*, is included to capture the spillovers that are proportional to a foreign presence. In addition to these variables, and in contrast to earlier studies, we include the labour productivity of the foreign affiliates in the industry, VA/L^f, to reflect spillovers from competition.[4]

Capital-intensity, labour quality, technology inputs, concentration and advertising are expected to have positive coefficients, although the fact that *TECH* and *ADV* are defined for industry totals (rather than for foreign and local firms separately) may disturb the results, as we shall see later. The hypotheses related to spillovers are concentrated on the variables *FOR* and VA/L^f. The coefficient of *FOR* should be positive if contagion type spillovers occur. Similarly, VA/L^f should have a positive impact if competition-related spillovers have an additional impact on local productivity (or rather, X-efficiency, since the other determinants of VA/L^d are exogenously given).

For simplicity, Equation (12.2) assumes that the labour productivity of foreign firms is determined by similar factors (except foreign share) to those of locally-owned firms. The coefficients b_1 to b_5 are expected to be positive, as for locally-owned firms, and the impact of local productivity, VA/L^d, should be positive if competition is important.[5]

To estimate the simultaneous Equations (12.1) and (12.2), we shall use the method of three-stage least squares – 3SLS. If simultaneous interactions take place, the 3SLS estimates are more efficient and consistent than the corresponding OLS estimates. Two-stage least squares – 2SLS – provide a somewhat simpler alternative estimation method, but we prefer 3SLS because it yields more efficient estimates of the parameters we are most interested in. Keeping in mind the functional relationship between LQ^f and LQ^d, it can be seen that Equation (12.1) is exactly identified, while Equation (12.2) is overidentified. The additional information about error correlations improves the 3SLS estimates for Equation (12.1) – that is, those related to spillovers, although both methods give identical estimates for Equation (12.2) (Maddala, 1977, pp. 484–5).

12.4   Empirical results

Test of endogeneity

Before moving on to the regression analysis, it is useful to examine whether a simultaneous model is necessary for the particular data set we are working with. The reason is that the simultaneity of the present model depends on the existence of competition between locally-owned firms and MNC affiliates, whereas earlier studies of the data set used here (see Chapter 10) have argued that the foreign affiliates in some industries are likely to operate in 'enclaves', in isolation from local competition. Failure to find any signs of simultaneity would, of course, constitute a strong argument against the model we use.

A convenient test for this purpose is suggested by Geroski (1982), who argues that two equations, such as Equations (12.1) and (12.2) above, are likely to be determined simultaneously (and OLS estimates biased and inconsistent) if the residual of the reduced form estimate of Equation (12.2) has a significant impact on the dependent variable in Equation (12.1). Thus we can test for endogeneity of VA/L^f by estimating Equation (12.1'):

$$VA/L^d = a_0 + a_1 K/L^d + a_2 LQ^d + a_3 TECH + a_4 HERF$$
$$+ a_5 ADV + a_6 VA/L^f + a_7 FOR + qR + e \qquad (12.1')$$

where R is the residual from the reduced form OLS estimate of VA/L^f.[6] If q is equal to zero, we should accept the null hypothesis that VA/L^f is exogenous.[7] If, on the other hand, q is significantly different from zero, VA/L^f is likely to be endogenous, and there is reason to use a multi-equation system to estimate the parameters.

Looking at the entire sample of 156 Mexican manufacturing industries, the 'Geroski test' does not offer any support for the hypothesis that VA/L^f is endogenous: q is not significantly different from zero at any reasonable level of confidence. However, we find clear signs of endogeneity when we exclude the industries where enclaves are most likely. Lacking detailed information about product differentiation, scale economies, and relations between foreign affiliates and their local competitors, it is obvious that we cannot accurately identify enclave industries. In line with Chapter 10, we have therefore assumed that the industries characterized by large foreign shares and large differences in labour productivity between foreign affiliates and locally-owned firms are those where enclaves are the most likely to occur. Thus we have excluded the forty industries where the ratio of VA/L^f to VA/L^d is larger than 4 or the foreign employment share is above 50 per cent. For this sub-sample, q is different from zero at the 5 per cent level of confidence.[8] Consequently, on the basis of the Geroski test, we expect the simultaneous model to yield better results for the 116 industries in this subsample than for the whole population.[9]

Regression results

The regression results for the entire sample of 156 industries are summarized in Table 12.1, and the results for the 116 industries in the subsample without enclaves can be found in Table 12.2. For comparison, both 3SLS and OLS estimations are provided.

Table 12.1 shows that 3SLS and OLS give similar estimates for all parameters when we look at the entire sample, which is consistent with the results of the Geroski test – the simultaneity bias appears to be unimportant. Looking first at local firms, in columns (1a) and (1b), both methods yield the expected positive coefficients for all variables except *TECH*, although only capital intensity, labour quality, and foreign presence appear to have significant effects. The lack of significance for *TECH*, *HERF* and *ADV* may be explained by the fact that these variables are defined for industry totals, rather than for local firms alone. Advanced technologies (or high patent and licence payments) and large advertising expenditures are more common among MNC affiliates, and the variables may therefore have low explanatory power for local firms.[10] Moreover, many of the largest firms in each industry are likely to be foreign affiliates, and the positive impact of concentration – whether it is related to the opportunities to engage in monopoly pricing or to the exploitation of economies of scale – may be more relevant for them than for local firms. Regarding spillovers, only a foreign presence appears to have a significant impact, which is in accordance with the Geroski test: if the simultaneous interactions between locals and MNCs are obscured, so perhaps are the effects of competition.

The parameter estimates for foreign firms, in columns (2a) and (2b), do not contain any surprises, except a significant negative coefficient for labour quality in the 3SLS estimation. Capital intensity, inputs of advanced technology, concentration and advertising all have similar positive coefficients in both columns, but the impact of local

Table 12.1 Results of 3SLS and OLS regressions: labour productivity in locally-owned and foreign firms in Mexican manufacturing, 1970 (156 industries with foreign firms)

	(1a)	(1b)		(2a)	(2b)
Method	3SLS	OLS		3SLS	OLS
Dependent variable	VA/L^d	VA/L^d		VA/L^f	VA/L^f
Constant	0.2254	0.2344	Constant	0.1855	0.2235
	(1.639)	(1.771)*		(1.840)*	(2.340)**
K/L^d	0.4222	0.4259	K/L^f	0.3654	0.3806
	(6.969)***	(7.573)***		(9.211)***	(10.13)***
LQ^d	0.1233	0.1223	LQ^f	−0.0958	−0.0724
	(1.756)*	(1.740)*		(1.738)*	(1.403)
TECH	−0.0196	−0.0172	TECH	0.1431	0.1439
	(0.948)	(1.031)		(12.58)***	(12.85)***
HERF	0.0329	0.0333	HERF	0.1147	0.1487
	(0.315)	(0.320)		(1.429)	(1.976)**
ADV	0.0189	0.0237	ADV	0.1134	0.1149
	(0.544)	(0.960)		(5.797)***	(5.964)***
FOR	0.1482	0.1502	VA/L^d	0.1736	0.0700
	(2.464)**	(2.444)**		(1.721)*	(1.092)
VA/L^f	0.0487	0.0274			
	(0.375)	(0.345)			
Adj. R^2		0.423			0.822
F-value		17.30			120.22
N	156	156		156	156

Notes: System weighted R-square for 3SLS estimations 0.75. All variables are normalized by division with the sample means. Estimated coefficients are shown together with the absolute value of the t-statistics in parentheses. *, ** and *** denote significance at the 10, 5, and 1 per cent levels of confidence (two-tailed tests).

competition appears to be more significant and larger in the 3SLS variant. It can also be noted that the explanatory power of the OLS estimation is remarkably high – adjusted R^2 is above 0.8. This is probably related to the highly significant impact of TECH and ADV on the productivity of foreign affiliates: dropping the variables from the equation for local firms – column (1b) – leaves adjusted R^2 unchanged, but dropping them from column (2b) halves adjusted R^2. This result also suggests that TECH and ADV mainly reflect the behaviour of foreign firms.

Table 12.2 shows the results for the subsample without enclaves. The first result to note is that all coefficients in the 3SLS estimation for local firms (column 3a), except those for TECH and ADV (which are perhaps not relevant for local firms), are significant at the 5 per cent level or better. Capital intensity and labour quality have the expected

Table 12.2   Results of 3SLS and OLS regressions: labour productivity in locally-owned and foreign firms in Mexican manufacturing, 1970 (116 industries, 'enclaves' excluded)

	(3a)	(3b)		(4a)	(4b)
Method	3SLS	OLS		3SLS	OLS
Dependent variable	VA/L^d	VA/L^d		VA/L^f	VA/L^f
Constant	0.2839	0.3688	Constant	0.0342	0.0227
	(3.468)***	(6.077)***		(0.271)	(0.187)
K/L^d	0.3044	0.3741	K/L^f	0.1906	0.1830
	(5.918)***	(11.89)***		(3.027)***	(3.114)***
LQ^d	0.1025	0.1282	LQ^f	−0.0042	−0.0131
	(2.315)**	(3.368)***		(0.051)	(0.168)
$TECH$	−0.0155	−0.0088	$TECH$	0.0318	0.0327
	(1.198)	(0.787)		(1.404)	(1.455)
$HERF$	−0.1227	−0.1292	$HERF$	0.1041	0.0992
	(2.335)**	(2.708)**		(1.149)	(1.109)
ADV	−0.0084	0.0013	ADV	0.0490	0.0489
	(0.552)	(0.100)		(1.919)*	(1.917)*
FOR	0.0588	0.0760	VA/L^d	0.5945	0.6266
	(2.221)**	(2.546)**		(3.916)***	(5.297)***
VA/L^f	0.3970	0.1897			
	(3.246)***	(4.596)***			
Adj. R^2		0.792			0.494
F-value		63.67			19.75
N	116	116		116	116

Notes: System weighted R-square for 3SLS estimations 0.73. All variables are normalized by division with the sample means. Estimated coefficients are shown together with the absolute value of the t-statistics in parentheses. *, ** and ***   denote significance at the 10, 5, and 1 per cent levels of confidence (two-tailed tests).

positive coefficients, but *HERF* carries a significant negative effect. The negative impact of *HERF* seems to confirm that local firms are less able to exploit economies of scale and engage in monopoly pricing because they are generally smaller than foreign firms, as discussed above. Both *FOR* and VA/L^f register significant positive coefficients, which supports our hypothesis that some spillovers may be related to a foreign presence, at the same time that others are determined by the behaviour of foreign affiliates. Moreover, there is a large difference between 3SLS and OLS estimates of the impact of VA/L^f on local productivity, in line with the Geroski test result that simultaneity is likely to bias the OLS estimation.

Columns (4a) and (4b), for foreign firms, are less successful in terms of their overall explanatory power. Only capital-intensity, advertising and local competition have significant effects, and adjusted R^2 is notably lower in column (4b) than in column (2b). The reduction in adjusted R^2 is probably related to the characteristics of the industries that were dropped from the original sample. The suspected foreign enclaves were not only marked by large market shares and high productivity relative to local firms, but also by high absolute productivity that seemed to be explained by large technology payments and large advertising expenditures (see Table A-12.1).[11]

Nevertheless, the finding that local productivity, VA/L^d, has a significant positive impact on foreign productivity in column (4a) suggests that the behaviour of affiliates is partly determined by the behaviour of local firms. Hence, the results from columns (3a) and (4a) together support the hypothesis that the productivities of foreign affiliates and local firms are determined simultaneously, and that there are endogenous spillovers from competition in addition to the spillovers that are proportional to a foreign presence.

12.5 Summary and conclusions

Earlier empirical studies have attempted to measure spillovers from foreign direct investment by estimating the effect of foreign presence on local productivity, with contradictory results. Some authors, such as Caves (1974), Globerman (1979a), and Blomström and Persson (1983) have argued that spillovers are important, whereas others – for example, Aitken and Harrison (1991) and Haddad and Harrison (1993) – have come to the opposite conclusion. We argued that a possible explanation for this discrepancy is that earlier studies may have failed to capture an important class of spillovers – the results of the competition between local firms and foreign affiliates – because these effects are not proportional to foreign presence but rather are related to investment decisions and learning efforts in both types of firm.

The purpose of this chapter was to examine empirically whether we could observe any signs of these spillovers from competition. To this end we constructed a simple simultaneous model based on data for the operations of foreign and domestic firms in Mexican manufacturing in 1970, and tested two hypotheses. Our first hypothesis was that the labour productivities of foreign and local firm are simultaneously determined because of competition. Our second stated that competition has an independent effect on the productivity of local firms, even after allowing for the spillovers that are proportional to a foreign presence. The results support both hypotheses, but only for a subsample of industries that excludes suspected 'enclaves', where foreign firms operate in isolation from local competition.

Before we move onto policy conclusions, it is necessary to consider briefly the shortcomings of the present model. First, capital intensity is an exogenous variable in the model we have used, which means that spillovers have an impact mainly on X-efficiency – that is, the part of productivity that is not explained by the amount of factor inputs. Yet the technology imports of affiliates probably depend on the level of competition in the host economy (see Chapter 14) and capital intensity should perhaps be endogenously determined in a more complete model. Second, the results indicate that the productivity levels of foreign and local firms are positively correlated, and we have interpreted this as a consequence of competition. However, it is also possible that there is some neglected factor which determines simultaneously the behaviour of foreign and local firms, and causes the correlation we are able to detect. Third, the model says nothing about the long-run characteristics of the interactions between local and foreign firms. Situations where both foreign and local firms 'work hard', and cases where both are 'lethargic', are equally consistent with the present results and hypotheses. Thus the model does not say anything explicitly about how to induce an equilibrium where both kinds of firm are active and productive, and where the rate of growth of the host country is maximized.

Nevertheless, some important policy conclusions follow from the finding that the behaviour of local firms is a determinant of the spillover benefits from FDI. Spillovers are likely to be less important in industries where competition is limited. Measures to support local technological capability and to stimulate competition between foreign affiliates and local firms should therefore complement the usual policies that aim to encourage inflows of FDI. At the same time, it must be stressed that more research is needed to examine second-best policy alternatives for those industries where locals cannot be expected to compete effectively with foreign affiliates in the short run.

Notes

1. Comparable data on the operations of foreign firms are not available for any other year, to the best of our knowledge.
2. Blomström and Persson (1983) define their proxy for labour quality in local firms only as the error term e, but we add the intercept a to make the comparison between LQ^d and LQ^f easier.
3. The Herfindahl index is calculated from plant-level data, and is defined as:

$$HERF = S(x_i/X)^2 \qquad i = 1, \ldots, n$$

where x_i is employment in the n individual plants, and X is total employment in the industry.

4. Caves (1974) also used VA/L^f as an explanatory variable, but not in order to measure spillovers. Instead, VA/L^f was included to capture the interindustry differences in technology and capital-intensity.

5. A more complete model ought to treat FOR as an endogenous variable, since the productivities of foreign and local firms are likely to be important determinants of the degree of foreign penetration. However, we treat FOR as an exogenous variable for two reasons. First, FOR is probably a function of *past* rather than *currrent* productivities: we only have data for one year. Second, FOR is also likely to depend heavily on FDI regulations, trade barriers, and other (institutional) variables for which we have no data.

6. The reduced form of Equation (12.2) is:

$$VA/L^f = b_0 + b_1 K/L^f + b_2 LQ^f + b_3 TECH + b_4 HERF + b_5 ADV$$
$$+ b_6 K/L^d + b_7 FOR + r \qquad (12.2')$$

and the residual R is the difference between the actual and estimated value for VA/L^f from this equation. LQ^d is not included in the equation, because it is a function of LQ^f and FOR.

7. Failure to reject the null hypothesis does not, in principle, rule out endogeneity, as noted by Geroski (1982, p. 150). VA/L^f may be endogenous if the covariance of e and m equals minus the variance of e times a_6; however, in this case, OLS estimates of VA/L^d are still consistent. Geroski also notes another caveat of which we must be aware: it is possible to confuse a misspecification of the model with endogeneity.

8. It can be noted that many of the industries dropped are such that superior marketing abilities and proprietary brand names and labels are likely to make up the competitive assets of foreign firms. Examples of the goods produced are perfumes and cosmetics, alcoholic beverages, cigars and cigarettes, chewing gum, instant coffee, snacks, clocks and watches, batteries, records, tapes, and photographic film. Some of the other industries in the subsample – for example, motor vehicles, office and computing machines, synthetic oils, synthetic fibres and tyres – may also be characterized by significant economies of scale. Hence, at least in this specific case, it does not seem implausible to associate high foreign shares and large productivity gaps with the term 'enclave'.

However, it should also be mentioned that there are many alternative ways to try to exclude possible enclave industries. For example, dropping only the industries with large foreign shares is sufficient to get mildly significant results from the Geroski test (but there is no evidence of endogeneity if we only drop industries with large productivity gaps between foreign affiliates and local firms). There are also signs of endogeneity if we exclude industries with large foreign shares together with high advertising or high technology payments. It can be seen from Table A-12.1 that these characteristics (large FOR, large productivity gaps, high $TECH$,

high *ADV*) coincide in the industries we have chosen to exclude from
the sample.
9. The more well-known Hausman test gives similar results. See Hausman
(1978) and Spencer and Berk (1981).
10. Fairchild (1977), in a study of twenty-five closely matched pairs of US
affiliates and local firms operating in Monterrey, Mexico, concludes that
four times as many affiliates as local firms used US patents or licences
in 1973. More comprehensive data on the use of patents and licences are
not available, and we do not know whether the differences between
affiliates and local firms are smaller or larger in our more heterogenous
sample.
11. The estimated coefficients of labour quality and *TECH* may also be dis-
torted by some multicollinearity (see Table A-12.2), but dropping either
of the variables has little effect on the other coefficient estimates, so the
figures presented in the table have not been adjusted for this.

Appendix

Table A-12.1   Descriptive statistics for Mexican manufacturing industries,
1970

Variable	Unit	Mean	Standard deviation	Minimum	Maximum
VA/L^d	000s pesos	54.77	35.56	12.97	259.89
		(49.51)	(21.13)	(15.27)	(120.22)
VA/L^f	000s pesos	100.22	95.92	11.76	726.74
		(80.20)	(44.65)	(11.76)	(327.77)
K/L^d	000s pesos	112.57	92.06	14.54	568.63
		(102.06)	(76.59)	(14.54)	(511.48)
K/L^f	000s pesos	196.98	207.80	11.84	2296.17
		(171.70)	(130.46)	(11.84)	(862.56)
LQ^f		0.33	0.23	0.06	1.63
		(0.31)	(0.21)	(0.06)	(1.63)
LQ^d		0.01	0.21	−0.35	1.39
		(0.03)	(0.19)	(−0.29)	(1.39)
HERF		0.43	0.19	0.19	1.00
		(0.37)	(0.16)	(0.19)	(1.00)
TECH	000s pesos	1.84	6.03	0	51.14
		(0.76)	(1.54)	(0)	(13.07)
ADV	000s pesos	2.34	5.39	0	37.51
		(1.47)	(2.32)	(0)	(14.94)
FOR		0.31	0.25	0.01	0.99
		(0.21)	(0.15)	(0.01)	(0.50)

Note: Figures in parentheses refer to the sub-sample of 116 industries that
excludes suspected enclaves.

Table A-12.2　Simple correlation coefficients for exogenous variables, 156 Mexican manufacturing industries with foreign firms present, 1970

	K/L^d	K/L^f	HERF	LQ^f	LQ^d	FOR	TECH	ADV
K/L^d	1.00							
K/L^f	0.38	1.00						
	(0.42)							
HERF	0.23	−0.01	1.00					
	(0.35)	(0.03)						
LQ^f	0.24	0.23	0.05	1.00				
	(0.36)	(0.31)	(0.07)					
LQ^d	0.11	0.22	−0.15	0.91	1.00			
	(0.27)	(0.27)	(−0.01)	(0.96)				
FOR	0.34	0.05	0.48	0.34	−0.08	1.00		
	(0.29)	(0.24)	(0.30)	(0.43)	(0.17)			
TECH	0.19	0.11	0.04	0.23	0.13	0.28	1.00	
	(0.06)	(0.14)	(0.11)	(0.55)	(0.50)	(0.33)		
ADV	0.22	0.59	−0.04	0.22	0.18	0.11	0.40	1.00
	(−0.03)	(0.00)	(−0.04)	(0.35)	(0.30)	(0.30)	(0.30)	
	K/L^d	K/L^f	HERF	LQ^f	LQ^d	FOR	TECH	ADV

Note:　Figures in parentheses refer to the sub-sample of 116 industries that excludes suspected enclaves.

13
Policies to Encourage Inflows of Technology through Foreign Multinationals

13.1 Introduction

The debate on the role of government policies for economic performance has, in recent years, turned from discussing the choice between free markets and government intervention to asking what types of intervention are good or bad. One reason is that almost all governments, irrespective of their political orientation, have chosen to play an active role in their economy (see, for example, Bardhan, 1990). However, the definition of successful intervention is still disputed, although an important lesson from the recent experience of several Asian economies seems to be that governments should make use of market forces in their efforts to influence the direction and character of economic growth: markets and competition need to be retained to discourage wasteful use of resources and to encourage learning and technical advances.

The distinction between good and bad intervention has also been noted in the trade policy debate. For example, Bhagwati (1988) argues that policies based on prescriptions rather than proscriptions generally produce the better economic performance. One reason is that the latter types of intervention tend to stifle initiative and hurt entrepreneurship and growth, whereas the former leave large areas untouched and also allow people to do what is not formally prescribed. Another reason is that proscriptions tend to divert resources into unproductive efforts to evade the rules.

A similar discussion is now emerging in the literature on foreign direct investment and technology transfer. Some of the main host country benefits of FDI are considered to stem from the inflows of new technology to affiliates of multinational firms, since these flows create a potential for technology spillovers to the host country's local firms (Caves, 1974; Globerman, 1979a; Mansfield and Romeo, 1980; Blomström, 1989; Kokko, 1992). What policy measures should host countries adopt to get the MNCs to transfer more technology, and to increase the potential for spillovers? The traditional view has been that different types of regulations are necessary. Many governments have therefore framed the environment within which multinationals operate by introducing various performance requirements for their behaviour. Special attention has been given to policies regarding technology transfer, and a number of measures intended to encourage or force multinational firms to increase their technology transfer have been introduced over the years, including requirements for local content and local R&D.

A different view on how to influence the multinationals' technology transfer has recently been suggested by Wang and Blomström (1992). They develop a theoretical model where the MNC affiliate's decision to import technology is explicitly related to profit maximization – that is, the affiliate imports technology until the marginal revenue of further import is equal to the marginal cost. Technology imports raise revenue (although at a diminishing rate) because the demand for MNC products is positively related to the technological gap between the affiliate and competing host country firms. However, there are also costs involved in each transfer operation (for example, for the training of local workers), and more modern technologies are increasingly expensive to transfer.

The model's implications for host country policies match those from the recent debate on government intervention in the trade literature. For example, Wang and Blomström (1992) point out that technology transfer requirements, which typically increase the affiliates' technology transfer costs, may have perverse effects and reduce technology imports, unless there are strong sanctions for those who do not abide by the rules. They also hypothesize that host country governments may increase the transfer of technology through foreign affiliates by making sure that they are exposed to local competition and by supporting domestic firms in their efforts to learn from the foreigners. Increased competitiveness in local firms means that the technology gap becomes narrower, which reduces the demand for the affiliates' products and gives them a reason to bring in new technology in order to restore their advantages. Analogously, government intervention that reduces the affiliates' transfer costs – for example, education policies that raise the host countries' learning capabilities and improve local labour skills, may encourage higher technology imports. In other words, policies making use of market forces may be preferable to direct intervention in the form of conventional technology transfer and performance requirements.

To the best of our knowledge there is no host government that has tried methodically to encourage foreign affiliates to import technology by using competition and education policies instead of formal requirements, so it is not possible to compare the effects of the various types of policy intervention. However, there is a large variation in requirements, competition, education and other characteristics across host countries, and it should be possible to observe systematic cross-country differences in the affiliates' technology imports, if these characteristics influence the marginal costs and benefits of technology transfer in the way hypothesized by the Wang–Blomström model. In this chapter we shall therefore examine how the technology imports of US majority-owned foreign affiliates in thirty-three host countries are related to proxies for the host countries' requirements, levels of local competition, and learning capabilities.[1] The results are intended to provide some insights about how host countries can persuade foreign-owned multinationals to bring more technology to their affiliates.

The chapter is organized as follows: Section 2 presents data, variables and statistical hypotheses; Section 3 reports the statistical results; and Section 4 summarizes and concludes the chapter.

13.2 Data, variables and statistical hypotheses

Dependent variables: measures of parent–affiliate technology transfers

The transfer of the parent MNC's proprietary technology can take different forms, including technical documentation, education and training of the affiliate's labour force, exchanges of technical personnel, shipments of machinery and equipment, and continuing communication to solve whatever problems occur in the production processes. Each transfer is likely to include several of these modes; yet only a few of the transfer forms are usually recorded. There are reasons to be cautious even when data are available. One problem is that not all parent companies have developed precise methods for pricing the technology that is supplied to affiliates. Another complication has to do with transfer pricing: intra-corporate technology payments are likely instruments for concealing repatriated profits and evading host country taxes, because market prices for the technologies are usually lacking.

The data on technology transfers used in this study are from the US Department of Commerce surveys of *US Direct Investment Abroad*, and refer to the manufacturing operations of majority-owned foreign affiliates (MOFAs) of US multinationals in thirty-three host countries in 1982 (US Department of Commerce, 1985).[2] We shall define several alternative proxies for the affiliates' technology imports, based on data for the US MOFAs' total payments for royalties and licence fees and their imports of capital equipment from the USA. In addition to the possible data problems mentioned above, two additional sources of errors should be noted. The data on the affiliates' royalties and licence payments include payments to non-affiliated persons (although intra-MNCs transactions make up 93 per cent of the total payments), and imports from all US sources are included in the data on capital equipment. The proxies therefore refer to the affiliates' technology imports from all sources rather than to transfers between parents and affiliates.

The total value of the payments for royalties and licence fees (*LICENSE*) by US MOFAs in the manufacturing sector in 1982 was US$ 3051 million. Out of this, US$ 2856 million were accounted for by affiliates in developed countries (including Europe, Canada, Japan, Australia, New Zealand and South Africa) and 195 million by affiliates in developing countries. In the same year, the US MOFAs' imports of capital equipment from the USA (*CAPIMP*) amounted to US$ 1358 million dollars, with US$ 874 million-worth of capital equipment going to developed country affiliates and US$ 484 million to developing countries. These data suggest that imports of capital equipment are the main mode of technology transfer for affiliates in developing countries, whereas affiliates in developed countries rely more on technologies that can be imported in the form of licences. One reason for this pattern may be that technologies embodied in machinery and equipment require less human capital and technical skills – that is, assets that are scarce in developing countries. Another reason may be that the choice between different modes of technology transfer is influenced by national rules for technology transactions. For example, restrictions on payments of royalties and licence fees are more common in developing countries, and may induce the affiliates to focus more on transactions involving capital equipment. It is also possible that the relatively high imports of capital equipment by affiliates in developing countries are a result of transfer pricing – that is, overinvoicing by the US parents. Because of data limitations, we can neither examine the gravity of the problem, nor make any meaningful corrections, but this possible source of error should be kept in mind when interpreting the statistical results.

Table 13.1 presents some rough measures of the 'intensity' of formal technology transfers in some industry and country groups for 1982. The variables *LICENSE/LABOR* and *CAPIMP/LABOR* proxy the technology imports per employee in US MOFAs, and the variables *LICENSE/SALES* and *CAPIMP/SALES* show technology imports as shares of the affiliates' total sales. On average, the payments of royalties and licence fees amounted to about US$ 900 per employee, or 1.1 per cent of the affiliates' sales, while the imports of capital equipment averaged US$ 400 per employee, or 0.5 per cent of sales. However, developing country affiliates spent more on capital equipment imports than on payments of royalties and licence fees. In fact, both *CAPIMP/SALES* and *CAPIMP/LABOR* were higher for

Table 13.1 Measures of US majority-owned foreign affiliates' payments of royalties and licence fees and imports of capital equipment, 1982 (weighted averages)

	License/ Sales	*License/ Labour* (US$)	*CAPIMP/ Sales*	*CAPIMP/ Labour* (US$)
Food products	0.0049	450	0.0020	183
Chemical products	0.0133	1 504	0.0018	197
Metal products	0.0049	334	0.0057	388
Machinery	0.0315	2 890	0.0106	969
Electrical equipment	0.0087	390	0.0055	246
Transport equipment	0.0009	90	0.0058	574
Other manufacturing	0.0118	761	0.0047	300
Total manufacturing	**0.0113**	**909**	**0.0050**	**405**
Total manufacturing, developed countries	**0.0130**	**1 234**	**0.0040**	**378**
Total manufacturing, developing countries	**0.0038**	**187**	**0.0095**	**464**

Source: Calculated from US Department of Commerce (1985), tables III.D.3, III.F.3, III.G.14, and III.H.12.

developing countries than for developed countries. It can be seen from Table 13.1 that the differences between industries are remarkably large for the *LICENSE* variables: the payments range from US\$ 90 per employee (or a tenth of a per cent of the value of sales) in transport equipment to US\$ 2890 per employee (or over 3 per cent of sales) in machinery. The variation in equipment imports is smaller, but still notable.

The cross-country data we shall use for the regression analysis are only available for total manufacturing, because numerous industry-level observations have been suppressed at source for reasons of confidentiality. Yet the large inter-industry differences illustrated by Table 13.1 suggest that the industry distribution of affiliates may show through in the figures for total manufacturing. For example, in Sweden, most US investment is in machinery, which clearly is the most 'licensing-intensive' industry group, and technology payments can be expected to be high for this reason alone. It is even possible that these industry effects dominate other explanations for cross-country differences in technology imports. To get around this problem, we have therefore constructed some alternatives to the simple *LICENSE* measure.

The first of these, termed *LICDIF*, attempts to measure the difference between actual licence payments and what we might 'expect' on the basis of the industry distribution of US MOFAs in each host country. The measure is constructed using data on average licence payments per employee (weighted by employment shares, from Table 13.1) and employment data for US affiliates (from US Department of Commerce, 1985).[3] To get a measure of expected licence payments for each country/industry group, we multiplied the affiliates' employment in each industry in each country by the average licence payment for that industry. An estimate of the total expected licence payment for each host country, taking into account its industry distribution of affiliates, was then obtained by summing across industries for each country. To get the variable *LICDIF*, finally, we subtracted these estimates from the actual licence payments of the host country. In contrast to the ratio of actual licence payments to labour, *LICDIF* is not automatically high if a large share of the country's affiliates are in 'licensing-intensive' industries, since the expected licence payment in this case is also high. Instead, *LICDIF* is hypothesized to be high only when the affiliates import more technology than 'normal'. Measures for *CAPDIF*, the difference between actual and expected imports of capital equipment, were calculated analogously.

The differences between developed and developing countries, in particular for payments of royalties and licence fees, are also strikingly large, as noted above. Differences in industry distribution explain part of this, but there may be other factors that depress the technology flows to developing countries. These include the weaker learning capability of developing countries, weak infrastructure, fragmented markets, political instability and a host of other matters for which we have no comprehensive information. For some of the tests, therefore, we have recalculated the dependent variables with separate expectations for developed and developing countries – in other words, the measures for expected licence payments from developing countries have been based on average licence payments from developing countries only. The resulting variables, which are corrected for both industry distribution and development status, are termed *LICDEV* and *CAPDEV*, and allow us to concentrate more directly on the effects of the host country characteristics for which we have data. All the measures have been scaled in two ways, – that is, divided by the affiliates' sales and employment, to provide several alternative proxies for technological effort. The six versions of the dependent variable are summarized in Table A-13.1.[4]

Explanatory variables: requirements, local competition and learning capability

Levels of economic development, political stability, technology transfer requirements, local competition, learning capability and a host of other characteristics are likely to vary across host countries. We hypothesized in the introduction that it should be possible to observe systematic cross-country differences in the MNC affiliates' technology imports if these host country characteristics influence the marginal costs and benefits of technology transfer, as argued by Wang and Blomström (1992). Since most of these features are difficult to measure empirically, we have restricted our analysis to proxies for three variables – technology transfer and performance requirements, local competition, and local learning capability – but even these suffer from some obvious weaknesses.[5]

First, to measure the host countries' technology transfer and performance requirements, we have calculated two proxies from US Department of Commerce (1985), table II.I.3. The first of these, labelled *TREQS*, focuses directly on technology transfer requirements, and measures the share of US affiliates in each host country in

1982 that were reported to operate under requirements to use the most advanced technology available, perform R&D locally, have access to the US parent's patents, or transfer skills to local personnel. We hypothesize that these requirements increase the affiliates' technology transfer costs, and we therefore expect *TREQS* to have a negative impact on the affiliates' imports of technology. However, the impact may not be very significant, for several reasons. Although the requirements captured by *TREQS* typically increase transfer costs, it is likely that they are sometimes backed up by strong sanctions, so that only the firms that in fact transfer significant quantities of technology are allowed to stay in operation. The effects of the requirements may sometimes be insignificant because many of the rules are ambiguous: the affiliate decides which technologies are viable; there may not be any direct connection between R&D and imports of new technology; and access to the parent's patents does not necessarily ensure transfer of technology. Most importantly, high levels of *TREQS* may sometimes be motivated by low imports of technology.

The alternative proxy *PREQS* reflects the share of affiliates that faced various quantitative performance requirements in 1982 (including import restrictions, minimum local content, and minimum local employment requirements). These requirements are likely to increase the costs of importing and using advanced technologies, and we hypothesize that *PREQS* will have a negative impact on technology transfer. It is possible that *PREQS* avoids some of the problems afflicting *TREQS*, and it may therefore be more suitable for our present purposes. One of its advantages is that the quantitative requirements reflected by *PREQS* are less ambiguous and easier to uphold than those included in *TREQS*; another is that local content requirements are typically not motivated by worries about low technology inflows to the affiliates of foreign MNCs, but rather by concerns about the employment and balance-of-payments effects of FDI.

Both *TREQS* and *PREQS* cover all non-bank affiliates of US parents with more than 10 per cent US ownership, rather than only the majority-owned affiliates included in the measures of technology imports. The general pattern, with Organization for Economic Cooperation and Development (OECD) countries and some South-East Asian economies registering the lowest formal requirements, and Latin-American and South Asian nations exhibiting the highest ones, is the one we would also expect for more comprehensive measures of technology transfer requirements.[6]

We have proxied local competition with two alternative measures of investment intensity in the host economy. The assumption is that investment reflects either new entrants into industry, or an upgrading of the technological level of existing firms, both of which increase competition and reduce the technology gap between the affiliate and local firms. The variables are *INV/OUTPUT* (the gross fixed capital formation/gross output ratio) and *INV/EMPL* (gross fixed capital formation per employee), and both cover the host countries' entire manufacturing sectors, excluding the US affiliates. They are based on data from various issues of the United Nations' *Industrial Statistics Yearbook* (united Nations, various years), and for the *INV/EMPL* variable, capital formation figures have been converted from local currency to US dollars and corrected for international differences in capital goods prices using data from Summers and Heston (1988). Investment by multinationals from countries other than the USA has not been subtracted, which means that 'local competitors' are defined as all non-US actors in the host country market, including MNC affiliates from other countries.[7] *INV/OUTPUT* and *INV/EMPL* are used interchangeably in the estimations: the variables provide alternative, although related, measures of competition, as seen by the simple correlation of about 0.5 (see Table A-13.2). The hypothesis from the theoretical model is that local competition reduces the technology gap and the demand for the affiliates' products, and increases the marginal revenue of further technology transfer. Hence, we expect the affiliates' technology imports to be positively related to our proxies for local competition.

To account for the cross-country differences in learning capabilities and labour skills, we use the variables *ED2ND* and *ED3RD*. They measure the share of the appropriate age-group in secondary and third-level education in each host country in 1980, and are taken from UNESCO's *Statistical Yearbook 1990* (UNESCO, 1990), table 3.2.[8] We expect both variables to have a positive influence on the affiliates' technology imports, because the marginal technology transfer costs are lower when the level of education is higher. However, it should be noted here that the small variance in *ED2ND* is likely to reduce its observed significance.

13.3   Statistical results

Payments for royalties and licence fees by MNC affiliates

The results of OLS estimations of the US MOFAs' licence payments are reported in Table 13.2. The dependent variables in equations (1)

Table 13.2   Results of OLS estimations: payments of royalties and license fees by affiliates, 1982[a]

Equation	Constant	*INV /EMPL*	*INV/ Output*	*PREQS*	*ED3RD*	$\bar{R}^2$	F	N
License/ Labour (1)	0.0907 (0.161)	0.9446 (3.099)***	– –	–0.5075 (2.575)**	0.6536 (1.695)	0.445	9.55	33
License/ Sales (2)	0.2016 (0.402)	– –	0.9250 (2.587)**	–0.5444 (3.140)***	0.4178 (1.375)	0.348	6.51	32
LICDIF/ Labour (3)	0.2058 (0.559)	0.6335 (3.178)***	– –	–0.3392 (2.632)**	0.4999 (1.982)*	0.477	10.71	33
LICDIF/ Sales (4)	0.7743 (5.080)***	– –	0.1610 (1.481)	–0.1512 (2.869)***	0.2158 (2.336)**	0.382	7.40	32
LICDEV/ Labour (5)	0.4102 (1.372)	0.4630 (2.858)***	– –	–0.0995 (0.950)	0.2263 (1.104)	0.252	4.59	33
LICDEV/ Sales (6)	0.4758 (1.971)*	– –	0.4249 (2.468)**	–0.1364 (1.634)	0.2356 (1.611)	0.223	3.96	32

Notes: a   All variables appearing in the regression equations are scaled by division with the sample means. Estimated coefficients are shown together with the absolute value of the t-statistic in parentheses. For definitions of variables and data sources, see Table A-13.1. *, ** and *** indicate significance at the 10, 5 and 1 per cent levels of confidence (two-tailed tests).

and (2) are based on the observed licence payments (*LICENSE*); equations (3) and (4) refer to variables that are adjusted for the industry distribution of affiliates (*LICDIF*); and those in equations (5) and (6) have also been adjusted for the host countries' development levels (*LICDEV*).

Looking first at the estimations with *LICENSE*, we find that our proxies for local competition and education are positively related to the affiliates' licence payments, whereas the effect of requirements seems to be negative. The coefficients for the two variants of the local competition proxy, *INV/EMPL* and *INV/OUTPUT*, are both highly significant, but the former performs better in terms of R^2. This holds for the other equations as well, and the reason is probably that *INV/EMPL* captures some of the differences between the countries' capital intensities: high rates of gross investment per employee are likely to be connected to high capital–labour ratios (simply because much capital must be replaced in every period), and also to high levels of technical skill that facilitate the affiliates' technology imports.

The coefficients for the requirement proxies *TREQS* and *PREQS* are both negative, but *TREQS* is seldom significantly different from zero, and it is therefore not shown in the table. This may suggest that the requirements captured by *TREQS* may sometimes include rules that force the affiliates to import technology irrespective of the costs, or that *TREQS* has little effect on the affiliates' costs of importing technology, as discussed earlier. Both *ED2ND* and *ED3RD* have the expected positive coefficients, but they are not highly significant.

However, it is difficult to draw firm conclusions from the results for *LICENSE*, although they seem to confirm some of our hypotheses. As discussed earlier, the cross-country differences in licensing intensity may be caused mainly by differences in the industry distribution of affiliates, and not by our explanatory variables. The observed effects of competition, education and requirements may therefore be related to decisions about industry localization rather than to the determinants of the affiliates' technology imports.

In equations (3) and (4) in Table 13.2, an attempt has been made to account for the cross-country differences in the industry distribution of affiliates. The explanatory power of the equations improves somewhat, and the coefficient for *ED3RD* becomes significant. However, *INV/OUTPUT* loses its significance. A possible reason for this is that the licence payments from developed and developing countries differ so much that local competition alone, as proxied by *INV/OUTPUT*, cannot explain the pattern. *INV/EMPL* contains some information about capital intensities, and may be more significant for that reason.

The major result of the crude adjustment for development levels in the variable *LICDEV* is that *INV/OUTPUT* becomes more efficient, whereas the estimated coefficients of *PREQS* and *ED3RD* become less significant, although their signs remain as expected. In equation (5) in Table 13.2, the coefficient of *INV/EMPL* is significant at the 1 per cent level, whereas those for *PREQS* and *ED3RD* are not significantly different from zero. In equation (6), the coefficient of the alternative competition proxy *INV/OUTPUT* is significant at the 5 per cent level, but the confidence levels for requirements and education are below 10 per cent. The reason why the proxies for education and requirements are not significant in these two equations is probably that their effects have already been captured by the adjustment for development levels in the dependent variable.

Summing up these results, there is fair support for the hypotheses that the affiliates' technology payments are positively related to the host countries' domestic investment levels and education levels, but negatively related to various performance requirements.

Imports of capital equipment by MNC affiliates

Before discussing the determinants of the affiliates' capital imports, it is necessary to make some additional comments on the relationship between imports of capital equipment and technology transfer in general. We already noted that affiliates in developing countries seem to prefer imports of capital equipment over imports of disembodied technologies – some possible reasons are that technologies embodied in machinery may require less human capital, which is scarce in developing countries, and that payments for capital equipment are seldom subject to the types of restriction that regulate payments of royalties and licence fees in many developing countries. These arguments imply that there may be some substitution between different modes of technology transfer, and that the effects of education and technology transfer requirements on the variable *CAPIMP* may be more complicated than those for *LICENSE*. For example, we have hypothesized that higher learning capability and labour quality in a host country encourage the foreign affiliates operating there to import more technology. However, these technology flows may not always occur as increased imports of capital equipment. A higher level of education may sometimes mean that it is easier to find local suppliers of advanced machinery and equipment – so that the needed machine technology can be imported in the form of blueprints – and *CAPIMP* may remain low although technology transfers in general are high. Similarly, low levels of education and relatively high imports of capital equipment may sometimes coincide if there are no local suppliers of machinery and all equipment has to be imported. This suggests a more complex case, with several effects pulling in different directions.

There are similar caveats also concerning the effects of technology transfer and performance requirements. Most technology transfer requirements aim to control the transfer of disembodied technology – for example, by demanding special training of the local labour force, and performance requirements are often initiated to reach some target level of local content or to restrict imports of intermediary goods for macroeconomic reasons. It is not clear whether these rules have any major effects on imports of machinery and equipment.

Table 13.3 presents some of the estimations for imports of capital equipment by US MOFAs. The dependent variables in equations (7) and (8) are based on the directly observable data for the affiliates' imports of capital equipment (*CAPIMP*), but has been adjusted for the industry mix of the affiliates operating in the host country in equation (9) (*CAPDIF*), and also for the host country's development level in equation (10) (*CAPDEV*). The results are weaker than those for the licence measures – most notably, R^2 is significantly lower – but the positive coefficient of local investment remains significant at the 10 per cent level for all variants of the equation. The coefficient of *PREQS* is positive in all estimations, although never significant. The signs of the coefficients of *TREQS* and the education proxies vary, but none of them is significantly different from zero.[9] Furthermore, there are only small differences between equation (7) and equations (9) and (10), which suggests that neither the industry distribution of affiliates nor the development level of the host country have any unambiguous impact on the affiliates' imports of capital equipment.

Thus there is some evidence that investment by local competitors may force the affiliates to higher imports of the kind of technology that is embodied in capital goods. The costs posed by the host

Table 13.3   Results of OLS estimations: imports of capital equipment from the USA by affiliates, 1982[a]

Equation	Constant	INV/ EMPL	INV/ OUTPUT	PREQS	ED3RD	$\bar{R}^2$	F	N
CAPIMP/ Labor (7)	0.1514 (0.288)	0.6329 (2.154)**	– –	0.1867 (0.947)	0.0289 (0.081)	0.081	1.88	31
CAPIMP/ Sales (8)	0.3995 (0.558)	– –	0.9594 (1.840)*	0.0566 (0.214)	–0.4154 (0.979)	0.084	1.88	30
CAPDIF/ Labor (9)	0.2277 (0.453)	0.5391 (1.919)*	– –	0.2623 (1.391)	–0.0291 (0.086)	0.082	1.90	31
CAPDEV/ Labor (10)	0.2393 (0.469)	0.5107 (1.792)*	– –	0.1407 (0.736)	0.1093 (0.317)	0.034	1.35	31

Notes: a   All variables appearing in the regression equations are scaled by division with the sample means. Estimated coefficients are shown together with the absolute value of the t-statistic in parentheses. For definitions of variables and data sources, see Table A-13.1.
* and **   indicate significance at the 10 and 5 per cent levels of confidence (two-tailed tests).

countries' performance and technology transfer requirements do not seem to discourage imports of capital equipment – if anything, there is a slight positive effect of requirements, that perhaps reflects the preference to import more embodied technology when the costs for other transfer modes are high. Differences in the level of education do not have any determinate effects on the imports of capital equipment. As discussed above, the reason may be that variations in the level of education are related to two opposite effects: the negative relationship between education and technology transfer costs may be balanced by a positive relationship between education and the availability of locally-produced capital equipment. Yet the weak fit of the model suggests that we have omitted some important determinants of affiliates' capital equipment imports, or that our proxies are weak measures of the affiliates' technology imports, because of transfer pricing or other data errors. In either case, it is clear that more detailed analyses of intra-MNC trade in machinery and equipment are necessary.

13.4   Concluding remarks

The purpose of this study has been to determine whether host countries aiming to maximize the inflows of technology through foreign multinationals have viable policy alternatives to formal technology transfer requirements. On the basis of a simple theoretical model of technology transfer, proposed by Wang and Blomström (1992), we hypothesized that policies making use of market forces may be preferable to conventional technology transfer requirements. For example, policies increasing the level of competition in the host country may erode the MNC affiliate's technological advantages, and force it to import new technology from its parent. Similarly, policies improving local learning capability and labour skills may reduce technology transfer costs and encourage imports of technology.

To test these hypotheses, we examined how cross-country differences in the technology imports of US affiliates in thirty-three host countries (calculated from data on the affiliates' payments for royalties and licence fees and their imports of capital equipment from the USA in 1982) were related to proxies for technology transfer requirements, local competition, and labour skills in the host countries. The results consistently showed that the technology imports of MNC affiliates increased with our proxies for the competitive pressure in the host economy. The technology transfers that were reflected by data on payments of royalties and licence fees were negatively related to performance requirements, but the requirements did not have any clear effect on imports of technologies embodied in machinery and equipment. Moreover, the host countries' levels of education seemed to have a positive impact on the affiliates' payments of royalties and licence fees, but no significant effect on the affiliates' imports of capital equipment.

A policy conclusion of these findings is that host country governments may choose to support local investment, competition and education rather than to rely on controls and direct supervision of FDI to secure inflows of technology to the affiliates of foreign MNCs. This conclusion applies in particular to flows of disembodied technologies that are reflected by the affiliates' payments of royalties and licence fees. One problem, of course, is that some of these policies – especially those that promote competition – may be contrary to measures commonly used by host countries to attract new MNCs – for example, import protection. In practice, it may therefore be necessary to weigh the benefits from larger inflows of technology to already present MNC affiliates against the possible costs in terms of forgone new investment from abroad.

Notes

1.   Several empirical studies have already recognized that some of these variables have an impact on technology transfer, but no comprehensive analyses have been published. For example, McFetridge (1987) has noted the negative impact of various requirements on the multinationals' technology transfer activities. Lake (1979) and our study in Chapter 14 demonstrate the positive effect of competition on technology transfer and diffusion, and Teece (1976) has shown that technology transfer costs are negatively related to the host country's level of education and labour skills.

2.   The surveys cover affiliates in about fifty individual countries, and the data are presented for aggregate manufacturing and seven broad industry groups. Gaps in the data have forced us to exclude many countries, and those remaining for the tests are Australia, Austria, Belgium, Canada, Chile, Colombia, Denmark, Ecuador, France, West Germany, Greece, Hong Kong, India, Indonesia, Ireland, Italy, Japan, Luxembourg, Malaysia, The Netherlands, New Zealand, Norway, Panama, Peru, The Philippines, Portugal, Singapore, South Korea, Spain, Sweden, Turkey, the United Kingdom, and Venezuela. Some estimations cover fewer countries because of missing observations.

3.   It was not possible to calculate *unweighted* average licence payments because of the many missing country/industry observations.

4. Technology transfer could also have been proxied with data on the affiliates' R&D expenditure, since local R&D often requires imports of technology and skills from the parent company. However, in Chapter 5 we showed that the size and income level of the host economy are the only host country characteristics that influence this proxy significantly, and we have therefore not included it among our dependent variables.

5. Some other factors influencing technology transfer costs and technology imports have been discussed in the literature. For example, Katrak (1991) argues that affiliates are likely to use more capital-intensive technologies if there are minimum-wage laws that cause wage rates to exceed the market equilibrium rates, or if over-valued exchange rates subsidize the use of imported equipment and intermediaries. We have not included these in the analysis for lack of appropriate data.

6. The well-known Decision 24 of the Andean Investment Code, instituted in 1970/71, prohibited payments of royalties and licence fees from wholly-owned affiliates to parents. If implemented strictly, this rule would have meant that the *LICENSE* variable was equal to zero for Bolivia, Colombia, Ecuador, Peru and Venezuela. However, the number of exceptions has been large, and there does not seem to be any significant differences in the use of royalties and licence fees between these countries and the rest of Latin America in the early 1980s; see Grosse (1989), pp. 113–31.

7. Our results may therefore capture some of the international competition between multinationals from different countries; see, for example, Graham (1991) and Sölvell (1987).

8. *ED2ND* and *ED3RD* measure levels of education in 1980, since data for 1982 were not available for all countries.

9. We also tested our regression model for a dependent variable constructed as the sum of *CAPIMP* and *LICENSE*, to examine how the differences in the 'aggregate' technology imports of US affiliates can be explained. The estimated equation (for the thirty-one countries where data were available), with the dependent variable Y defined as the ratio $(CAPIMP + LICENSE) / LABOR$, and with t-statistics in parentheses, is:

$$Y = -0.07 + 1.00 \; INV/EMPL - 0.32 \; PREQS + 0.38 \; ED3RD$$
$$(0.18) \quad (4.72)^{***} \qquad (2.22)^{**} \qquad (1.50)$$

It can be seen that the impact of local competition (as measured by *INV/EMPL*) appears to be even more significant here than in any of the other estimations. The negative coefficient of *PREQS* is also significant, but that of *ED3RD* is not, although it has the expected positive sign. Moreover, there are notable improvements in the overall fit of the equation: R^2 increases to 0.55, and the F-value to 13.47.

Appendix

Table A-13.1 List of variables and data sources

Dependent variables: proxies for the technology imports of US MOFAs

LICENSE	Payments of royalties and licence fees to the USA by US MOFAs in host country *i*, 1982
LICDIF	Difference between *LICENSE* and expected licence payments, defined for each country *i* as: $LICENSE_i - \Sigma_j (LABOR_{ij}* AVELIC_j)$, where $LABOR_{ij}$ is the employment in country *i*'s industry *j* and $AVELIC_j$ is the unweighted average licence payment per employee in industry *j*, $\Sigma_i LICENSE_{ij}/\Sigma_i EMPL_{ij}$
LICDEV	As *LICDIF*, but *AVELIC* calculated separately for developed and developing countries
CAPIMP	Imports of capital equipment from the USA by US MOFAs in host country *i*, 1982
CAPDIF	Difference between *CAPIMP* and expected imports of capital equipment, calculated as *LICDIF*
CAPDEV	As *CAPDIF*, but average capital imports calculated separately for developed and developing countries

Independent variables

INV/EMPL	Gross fixed investment per employee in each host country's manufacturing sector 1982 (excluding US MOFAs), corrected for international price differences for capital goods. Proxy for local competition (*Industrial Statistics Yearbook*, various; Summers and Heston, 1988)
INV/OUTPUT	Ratio of gross fixed investment to gross output in each host country's manufacturing sector 1982 (excluding US MOFAs). Proxy for local competition (*Industrial Statistics Yearbook*, various)
TREQS	Share of US affiliates in each host country facing various technology transfer requirements 1982 (US Department of Commerce, 1985)
PREQS	Share of US affiliates in each host country facing various performance requirements 1982 (US Department of Commerce, 1985)
ED2ND	Percentage of age group (13–18) in secondary level education (1980) in each host country. Proxy for labour skills (UNESCO, 1990)
ED3RD	Percentage of age group (18–24) in third-level education (1980) in each host country. Proxy for labour skills (UNESCO, 1990)

Source: Basic data from US Department of Commerce, 1985. Data sources in parentheses in table.

Table A-13.2   Simple correlation coefficients for independent variables[a]

	INV/EMPL	INV/OUTPUT	ED2ND	ED3RD	PREQS	TREQS
INV/EMPL	1.00					
INV/OUTPUT	0.52	1.00				
ED2ND	0.12	−0.33	1.00			
ED3RD	0.20	−0.08	0.67	1.00		
PREQS	−0.04	0.36	−0.75	−0.39	1.00	
TREQS	−0.06	0.55	−0.64	−0.49	0.52	1.00

Notes: [a]   There are 33 observations for all variables except *INV/OUTPUT* (N = 32). For data sources and definitions of variables, see Table A-13.1.

14
Host Country Competition, Labour Skills, and Technology Transfer by Multinationals

14.1 Introduction

In Chapter 13, we examined aggregated data on the technology imports of US affiliates in thirty-three host countries, and found some weak support for the hypotheses proposed by Wang and Blomström (1992). Our results showed that the affiliates' technology imports were positively related to the income level of the host country and (crude proxies for) the competitive pressure in the host economy, but negatively related to the level of distortions and various host country performance requirements. In this chapter, we use more detailed data from a single host country, Mexico, to analyze how the technology imports of foreign firms are related to various industry characteristics. We are particularly interested in the hypotheses that market rivalry and availability of skilled labour may encourage the multinationals to bring more technology to their foreign operations.[1]

The chapter is organized as follows: Section 2 describes the data and introduces our empirical model; Section 3 reports the statistical results; and Section 4 presents the conclusions.

14.2 Data, definition of variables and statistical model

The data for this study are taken from unpublished worksheets provided by the Dirección de Estadísticas de la Secretaría de Industria y Comercio in Mexico, collected in connection with the Mexican Census of Manufactures, and refer to industry characteristics and operations in 1970 and 1975. Some supplementary information has been taken

221

from US Department of Commerce (1985). The Mexican data are gathered at the plant level, and aggregated into 230 4-digit manufacturing industries in 1970, and 235 industries in 1975. The change in the classification system between 1970 and 1975 (and missing information for some of the variables) has forced us to drop a number of industry observations from the estimations (more specifically, all 4-digit industries that were divided into two or more classes in 1975 were excluded, as were all industries without foreign firms). Consequently, the sample includes 144 4-digit industries.

For these industries we have information on capital stocks, employment, wages, gross output, payments for imported patents, trade marks, and technical assistance, advertising expenditures, and shares of white-collar and blue-collar workers. Apart from the last two characteristics, the data are available separately for foreign and domestic firms. A plant is included in the foreign category if 15 per cent or more of its shares are owned by foreigners. (Thus we are not able to separate between joint ventures and majority-owned foreign affiliates.) The category 'domestic firms' includes private as well as state-owned plants.[2] The data from the US Department of Commerce surveys of US FDI refer to the average licence payments per employee in the world-wide operations of US affiliates in 1982.

Using these data, we can now formulate a statistical model to test the hypotheses that the availability of skilled labour and local competition encourage foreign firms to import technology. We shall use data on the foreign firms' technology payments abroad to construct a proxy for their total technology imports, which makes up our dependent variable. Data on the share of white-collar employees in the industry's labour force or the wage payments by foreign firms will approximate the availability of skilled labour. Growth rates of domestic firms' output, capital stocks and market shares serve as crude proxies for local competition. In addition to these factors, we need to control for the variation in technology imports that stems from basic differences in technology: data on the domestic firms' technology payments, the average licence payments in US industries, and the advertising expenditures of Mexican industries are used for this purpose.

Equation (14.1) summarizes the function we shall estimate and the expected effects (with *SKILL* and *COMP* denoting several alternative proxies for the availability of skilled labour and the level of local competition), while the following paragraphs define the variables in closer detail:

$$PAT^f = f(PAT^d, USLIC, ADV, SKILL, COMP)$$
$$(+)\qquad (+)\qquad (+)\qquad (+)\qquad (+) \qquad\qquad (14.1)$$

The dependent variable, PAT^f, measures the foreign firms' average payments per employee for imported patents, trade marks, and technical assistance in 1975. This measure underestimates the affiliates' true technology imports, since much technology is transferred through machinery, equipment and personnel, but we assume that it is an accurate reflection of the imports of disembodied technology. A problem is that the proxy may capture some degree of transfer pricing activities if foreign parents over-invoice the technology transactions with affiliates – because of data limitations, we can neither examine the gravity of the problem, nor make any meaningful corrections.

PAT^d is the corresponding measure for domestic firms, and it is included as a control variable to account for the industry-specific variation in the imports of disembodied technology: some industries are more dependent on imported patents, trade marks and technical assistance because of the industry's technological characteristics, irrespective of the level of competition or labour skills in the host country. The assumption is that the patent payments of the local firms reflect these features, so its expected effect is positive.

An alternative proxy for these industry characteristics is $USLIC$. It measures the average patent and licence payments per employee of all foreign affiliates of US MNCs in 1982, and it has an expected positive impact on PAT^f. However, the US data are not available at the 4-digit level of aggregation, so the Mexican industries have been classified into sixteen groups depending on the size of the average patent payments in corresponding US 2-digit industries. Hence there is reason to be cautious with the interpretation of the results. A further problem with the variable is that it was not possible to find US 2-digit equivalents for all Mexican industries, because of the differences in the national classification schemes, so $USLIC$ is defined only for 142 of the industries in the sample. It is nevertheless interesting to use $USLIC$ in some estimations: when it is included, PAT^d can be interpreted as a proxy for local competition, rather than a control variable.

A third control variable is ADV, which measures the ratio of each industry's advertising expenditures to gross output in 1970 (data for 1975 were not available). It is intended to account for the cases where trade marks are commonly used, and where the PAT^f variable can be expected to be high for that reason alone.

LQ, labour quality, is our first proxy for the availability of skilled labour. It measures the ratio of white-collar to blue-collar workers in each Mexican industry 1970 (1975 data were not available) and assumes that the share of white-collar workers reflects some of the labour skills that are needed to use the types of disembodied technologies in question. The higher the level of labour skills, the lower the costs for transferring and adapting technology: hence, the expected effect is positive. $WAGE^f$, the ratio of the foreign firms' wage payments to their employment in 1970, is an alternative proxy for labour skills: the underlying assumption is that labour with more advanced skills earns higher wages. However, wage rates are highly correlated with capital–labour ratios, so we run the risk of capturing spurious correlations between capital intensities and technology payments when this variable is used.

Our first proxy for local competition is termed ΔK^d, and it measures the relative increase (as a percentage of the 1970 value) in the real capital stock of domestic firms between 1970 and 1975. The hypothesis is that industries with higher rates of domestic investment during the period have become more competitive. One reason may be that a larger share of the total capital stock in these industries is made up of 'new' and more efficient vintages of machinery and equipment. High investment figures may also signal the entry of many new local firms into the industry, and/or rapid growth in the size of existing firms: both of these circumstances are likely to translate into more intensive competition.[3]

Our second proxy for local competition, ΔGO^d, measures the percentage increase in real gross output in domestic firms in the 1970–5 period.[4] As above, we assume that industries where local output increases faster are also those where competition is becoming tougher – what separates this variable from ΔK^d is that it also reflects the efficiency of investment.

One of the shortcomings of both proxies is that shifts in demand may stimulate investment and output in some sectors, so that both ΔK^d and ΔGO^d increase, although the level of competition remains unchanged.[5] We have therefore included a measure of the change in the domestic firms' market share, ΔMS^d, as a third proxy for competition. The assumption is that increases in the local firms' market shares reveal that the competition facing foreign affiliates is becoming stiffer. Yet it should be noted that this is also a crude measure, since the observed changes in market shares may fail to reflect the true extent of competition in the market place. For instance, ΔMS^d will remain low if the MNC affiliates are able to respond successfully to local challenges and hold on to their market shares – for example, by upgrading their technology and productivity.[6]

All the variables used in the estimations are normalized by division with the sample means, the variable definitions are summarized in Table A-14.1, and Table A-14.2 presents simple correlations between the independent variables.

14.4   Statistical results

Table 14.1 reports some of our estimation results. We have used ordinary least squares to estimate linear, additive versions of the different variants of our regression model. Regression equations in columns (1), (2) and (4) refer to the full sample of 144 industries, whereas the equations in columns (3) and (5) cover fewer observations because of missing values for the variables ΔMS^d and $USLIC$. The estimation results provide strong support for the hypotheses regarding the foreign firms' technology imports that were summarized in Equation (14.1) above. All coefficient estimates have the expected signs, the model appears to explain nearly half of the variation in the dependent variable, and the significance levels for most estimates are high.

Regression equations in columns (1), (2) and (3) estimate our basic model, where PAT^d and ADV are included to control for the industry-specific variation in the use of foreign patents and trade marks; LQ accounts for the effects of differences in availability of skilled labour; and ΔK^d, ΔGO^d and ΔMS^d are used as proxies for local competition. There are only small differences in the estimates between the regression equations, and both labour quality and local competition appear to have significant positive effects. The high positive correlation between the competition proxies (particularly ΔK^d and ΔMS^d) and PAT^d may disturb the results (see Table A-14.2), but we believe that multicollinearity is a minor problem, since small random changes in the sample size have little effect on the coefficient estimates.

In the regression equation in column (4), we have included the variable $WAGE^f$ instead of LQ, as a proxy for the availability of labour skills, without any significant changes in the results. All the alternative

Table 14.1   Results of OLS regressions: payments to countries abroad for patents fees, trade marks and technical assistance by foreign firms in Mexican manufacturing industries, 1975

	(1)	(2)	(3)	(4)	(5)
Constant	−0.147	−0.183	−0.212	−0.175	−0.259
	(0.88)	(1.06)	(1.10)	(0.88)	(1.46)
PAT^d	0.119	0.147	0.159	0.110	0.124
	(2.50)**	(3.11)***	(2.94)***	(2.24)**	(2.61)**
$USLIC$	–	–	–	–	0.179
	–	–	–	–	(1.79)*
ADV	0.126	0.237	0.207	0.174	0.121
	(1.77)*	(3.25)***	(2.59)**	(2.45)**	(1.72)*
LQ	0.611	0.555	0.643	–	0.537
	(4.36)***	(3.86)***	(4.11)***	–	(3.61)***
$WAGE^f$	–	–	–	0.606	–
	–	–	–	(3.41)***	–
ΔK^d	0.292	–	–	0.285	0.298
	(6.07)***	–	–	(5.78)***	(6.18)***
ΔGO^d	–	0.242	–	–	–
	–	(5.35)***	–	–	–
ΔMS^d	–	–	0.204	–	–
	–	–	(3.47)***	–	–
Adj. R^2	0.45	0.43	0.38	0.43	0.46
F-value	30.50	27.46	21.11	27.44	25.33
N	144	144	132	144	142

Notes: The dependent variable is PAT^f. All variables are normalized by division with the sample means. Estimated coefficients are shown together with the absolute value of the t-statistics in parentheses. *, ** and ***   denote significance at the 10, 5 and 1 per cent levels of confidence (two-tailed tests). For definitions of variables, see Table A-14.1.

competition proxies yield similar results, and therefore only the function with ΔK^d is shown in the table.

The equation in column (5) introduces $USLIC$ as a control variable for the industries where disembodied technology is used more frequently. This allows us to interpret PAT^d as an additional proxy for local competition: the hypothesis is that it may mark industries where local firms are particularly active in importing technology, and where foreign firms are also forced to innovate and import technology in order to retain their market shares. $USLIC$ appears to have the expected positive impact, and both PAT^d and the other proxies for local competition (only ΔK^d is shown in the table) have significant positive effects. In other words, the equation in column (5) offers some additional support to the hypothesis that local competition matters.

The results (especially using ΔK^d as a proxy for local competition) are robust to small changes in the sample, but we have also estimated the model for different groups of industries.[7] The reason is that the relationships between foreign and local firms may differ between industries, depending on product and technology characteristics. For example, it is possible that local competition (as we have defined it) is a more important determinant of the affiliates' decisions in industries where technology is simpler and more accessible for local firms. We have therefore divided the industries into three groups according to product characteristics – that is, consumer goods, intermediates, and durables and capital goods. The barriers to entry in the form of capital requirements are highest in the durable and capital goods industries, and it also seems reasonable to assume that these industries employ more advanced technologies.

Table 14.2 shows the results of some of our estimations for the three industry groups. Only equations using ΔK^d as a proxy for local competition are shown, since the alternative variables yield very similar results. The main finding is that the estimated effects of both local competition and education are significant in the consumer and intermediate goods industries (equations in columns (6) and (7)), but only education has a significant impact in the durable and capital goods industries (equation in column (8)). One possible interpretation of the lack of significance for the local competition proxy in the equation in column (8) is that it is more difficult for local Mexican firms to put pressure on foreign-owned multinationals in durable and capital-goods industries, because the minimum technology levels are harder to reach. The large estimated effect for labour quality in the durable and capital goods industries may also imply that access to skilled labour is more important the more advanced the technology, but the small sample size precludes more reliable conclusions.

14.4   Concluding comments

Although there appears to be a wide consensus that multinationals may act as an important bridge between advanced and less advanced countries in the geographical diffusion of technology, there seems to be less agreement on what policy measures countries hosting

Table 14.2   Results of OLS regressions: payments to countries abroad for patents fees, trade marks and technical assistance by foreign firms in Mexican manufacturing industries, 1975, by product groups

	Consumer goods (6)	Intermediate goods (7)	Durables and capital goods (8)
Constant	−0.133	−0.231	0.061
	(0.55)	(0.84)	(0.14)
PAT^d	0.144	0.034	−0.170
	(1.98)*	(0.39)	(0.79)
ADV	0.240	−0.028	−0.206
	(1.83)*	(0.30)	(1.90)*
LQ	0.471	0.979	0.957
	(2.59)**	(3.94)***	(2.27)**
ΔK^d	0.277	0.246	0.358
	(3.87)***	(3.56)***	(1.62)
Adj. R^2	0.47	0.39	0.15
F-value	16.09	8.84	2.05
N	68	51	25

Notes: The dependent variable is PAT^f. All variables are normalized by division with the sample means. Estimated coefficients are shown together with the absolute value of the t-statistics in parentheses. *, ** and ***   denote significance at the 10, 5 and 1 per cent levels of confidence (two-tailed tests). For definitions of variables, see Table A-14.1.

multinationals should adopt to get these firms to transfer more (and more advanced) technologies.

In this chapter, we have employed detailed (unpublished) data from Mexican manufacturing industries to examine some determinants of the technology imports of the foreign MNCs operating there in 1975. Departing from a theoretical framework suggested by Wang and Blomström (1992), we specified an empirical model where the foreign affiliates' technology imports were related to proxies for local competition, availability of skilled labour, and other industry characteristics. The results of our OLS estimations show that there is a statistically significant positive association between the technology imports of foreign affiliates and local competitors' investment and output growth. Moreover, the level of technology imports is positively correlated with our proxy for labour skills in the affiliates' industries. The effects of the competition proxies are particularly strong for consumer goods and intermediates, which suggests that foreign multinationals are especially sensitive to the local market environment when barriers to entry in the form of advanced technology or high capital requirements are relatively low.

The analysis leads us to conclude that government policies aiming to create a competitive climate and improve labour quality may indeed be relevant alternatives to the formal requirements that have often been used to promote inflows of modern technology. However, the technology policies of many countries still focus on administrative controls and direct technology transfer requirements, rather than market conditions.

Notes

1. The effects of local competition are most likely to concern foreign affiliates producing for the host country's local market, whereas the technology imports of export-orientated affiliates are probably determined by other factors. This distinction is not a major problem in the Mexican case, since the foreign multinationals were heavily orientated towards the local market during the period in study, as shown by, for example, Peres Nuñez (1990) and Fajnzylber and Martínez Tarragó (1976).
2. The 1970 data are available separately for private and state-owned Mexican firms, but the two groups are merged here, because the 1975 data do not make this distinction.
3. It should be noted that the capital stock data for 1970 and 1975 are not directly comparable. The 1970 data for local firms are defined as *capital invertido*, which is the book value of net property, plant and equipment plus intangible capital; for 1975, local capital stock is defined as *activos fijos brutos*, which is the gross value of property, plant and equipment. We have therefore made some transformations of the 1975 data. The 1970 database includes both variants of the capital stock for industry totals, and we calculated industry-specific ratios between the two measures. These were then used to transform the *activos fijos* data for 1975 into *capital invertido* proxies, which were deflated using the wholesale price index. There is a significant absolute difference between the two measures, but there is also a high simple correlation between them, at about 0.9. Hence the regression results are similar for both proxies.
4. We have used industry-specific price indices rather than the wholesale price index to deflate the 1975 data for gross output, but the choice of deflator does not have any significant impact on the regression results.
5. However, the correlation between gross output per industry in 1970 and gross output per industry in 1975 is above 0.95, which suggests that there have only been small shifts in demand between industries.
6. Competition is inherently difficult to measure in aggregate cross-section studies of this type, and we have therefore tested several additional variables – for example, measures of changes in productivity and capital intensity in local firms. The results did not differ much from those presented in Tables 14.1 and 14.2. Other possible proxies for competition focus on changes in concentration and market structure, but we could not find any significant effects of these in the Mexican data. One

possible reason is that the concentration measures in small economies such as Mexico reflect economies of scale and specialization rather than competition and the market power of large firms (Blomström, 1989).

7. The significance levels for the estimated effects of ΔGO^d and ΔMS^d fall when the observations with the highest increases in local output and local market shares are dropped, but the changes in the size of the coefficient are small.

Appendix

Table A-14.1   Definitions of variables

Dependent variables

PAT^f Average payments per employee for imported patents, trade marks, and technical assistance, foreign firms, 1975. Proxy for technology imports

Independent variables

PAT^d Average payments per employee for imported patents, trade marks and technical assistance, domestic firms, 1975. Used as control variable

$USLIC$ Average payments per employee of licence fees by US manufacturing affiliates. Defined for 16 2-digit (US SIC) industries, 1982. Used as control variable (Source: US Department of Commerce, 1985)

ADV Ratio of advertising expenditure to gross output, industry totals, 1970. Used as control variable

LQ Ratio of white-collar workers to blue-collar workers, industry totals, 1970. Proxy for availability of skilled labour

$WAGE^f$ Ratio of wage payments to employment, foreign firms, 1970. Proxy for availability of skilled labour

ΔK^d Increase (per cent) in real capital stock 1970–5, domestic firms; 1975 data transformed from *activos fijos brutos* to *capital invertido* with industry-specific ratios from 1970, and deflated by the wholesale price index. Proxy for local competition

ΔGO^d Increase (per cent) in real gross output 1970–5, domestic firms; 1975 data deflated by industry-specific price indices. Proxy for local competition

ΔMS^d Increase (per cent) in the market share of domestic firms 1970–5. Proxy for local competition

---

Sources: Data for dependent variables from unpublished worksheets provided by the Dirección de Estadísticas de la Secretaría de Industria y Comercio in Mexico; data for independent variables from same source, unless otherwise stated.

Table A-14.2   Simple correlation coefficients for exogenous variables, Mexican manufacturing industries, 1970–5

	PAT^d	$USLIC$	ADV	LQ	$WAGE^f$	ΔK^d	ΔGO^d	ΔMS^d
PAT^d	1.00							
$USLIC$	0.00	1.00						
ADV	0.18	0.09	1.00					
LQ	0.19	0.32	0.27	1.00				
$WAGE^f$	0.28	0.16	0.16	0.50	1.00			
ΔK^d	0.45	−0.03	0.19	0.13	0.19	1.00		
ΔGO^d	0.27	0.02	−0.06	0.12	0.18	0.46	1.00	
ΔMS^d	0.48	−0.04	−0.03	0.07	0.18	0.24	0.79	1.00
	PAT^d	$USLIC$	ADV	LQ	$WAGE^f$	ΔK^d	ΔGO^d	ΔMS^d

Notes: There are 144 observations for all variables except $USLIC$ (N = 142) and ΔMS^d (N = 132).

Bibliography

Abramovitz, M. (1986) 'Catching Up, Forging Ahead, and Falling Behind', *Journal of Economic History*, vol. 46, pp. 385–406.

Aitken, B. and Harrison, A. (1991) 'Are There Spillovers from Foreign Direct Investment? Evidence from Panel Data for Venezuela', Mimeo, MIT and the World Bank, November.

Aitken, B., Hanson, G. D. and Harrison, A. (1994) *Spillovers, Foreign Investment, and Export Behavior*. NBER Working Paper No. 4967, December.

Andersson, T. (1993) *Utlandsinvesteringar och policy-implikationer*, SOU, 1993:16, Stockholm: Allmänna Förlaget.

Andersson, T., Fredriksson, T. and Svensson, R. (1996) *Multinational Restructuring, Internationalization and Small Economies. The Case of Sweden*, London: Routledge.

Balassa, B. (1986) 'Intra-Industry Specialization. A Cross-Country Analysis', *European Economic Review*, vol. 30, pp. 27–42.

Balasubramanyam, U. N. (1973) *International Transfer of Technology to India*, New York: Praeger.

Bardhan, P. (1990) 'Symposium on the State and Economic Development', *Journal of Economic Perspectives*, vol. 4, pp. 3–7.

Beamish, P. W. (1988) *Multinational Joint Ventures in Developing Countries*, London: Routledge.

Behrman, J and Fischer, W. (1980) *Overseas R&D Activities of Transnational Companies*, Cambridge, Mass.: Oelgeschlager, Gunn & Hain.

Behrman, J. and Wallender, H. (1976) *Transfer of Manufacturing Technology within Multinational Enterprises*, Cambridge, Mass.: Ballinger.

Bergsman, J. (1974) 'Commercial Policy, Allocative Efficiency and "X-efficiency"', *Quarterly Journal of Economics*, vol. 86, pp. 409–33.

Bernstein, J. I. (1988) 'Cost of Production, Intra- and Interindustry R&D Spillovers: Canadian Evidence', *Canadian Journal of Economics*, vol. 21, pp. 324–47.

Bernstein, J. I. (1989) 'The Structure of Canadian Interindustry R&D Spillovers, and the Rates of Return to R&D', *Journal of Industrial Economics*, vol. 37, pp. 315–28.

Berry, C. H. (1971) 'Corporate Growth and Diversification', *Journal of Law and Economics*, October.

Bhagwati, J. (1988) *Protectionism*, Cambridge, Mass.: MIT Press.

Blomström, M. (1986a) 'Foreign Investment and Productive Efficiency: The Case of Mexico', *Journal of Industrial Economics*, vol. 15, pp. 97–110.

Blomström, M. (1986b) 'Multinationals and Market Structure in Mexico', *World Development*, vol. 14, pp. 523–30.

232

Blomström, M. (1989) *Foreign Investment and Spillovers*, London: Routledge.

Blomström, M. (1990) *Transnational Corporations and Manufacturing Exports from Developing Countries*, New York: United Nations.

Blomström, M. (1991) 'Host Country Benefits of Foreign Investment', in D. G. McFetridge (ed.), *Foreign Investment, Technology and Economic Growth*, Toronto and London: Toronto University Press.

Blomström, M. and Kokko, A. (1994) 'Home-Country Effects of Foreign Direct Investment: Sweden', in S. Globerman (ed.), *Canadian-Based Multinationals*, Calgary: University of Calgary Press.

Blomström, M. and Kokko, A. (1997) 'Sweden', in J. Dunning (ed.), *Governments, Globalization, and International Business*, Oxford University Press.

Blomström, M. and Lipsey, R. E. (1989) 'The Export Performance of US and Swedish Multinationals', *Review of Income and Wealth*, vol. 35, pp. 245–64.

Blomström, M. and Lipsey, R. E. (1993) 'Foreign Firms and Structural Adjustment in Latin America. Lesson from the Debt Crisis', in G. Hansson (ed.), *Trade, Growth, and Development. The Role of Politics and Institutions*, London: Routledge.

Blomström, M. and Meller, P. (eds) (1991) *Diverging Paths: Comparing a Century of Scandinavian and Latin American Economic Development*, Baltimore, Md: Johns Hopkins University Press.

Blomström, M. and Persson, H. (1983) 'Foreign Investment and Spillover Efficiency in an Underdeveloped Economy: Evidence from the Mexican Manufacturing Industry', *World Development*, vol. 11, pp. 493–501.

Brander, J. A. and Spencer, B. J. (1985) 'Export Subsidies and International Market Share Rivalry', *Journal of International Economics*, vol. 18, pp. 83–100.

Brash, D. T. (1966) *American Investment in Australian Industry*, Cambridge, Mass.: Harvard University Press.

Braunerhjelm, P. and Ekholm, K. (eds.) (1998) *The Geography of Multinational Firms*, Norwell, Mass.: Kluwer.

Braunerhjelm, P. and. Svensson, R. (1996) 'Host Country Characteristics and Agglomeration in Foreign Direct Investment', *Applied Economics*, vol. 28, pp. 833–40.

Buckley, P. and Casson, M. (1976) *The Future of the Multinational Enterprise*, London: Macmillan.

Buckley, P. and Pearce, R. D. (1979) 'Overseas Production and Exporting by the World's Largest Enterprises', *Journal of International Business Studies*, vol. 10, pp. 9–20.

Cantwell, J. (1989) *Technological Innovation and Multinational Corporations*, Oxford: Basil Blackwell.

Cantwell, J. (ed.) (1994) *Transnational Corporations and Innovatory Activities*, United Nations Library on Transnational Corporations, vol. 17, London: Routledge.

Cantwell, J. (1995) 'The Globalization of Technology: What Remains of the Product Cycle Model?', *Cambridge Journal of Economics*, vol. 19, pp. 155–174.

Cantwell. J. and Hodson, C. (1991) 'Global R&D and UK Competitiveness', in M. Casson (ed.), *Global Research Strategy and International Competitiveness*, Oxford and Cambridge: Basil Blackwell.

Casson, M. (1979) *Alternatives to the Multinational Enterprise*, London: Macmillan.

Casson, M. (1986) *Multinationals and World Trade. Vertical Integration and the Division of Labour in World Industries*, London: Allen & Unwin.

Caves, R. E. (1971) 'International Corporations: The Industrial Economics of Foreign Investment', *Economica*, vol. 38, pp. 1–27.

Caves, R. E. (1974) 'Multinational Firms, Competition and Productivity in Host-Country Markets', *Economica*, vol. 41, pp. 176–93.

Caves, R. E. (1996) *Multinational Enterprise and Economic Analysis* (2nd edn), New York: Cambridge University Press.

Caves, R. E. and Mehra, S. (1986) 'Entry of Foreign Multinationals into US Manufacturing Industries, in M. Porter (ed.), *Competition in Global Industries*, Boston, Mass.: Harvard Business School Press.

Chen, E. K. Y. (1983) *Multinational Corporations, Technology and Employment*, London: Macmillan.

Cheng, L. (1984) 'International Competition in R&D and Technological Leadership: An Examination of the Posner-Hufbauer Hypothesis', *Journal of International Economics*, vol. 17, pp. 15–40.

Cheng, L. (1987) 'Optimal Trade and Technology Policies: Dynamic Linkages', *International Economic Review*, vol. 28, pp. 757–76.

Chesnais, F. (1988) 'Multinational Enterprises and the International Diffusion of Technology', in G. Dosi *et al.* (eds.), *Technical Change and Economic Theory*, London and New York: Pinter.

Chow, G. C. (1960) 'Tests of Equality between Sets of Coefficients in Two Linear Regressions', *Econometrica*, vol. 28, no. 3, pp. 591–605.

Coase, R. H. (1937) 'The Nature of the Firm, *Economica*, vol. 4, pp. 386–405.

Corden, W. M. (1967) 'Protection and Foreign Investment', *Economic Record*, vol. 43, pp. 209–32.

Culem, C. and Lundberg, L. (1986) 'The Product Pattern of Intra-Industry Trade: Stability among Countries and over Time', *Weltwirtschaftliches Archiv*, vol. 122, pp. 113–29.

Das, S. (1987) 'Externalities, and Technology Transfers through Multinational Corporations: A Theoretical Analysis', *Journal of International Economics*, vol. 22, pp. 171–82.

Davidson, W. H. (1980) *Experience Effects in International Investment and Technology Transfer*, Ann Arbor, Mich.: UMI Research Press.

Deane, R. S. (1970) *Foreign Investment in New Zealand Manufacturing*, Wellington: Sweet and Maxwell.

Dunning, J. H. (1958) *American Investment in British Manufacturing*, London: George Allen & Unwin.

Dunning, J. H. (1974) 'Multinational Enterprises and the Trade Flows of Less Developed Countries', *World Development*, vol. 2, pp. 131–8.

Dunning, J. H. (1981) 'Explaining the International Direct Investment Position of Countries: Towards a Dynamic or Developmental Approach', *Weltwirtschaftliches Archiv*, vol. 117, pp. 30–64.

Dunning, J. H. (1993) *Multinational Enterprises and the Global Economy*, Reading, Mass.: Addison-Wesley.

Dunning, J. H. and Pearce, R. D. (1981) *The World's Largest Industrial Enterprises*, Farnborough: Gower.

Edwards, S. and Savastano, M. (1988) 'Latin America's Intraregional Trade: Evolution and Future Prospects', NBER Working Paper No. 2738 (October).

Estados Unidos Mexicanos (1973) *IX Censo Industrial 1971: Tomo 1*, Secretaría de Industria y Comercio, Mexico City.

Evans, P. B. (1977) 'Direct Investment and Industrial Concentration', *Journal of Development Studies*, vol. 13, pp. 373–85.

Evans, P. (1979) *Dependent Development: The Alliance of Multinational, State and Local Capital in Brazil*, Princeton NJ: Princeton University Press.

Fagre, N. and Wells, L. T. Jr (1982) 'Bargaining Power of Multinationals and Host Governments', *Journal of International Business Studies*, pp. 9–24

Fairchild, L. (1977) 'Performance and Technology of United States and National Firms in Mexico', *Journal of Development Studies*, vol. 14, pp. 14–34.

Fairchild, L. and Sosin, K. (1986) 'Evaluating Differences in Technological Activity between Transnational and Domestic Firms in Latin America', *Journal of Development Studies*, vol. 22, pp. 697–708.

Fajnzylber, F. and Martínez Tarragó, T. (1976) *Las empresas transnacionales*, Mexico City: Fondo de Cultura Económica.

Findlay, R. (1978) 'Relative Backwardness, Direct Foreign Investment, and the Transfer of Technology: A Simple Dynamic Model', *Quarterly Journal of Economics*, vol. 92, pp. 1–16.

Fishwick, F. (1982) *Multinational Companies and Economic Concentration in Europe*, Farnborough: Gower.

Forsyth, D. (1972) *US Investment in Scotland*, New York: Praeger.

Frischtak, C. R. and Newfarmer, R. S. (eds.) (1994) *Transnational Corporations: Market Structure and Industrial Performance*, United Nations Library on Transnational Corporations, vol. 15, London: Routledge.

Gabriel, P. P. (1967) *The International Transfer of Corporate Skills: Manager Contracts in Less Developed Countries*, Cambridge, Mass.: Harvard University Press.

Geroski, P. A. (1982) 'Simultaneous Equations Models of the Structure – Performance Paradigm', *European Economic Review*, vol. 19, pp. 145–58.

Gerschenberg, I. (1987) 'The Training and Spread of Managerial Know-How: A Comparative Analysis of Multinational and Other Firms in Kenya', *World Development*, vol. 15, pp. 931–9.

Globerman, S. (1979a) 'Foreign Direct Investment and "Spillover" Efficiency Benefits in Canadian Manufacturing Industries', *Canadian Journal of Economics*, vol. 12, pp. 42–56.

Globerman, S. (1979b) 'A Note on Foreign Ownership and Market Structure in the United Kingdom', *Applied Economics*, vol. 11, pp. 35–42.

Globerman, S., Kokko, A. and Sjöholm, F. (2000) 'International Technology Diffusion: Evidence from Swedish Patent Data', *Kyklos*.

Goldsbrough, D. J. (1981) 'International Trade of Multinational Corporations and its Responsiveness to Changes in Aggregate Demand and Relative Prices', *IMF Staff Papers*, vol. 28, pp. 573–99.

Graham, E. M. (1991) 'Strategic Management and Transnational Firm Behaviour: A Formal Approach', in C. N. Pitelis and R. Sugden (eds), *The Nature of the Transnational Firm*, London: Routledge, pp. 155–67.

Griliches, Z. (1992) 'The Search for R&D Spillovers', *Scandinavian Journal of Economics*, vol. 94, Supplement, pp. 29–47.

Grosse, R. (1989) *Multinationals in Latin America*, London: Routledge.

Haddad, M. and Harrison, A. (1991) 'Are There Positive Spillovers from Direct Foreign Investment', mimeo, Harvard University and World Bank, September.

Haddad, M. and Harrison, A. (1993) 'Are There Positive Spillovers from Direct Foreign Investment? Evidence from Panel Data for Morocco', *Journal of Development Economics*, vol. 42, pp. 51–74.

Håkansson, L. (1980) *Multinationella företag. FOU-verksamhet. Tekniköverföring och Företagstillväxt*. SIND 1980: 4, Stockholm: Liber Förlag.

Håkansson, L. (1983) 'R&D in Foreign Owned Subsidiaries in Sweden', in W. H. Goldberg (ed.), *Government and Multinationals. The Policy of Control versus Autonomy*, Cambridge, Mass.: Oelgeschlager, Gunn and Hain.

Halbach, A. J. (1989) 'Multinational Enterprises and Subcontracting in the Third World: A Study of Inter-Industrial Linkages', Multinational Enterprises Programme, Working Paper No. 58, Geneva: International Labour Office.

Hausman, J. A. (1978) 'Specification Tests in Econometrics', *Econometrica*, vol. 46, pp. 1251–71.

Havrylyshyn, O. and Civan, E. (1985) 'Intra-Industry Trade among Developing Countries', *Journal of Development Economics*, vol. 18, pp. 253–71.

Helleiner, G. K. (1979) 'Transnational Corporations and Trade Structure: The Role of Intra-Firm Trade', in H. Giersch (ed.) *On the Economics of Intra-Industry Trade*, Tübingen: Mohr, pp. 159–81.

Helleiner, G. K. and Lavergne, R. (1980) 'Intra-Firm Trade and Industrial Exports to the US', *Oxford Bulletin of Economics and Statistics*, vol. 41, pp. 297–311.

Hill, H. (1982) 'Vertical Inter-Firm Linkages in LDCs: A Note on the Philippines', *Oxford Bulletin of Economics and Statistics*, vol. 44, pp. 261–71.

Hirschey, R. and Caves, R. (1983) 'Research and Transfer of Technology by Multinational Enterprises', *Oxford Bulletin of Economics and Statistics*, vol. 43, pp. 115–30.

Hjalmarsson, L. (1991) 'The Scandinavian Model of Industry Policy', in M. Blomström and P. Meller (eds.), *Diverging Paths: Comparing a Century of Scandinavian and Latin American Economic Development*, Washington DC and Baltimore, Md: Inter-American Development Bank and Johns Hopkins University Press.

Hone, A. (1974) 'Multinational Corporations and Multinational Buying Groups: Their Impact on the Growth of Asia's Export of Manufactures – Myths and Realities', *World Development*, vol. 2, pp. 145–9.

Horstmann, I. and Markusen, J. (1987) 'Strategic Investment and the Development of Multinationals', *International Economic Review*, vol. 28, pp. 109–21.

Horstmann, I. and Markusen, J. (1989) 'Firm-Specific Assets and the Welfare Effects of Direct Foreign Investment', *Economica*, vol. 56, pp. 41–8.

Hymer, S. H. (1960) *The International Operations of National Firms: A Study of Direct Foreign Investment*, Ph. D. dissertation, MIT, Cambridge, Mass. (published by MIT Press, 1976).

Jenkins, R. (1990) 'Comparing Foreign Subsidiaries and Local Firms in LDCs: Theoretical Issues and Empirical Evidence', *Journal of Development Studies*, vol. 26, pp. 205–28.

Jensen, R. and Thursby, M. (1986) 'A Strategic Approach to the Product Life Cycle', *Journal of International Economics*, vol. 21, pp. 269–84.

Kamien, M. I. and Schwartz, N. L. (1982) *Market Structure and Innovation*, New York: Cambridge University Press.

Katrak, H. (1991) 'Market Rivalry, Government Policies and Multinational Enterprise in Developing Countries', in P. J. Buckley and J. Clegg (eds), *Multinational Enterprises in Less Developed Countries*, London: Macmillan, pp. 92–110.

Katz, J. M. (1969) *Production Functions, Foreign Investment and Growth*, Amsterdam: North-Holland.

Katz, J. M. (1984) 'Domestic Technological Innovations and Dynamic Comparative Advantage: Further Reflections on a Comparative Case Study Program', *Journal of Development Economics*, vol. 16, pp. 13–38.

Katz, J. M. (1987) *Technology Creation in Latin American Manufacturing Industries*, New York: St Martin's Press.

Keesing, D. B. and Lall, S. (1992) 'Marketing Manufactured Exports from Developing Countries: Learning Sequences and Public Support', in G. G. Helleiner (ed.), *Trade Policy, Industrialization, and Development: New Perspectives*, Oxford: Clarendon Press.

Kindleberger, C. P. (1969) *American Business Abroad: Six Lectures on Direct Investment*, New Haven, Conn.: Yale University Press.

Knickerbocker, F. T. (1976) 'Market Structure and Market Power Consequences of Foreign Direct Investment by Multinational Companies', Occasional Paper No. 8, Washington, DC: Center for Multinational Studies.

Kogut, B. and Chang, S. J. (1991) 'Technological Capabilities and Japanese Foreign Direct Investment in the United States', *Review of Economics and Statistics*, vol. 41, pp. 401–14.

Koizumi, T. and Kopecky, K. J. (1977) 'Economic Growth, Capital Movements and the International Transfer of Technical Knowledge', *Journal of International Economics*, vol. 7, pp. 45–65.

Kokko, A. (1992) *Foreign Direct Investment, Host Country Characteristics and Spillovers*, Stockholm: Economic Research Institute, Stockholm School of Economics.

Kokko, A., Tansini, R. and Zejan, M. (1997) 'Trade Regimes and Spillover Effects of FDI: Evidence from Uruguay', Mimeo, Stockholm School of Economics (June).

Lake, A. W. (1979) 'Technology Creation and Technology Transfer by Multinational Firms', in R. G. Hawkins (ed.), *Research in International Business and Finance, vol. 1: The Economic Effects of Multinational Corporations*, Greenwich: JAI Press.

Lall, S. (1973) 'Transfer Pricing by Multinational Manufacturing Firms', *Oxford Bulletin of Economics and Statistics*, vol. 35, pp. 173–95.

Lall, S. (1978a) 'The Pattern of Intra Firm Exports by US Multinationals', *Oxford Bulletin of Economics and Statistics*, vol. 40, pp. 209–22.

Lall, S. (1978b) 'Transnationals, Domestic Enterprises and Industrial Structure in LDCs: A Survey', *Oxford Economic Papers*, vol. 30, pp. 217–48.

Lall, S. (1979a), 'The International Allocation of Research Activity by US Multinationals', *Oxford Bulletin of Economics and Statistics*, vol. 41, pp. 313–31.

Lall, S. (1979b) 'Transfer Pricing and Developing Countries: Some Problems of Investigation', *World Development*, vol. 7, pp. 59–71.

Lall, S. (1979c) 'Multinationals and Market Structure in an Open Developing Economy: The Case of Malaysia', *Weltwirtschaftliches Archiv*, vol. 115, pp. 325–50.

Lall, S. (1980a) 'Vertical Interfirm Linkages in LDCs: An Empirical Study', *Oxford Bulletin of Economics and Statistics*, vol. 42, pp. 203–26.

Lall, S. (1980b) 'Developing Countries as Exporters of Industrial Technology', *Research Policy*, vol. 9, pp. 24–52.

Lall, S. (1982) 'The Monopolistic Advantages of Multinationals: Lessons from Foreign Investment in the US', *The Economic Journal*, vol. 92, pp. 668–83.

Lall, S. (1985) *Multinationals, Technology and Exports*, London: Macmillan.

Langdon, S. (1981) *Multinational Corporations in the Political Economy of Kenya*, London: Macmillan.

Lapan, H. and Bardhan, P. (1973) 'Localized Technical Progress and Transfer of Technology and Economic Development', *Journal of Economic Theory*, vol. 6, pp. 585–95.

Lecraw, D. J. (1984) 'Bargaining Power, Ownership, and Profitability of Transnational Corporations in Developing Countries', *Journal of International Business Studies*, vol. 15, pp. 27–43.

Leibenstein, H. (1966) 'Allocative Efficiency vs. X-efficiency', *American Economic Review*, vol. 56, pp. 392–415.

Leibenstein, H. (1980) 'X-efficiency, Intrafirm Behaviour, and Growth', in S. Maital and N. Meltz (eds), *Lagging Productivity Growth*, Cambridge, Mass.: Ballinger.

Lim, L. Y. C. and Pang, E. F. (1982) 'Vertical Linkages and Multinational Enterprises in Developing Countries', *World Development*, vol. 10, pp. 585–95.

Lindsey, C. N. (1989) 'Commodities, Technology, and Trade: Transnational Corporations and Philippine Economic Development. *Philippine Review of Economics and Business*, vol. 26, pp. 67–108.

Lipsey, R. E. (1984) 'Recent Trends in US Trade and Investment', in N. Miawaki (ed.), *Problems in Advanced Economies*, Heidelberg: Springer-Verlag.

Lipsey, R. E., Molinari, L. and Kravis, I. B. (1991) 'Measures of Prices and Price Competitiveness in International Trade in Manufactured Goods', in P. Hooper and J. D. Richardson (eds), *International Economic Transactions*, University of Chicago Press.

Lopez, J. (1991) 'Contractive Adjustment in Mexico 1982–1989', *Banca Nazionale del Lavoro Quarterly Review*, vol. 178.

MacDougall, G. D. A. (1960) 'The Benefits and Costs of Private Investment from Abroad: A Theoretical Approach', *Economic Record*, vol. 36, pp. 13–35.

Maddala, G. (1977) *Econometrics*, Tokyo: McGraw-Hill International.

Maddison, A. and van Ark, B. (1989) 'International Comparisons of Purchasing Power, Real Output, and Labour Productivity: A Case Study of Brazilian, Mexican, and US Manufacturing', *Review of Income and Wealth*, vol. 35, pp. 1–30.

Mansfield, E. and Romeo, A. (1980) 'Technology Transfer to Overseas Subsidiaries by US-Based Firms', *Quarterly Journal of Economics*, vol. 95, pp. 737–50.

Mansfield, E., Teece, D. and Romeo, A. (1979) 'Overseas Research and Development by US-Based Firms', *Economica*, vol. 46, pp. 187–96.

McAleese, D. and McDonald, D. (1978) 'Employment Growth and Development of Linkages in Foreign-Owned and Domestic Manufacturing Enterprises', *Oxford Bulletin of Economics and Statistics*, vol. 40, pp. 321–39.

McFetridge, D. G. (1987) 'The Timing, Mode and Terms of Technology Transfer: Some Recent Findings', in A. E. Safarian and G. Y. Bertin (eds), *Multinationals, Governments and International Technology Transfer*, London: Croom Helm.

McManus, J. C. (1972) 'The Theory of the International Firm', in G. Paquet (ed.), *The Multinational Firm and the Nation State*, Don Mills, Ontario: Collier-Macmillan, pp. 66–93.

Musgrave, J. C. (1986) 'Fixed Reproducible Tangible Wealth in the United States: Revised Estimates', *Survey of Current Business*, vol. 66, pp. 51–75.

Nadiri, M. I. (1991a) 'Innovations and Technological Spillovers', Mimeo, New York University and NBER (September).

Nadiri, M. I. (1991b) 'US Direct Investment and the Production Structure of the Manufacturing Sector in France, Germany, Japan, and the U.K.', Mimeo, New York University and NBER (December).

Newfarmer, R. S. (1979) 'Oligopolistic Tactics to Control Markets and the Growth of TNCs in Brazil's Electrical Industry', *Journal of Development Studies*, vol. 15, pp. 108–40.

Pack, H. (1974) 'The Employment–Output Tradeoff in LDCs – A Microeconomic Approach', *Oxford Economic Papers*, vol. 26, pp. 388–404.

Page, J. M. (1980) 'Technical Efficiency and Economic Performance: Some Evidence from Ghana', *Oxford Economic Papers*, vol. 32, pp. 319–39.

Pagoulatos, E. and Sorensen, R. (1975) 'Two-Way International Trade: An Econometric Analysis', *Weltwirtschaftliches Archiv*, vol. 111, pp. 454–65.

Patel, P. and Pavitt, K. (1994) 'Technological Competencies in the World's Largest Firms: Characteristics, Constraints and Scope for Managerial Choice', mimeo.

Pearce, R. D. (1982) 'Overseas Production and Exporting Performance: An Empirical Note', Discussion Papers in International Investment and Business Studies, No. 64, University of Reading.

Peres Nuñez, W. (1990) *Foreign Direct Investment and Industrial Development in Mexico*, Paris: OECD Development Centre.

Plasschaert, S. R. F. (1979) *Transfer Pricing and Multinational Corporations: An Overview of Concepts, Mechanisms and Regulations*, New York: Praeger.

Porter, M. E. (1990) *The Competitive Advantage of Nations*, New York: The Free Press.

Reuber, G. L., with H. Crookell, M. Emerson, and G. Gallais-Hamonno (1973) *Private Foreign Investment in Development*, Oxford: Clarendon Press.

Riedel, J. (1975) 'The Nature and Determinants of Export-Oriented Direct Foreign Investment in a Developing Country: A Case Study of Taiwan', *Weltwirtschaftliches Archiv*, vol. 111, pp. 505–28.

Romer, P. (1990) 'Endogenous Technological Change', *Journal of Political Economy*, vol. 98, pp. 71–102.

Ronstadt, R. (1977) *Research and Development Abroad by US Multinationals*, New York: Praeger.

Rosenberg, N. (1976) *Perspectives on Technology*, New York: Cambridge University Press.

Rosenbluth, G. (1970) 'The Relation between Foreign Control and Concentration in Canadian Industry', *Canadian Journal of Economics*, vol. 3, pp. 14–38.

Rugman, A. and Eden, L. (eds) (1985) *Multinationals and Transfer Pricing*, London: Croom Helm.

Safarian, A. E. (1966) *Foreign Ownership of Canadian Industry*, Toronto: McGraw-Hill.

Sleuwaegen, L. (1985) 'Monopolistic Advantages and the International Operations of Firms: Disaggregated Evidence from US-Based Multinationals', *Journal of International Business Studies*, vol. 16, pp. 125–33.

Sölvell, Ö. (1987) *Entry Barriers and Foreign Penetration: Emerging Patterns of International Competition in Two Electrical Engineering Industries*, Stockholm: Institute of International Business, Stockholm School of Economics.

Sölvell, Ö., Zander, I. and Porter, M. (1991) *Advantage Sweden*, Stockholm: Norstedts.

Spencer, B. J. and Brander, J. A. (1983) 'International R&D Rivalry and Industrial Strategy', *Review of Economic Studies*, vol. 50, pp. 707–22.

Spencer, D. E. and Berk, K. N. (1981) 'A Limited Information Specification Test', *Econometrica*, vol. 49, pp. 1079–85.

Stopford, J. M. and Wells, L. T. Jr (1972) *Managing the Multinational Enterprise: Organization of the Firm and Ownership of the Subsidiaries*, New York: Basic Books.

Summers, R. and Heston, A. (1988) 'A New Set of International Comparisons of Real Product and Prices: Estimates for 130 Countries, 1950–1985', *Review of Income and Wealth*, Series 34, pp. 1–26.

Swan, P. L. (1973) 'The International Diffusion of an Innovation', *Journal of Industrial Economics*, vol. 22, pp. 61–9.

Swedenborg, B. (1979) *The Multinational Operations of Swedish Firms. An Analysis of Determinants and Effects*, Stockholm: Industriens Utredningsinstitut.

Swedenborg, B. (1982) *Svensk Industri i Utlandet. En Analys av Drivkrafter och Effekter*, Stockholm: Industriens Utredningsinstitut.

Swedenborg, B. (1985) 'Sweden' in J. Dunning (ed.), *Multinational Enterprises, Economic Structure and International Competitiveness*, Chichester: John Wiley/IRM Series on Multinationals.

Swedenborg, B., Johansson-Grahn, G. and Kinnwall, M. (1989) *Den svenska industrins utlandsinvesteringar 1960–1986*, Stockholm: Industriens Utredningsinstitut.

Teece, D. (1976) *The Multinational Corporation and the Resource Cost of International Technology Transfer*, Cambridge, Mass.: Ballinger.

Teece, D. (1981) 'The Market for Expertise and the Efficient International Transfer of Technology', *The Annals of the American Academy of Political and Social Science*, vol. 458, pp. 81–96.

Teece, D. (1982) 'A Transaction Cost Theory of Multinational Enterprises', University of Reading Discussion Paper in International Investment and Business Studies No. 66.

Teitel, S. (1984) 'Technology Creation in Semi-Industrial Economies', *Journal of Development Economics*, vol. 6, pp. 39–61.

Tilton, J. E. (1971) *The International Diffusion of Technology: The Case of Semi-conductors*, Washington DC: Brookings Institution.

Tolentino, P. E. E. (1993) *Technological Innovation and Third World Multinationals*, London: Routledge.

US Department of Commerce (1981) *US Direct Investment Abroad, 1977*, Washington DC: US Government Printing Office.

US Department of Commerce (1985) *US Direct Investment Abroad: 1982*, Washington DC: US Government Printing Office.

UNCTC (1981) *Transnational Corporation Linkages in Developing Countries: The Case of Backward Linkages via Subcontracting*, New York: United Nations Centre on Transnational Corporations.

UNESCO (1990) *Statistical Yearbook 1990*, Paris: UNESCO.

UNIDO (1993) *Industry in a Changing World*, New York: United Nations.

United Nations (various years) *Industrial Statistics Yearbook*, New York: United Nations.

Vaitsos, C. V. (1974) *Inter-Country Income Distribution and Transnational Corporations*, Oxford: Clarendon Press.

Vernon, R. (1977) *Storm over the Multinationals. The Real Issues*, Cambridge, Mass.: Harvard University Press.

Vertinski, I. and Raizada, R. (1994) 'MacMillan Bloedel: Foreign Investment Decisions and Their Welfare Consequences', in S. Globerman (ed.), *Canadian-Based Multinationals*, Calgary: University of Calgary Press.

Wang, Y. and Blomström, M. (1992) 'Foreign Investment and Technology Transfer: A Simple Model', *European Economic Review*, vol. 36, pp. 137–55.

Wasow, B. and Hill, H. (1986) *The Insurance Industry in Economic Development*, New York: New York University Press.

Watanabe, S. (1983a) 'Technical Co-operation between Large and Small Firms in the Filipino Automobile Industry', in S. Watanabe (ed.), *Technology Marketing and Industrialization: Linkages between Small and Large Enterprises*, New Delhi: Macmillan.

Watanabe, S. (1983b) 'Technological Linkages through Subcontracting in Mexican Industries', in S. Watanabe (ed.), *Technology Marketing and Industrialization: Linkages between Small and Large Enterprises*, New Delhi: Macmillan.

White, L. J. (1976) 'Appropriate Technology, X-inefficiency and the Competitive Environment: Some Evidence from Pakistan', *Quarterly Journal of Economics*, vol. 90, pp. 575–89.

Wilson, B. D. (1980) 'The Propensity of Multinational Companies to Expand through Acquisitions', *Journal of International Business Studies*, vol. 11, pp. 59–65.

Yoshihara, K. (1988) *The Rise of Ersatz Capital in South-East Asia*, Oxford: Oxford University Press.

Zander, I. (1994) *The Tortoise Evolution of the Multinational Corporation – Foreign Technological Activity in Swedish Multinational Firms 1890–1990*, Stockholm: Institute of International Business, Stockholm School of Economics.

Index